Faithful fictions

The author and publisher gratefully acknowledge and thank the following for permission to reproduce the photographs on the front cover. In order from the top these are:
Evelyn Waugh: Mark Gerson Photography
Muriel Spark: Times Newspapers Ltd
Graham Greene: Times Newspapers Ltd
David Lodge: Andrew Douglas.

Faithful fictions

The Catholic novel in British literature

Thomas Woodman

Open University Press
Milton Keynes · Philadelphia

Open University Press
Celtic Court
22 Ballmoor
Buckingham
MK18 1XW

and
1900 Frost Road, Suite 101
Bristol, PA 19007, USA

First Published 1991

Copyright © Thomas Woodman 1991

All rights reserved. No part of this publication may be
reproduced, stored in a retrieval system or transmitted
in any form or by any means, without written permission
from the publisher.

British Library Cataloguing in Publication Data

Woodman, Thomas
   Faithful fictions: the Catholic novel in British
   literature.
   I. Title
   823.009

   ISBN 0-335-09638-7

Library of Congress Cataloging-in-Publication Number Available

Typeset by Rowland Phototypesetting Ltd
Bury St Edmunds, Suffolk
Printed in Great Britain by
St Edmundsbury Press Ltd, Bury St Edmunds, Suffolk

Contents

Preface	vii
Introduction	ix
Part one A chronological survey	1
1 The nineteenth-century Catholic novel	3
2 Catholic fiction 1900–45	17
3 Consolidation and change 1945–present	31
Part two The Catholic 'difference'	45
4 'This alien land'	47
5 Catholic chic	61
Part three The Church and the world	79
6 Images of the Church and the world	81
7 'Mixing themselves up in politics'	96
Part four 'A drama of good and evil that other writers do not see'	109
8 Good and evil: the providential plot	111
9 'The sorrowful mysteries'	128
10 Sin, sex and adultery	145
11 Conclusions	161
Notes	165
Selected bibliography	174
Selective glossary of Catholic and theological terminology	184
Index	186

Preface

Despite their minority status British Catholics have written a very large number of novels in a wide variety of modes. This is the first book to survey the range of this fiction and consider what generalizations, if any, can be made about it. Many of these works, naturally enough, are of no great literary merit, but they cast light on the greater achievements and are revealing from a sociological or theological perspective. It will be understood, of course, that I make no claims to have included every British Catholic novel and novelist of possible interest.

Ray Cunningham of the Open University Press has always been most encouraging about this project. Bernard Bergonzi has kindly sent me photocopies and suggestions and Max Steiger of Condé Nast Publications has also supplied useful material. I am grateful to David Lodge for permission to use information from his University of London MA thesis on British Catholic fiction and to quote various passages from *How Far Can You Go?*, a novel which has a special centrality in describing what has happened to Catholicism since the sixties.

In more general terms I am conscious of having learnt much about Catholicism from the Dominican community at Blackfriars, Oxford. I also, of course, owe very special debts of gratitude to my mother and to my wife Rosemary.

Introduction: 'Practically a Protestant form of art?'

Sir Hugh Walpole once wrote that he was opposed to the spread of Roman Catholicism because it would be bad for the novel. In another well-known comment George Orwell wrote that:

> The atmosphere of orthodoxy is always damaging to prose; and above all it is completely ruinous to the novel, the most anarchical of all forms of literature. How many Roman Catholics have been good novelists? Even the handful one could name have usually been bad Catholics. The novel is practically a Protestant form of art; it is a product of the free mind, of the autonomous individual.[1]

Extreme though these views may seem, there is a sense in which the critical consensus about the novel that existed for many years might have been held to support them. 'The novel', wrote Georg Lukács resoundingly, 'is the epic of a world that has been abandoned by God.' According to Peter Faulkner it is the 'one secular literary form'. Ian Watt's influential *The Rise of the Novel* (1957) presented the most detailed case for the genre as essentially realistic, its origins profoundly linked to the development of the modern secular world.[2] Increased prosperity and middle-class literacy had given a far greater proportion of people the opportunity to lead reasonably comfortable and fulfilling lives. What especially appealed to such readers were fictionalized yet realistic life stories of heroes and heroines with whom they could identify, whose adventures they found to be both more thrilling and significant than their own and yet in some ways parallel to them.

The development of the novel is thus bound up with increasing democratization, with a degree of improvement in the education and status of women and, indeed, with the whole liberal bourgeois ethos of the modern world. Its realm is social life and personal relations in a pluralist society. Lawrence Lerner says that 'there is clearly a link between individual characterization and the humanist tradition: before we promoted the individual to be the touchstone of our moral values, we did not make him the unit of literary creation either.' W. J. Harvey likewise emphasizes the importance of character, individualism and social pluralism. Since the realistic novel has to be regarded as the central classic tradition of English fiction, the novelist is almost by definition 'liberal, pluralist, foxy; his typical subject is the partial, the limited, the relative, the imperfect – in other words, the merely human rather than the overarching non-human absolutes.'[3]

A kind of agnosticism is thus seen as built into the very core of the genre. Human beings have come to find the central meaning of their lives in their own individual, time-bound, necessarily partial and imperfect experiences rather than in 'the revealed plots that appeared to subsume transitory human time to the timeless'. The rise of the novel is related quite specifically to the 'declining authority' of these 'proverbial plots' of revealed religion; it is a side-product of the process by which history replaces theology as the main mode of organizing and understanding human experience.[4] Writers who continue what Harvey calls a 'monist' mode where 'metaphysical or final issues' arise and 'where a total commitment to one ideology is envisaged' may produce 'a *kind* of fiction – romance, fable, the novel of ideas', but not the central form.[5]

Recent critical theory, of course, has reversed many of the old orthodoxies about the novel. The origins of the genre have once again become a matter of considerable debate. Elements of romance from which the novel was once distinguished are now recognized to be endemic within the 'new' form. More crucially, contemporary criticism has come to recognize that 'realism' is itself essentially an illusion, the product of art. Post-modernist fictions that constantly stress their own artificiality have come now to replace the classic realist text as in a sense the definitive form.[6]

The image of international Roman Catholicism has itself undergone a dramatic change since the Second Vatican Council. The Church now pays far more respect to the individual conscience, and Catholic political perspectives have also been transformed. Yet for a long period the Catholic tradition had appeared powerfully authoritarian and reactionary, and it was understandable that it should be seen as set against all the social and political developments on which the genre of the novel was held to depend.

Of course Catholics all over the world have written fiction. A recent, very incomplete bibliography of 'The Catholic Novel' lists over seventeen hundred examples as well as a variety of criticism.[7] Despite what Orwell says, a case could be made for the view that the art and culture of the Catholic tradition actually make it a more fertile ground for the novel than other forms of Christianity.

Even in Britain, despite the minority status of the religion, Catholics and Catholicism have had a considerable presence in the fiction. When the *Sunday Times* ran a readers' poll in 1989 to find out what were regarded as the indispensable 'classic' fictions, three of the twelve works selected, for what it's worth, were by English Catholics: Evelyn Waugh's *Brideshead Revisited* (1945), Graham Greene's *The Power and the Glory* (1940) and Tolkien's *The Lord of the Rings* (1954–5).[8] The reputations of Waugh, Greene and Muriel Spark have

Introduction

never stood higher, and all three are regarded as the authors of specifically 'Catholic' novels for at least a part of their careers. Some very distinguished British Catholics have written fiction, including two cardinals, Wiseman and Newman. To the names already mentioned could be added Chesterton and Belloc, Maurice Baring, Frederick Rolfe (Baron Corvo), Compton Mackenzie, A. J. Cronin and Antonia White, for example. Among contemporaries there are George Mackay Brown, David Lodge, Piers Paul Read, Beryl Bainbridge, Alice Thomas Ellis. If the net were to be cast wider other major figures could be included. Ronald Firbank and Ford Madox Ford were converts. Joseph Conrad was certainly brought up as a Catholic. So was George Moore, though he had left the Church by the time most of his major fiction on Catholic subjects was written.

Problems of classification grow by the moment, however. There are different degrees and levels of commitment. Ford Madox Ford's period as a practising Catholic seems to have been brief, yet a socio-political version of Catholicism contributes to his quasi-feudal ideology. Even in his best-known works there is evidence of a certain inwardness with the experience of British Catholics. Anthony Burgess is another problematic case since he is not a Christian believer, yet claims that he has always written from a Catholic perspective. It is often forgotten that G. K. Chesterton on the other hand, an indisputably 'Catholic' writer, was not converted specifically to Roman Catholicism until 1922 after most of his novels had already been written.

Many attempts have been made to define 'the Catholic novel'. Albert J. Menendez in the bibliography referred to above takes any novel on a Catholic theme or subject, whether by a Catholic or not, to be a 'Catholic novel' (though he excludes anti-Catholic works). At the other extreme a group of influential critics work with a much more rigorist conception. In their view the Catholic novel properly so considered is a violently pessimistic work written in reaction against the humanist values of the modern world. The mode is seen as originating in the French Catholic revival of the late nineteenth century, which had pronounced decadent overtones, and held to continue in the works of George Bernanos, François Mauriac and in this country Graham Greene.[9]

It is obvious, however, that this very narrow definition does not tell the whole story. The works of such well-known Catholic writers as Compton Mackenzie and A. J. Cronin bear little relation to it. Catholicism is a rich and complex system, and there are many different ways of being a Catholic. The fiction naturally reflects this. I have tended towards the inclusive rather than the exclusive approach in what follows, and I have not made any pretence at absolute theoretical consistency in solving all the problems of classification. I take a Catholic novel to be one that deals with specifically Catholic themes or subject matter or indeed with any themes or subject matter from a distinctively Catholic perspective and with a sufficient degree of inwardness. It is often said that Catholicism is analogous to Judaism in that it is a sub-culture as well as a religion. Writers who have ceased to be practising Catholics may well retain a distinctively Catholic perspective (the 'Once a Catholic always a Catholic' principle), and I have seen no reason to exclude their works unless they have moved into outright hostility (as with George Moore's *The Lake* (1905), for example) or relative indifference (as seems to me the case with Conrad).[10] By the same token I have assumed that non-Catholics, even if very sympathetic, will not have been immersed in the emotional associations of Catholicism in the same way as those who have experienced it from within, and I have used their novels only as incidental illustrations of particular points.

Needless to say the word 'British' also presents its own problems of definition. Much of what I have to say specifically concerns the problems of *English* Catholicism – the paradox, for example, of an alien minority status that is also combined with the 'pervasive English snobbery' identified by Piers Paul Read.[11] The cultural situation of Northern Ireland is obviously a unique one, and Welsh Catholicism has little presence in English-language fiction. The context of Scottish Catholicism is also very different from the English version, but there are interesting analogies all the same. It would obviously be impossible to survey British Catholic fiction and ignore the contributions made by Compton Mackenzie, A. J. Cronin, Bruce Marshall, Muriel Spark and George Mackay Brown. I have included writers from Southern Ireland only when they have lived in England for a long period and written primarily on English rather than Irish themes. Similar criteria have led to the inclusion of several American expatriates such as Pearl Craigie (John Oliver Hobbes), Henry Harland and Anne Redmon.

It is as well to recognize that some commentators would deny any real unity to British Catholicism anyway, since it has undergone so many changes and consists of such different strands – 'at least four cliques all blackguarding each other half the time', according to Waugh's Sebastian Flyte.[12] Nor does any very clear intertextual tradition emerge either. Greene praises Rolfe, but the latter can hardly be said to have founded a literary school. Antonia White refers to Robert Hugh Benson's *The Conventionalists* (1908) at a significant point in *The Lost Traveller* (1950). Waugh makes more central use of a motif from Chesterton in *Brideshead Revisited* when Cordelia says that though half the family has left the faith:

> 'God won't let them go for long, you know. I wonder if you remember the story mummy read us the evening Sebastian first got drunk – I mean the *bad* evening. "Father Brown" said something like "I caught him" (the thief) "with an unseen hook and an invisible line which is long enough to let him wander to the ends of the world and still to bring him back with a twitch upon the thread."'[13]

Here certainly is a theme that echoes and re-echoes throughout Catholic fiction, and the oracular last phrase appropriately becomes the subtitle of the whole final section of the novel.

Later writers such as Gabriel Fielding, Piers Paul Read and David Lodge obviously reveal the influences of Waugh and Greene. Yet the distinctive form of the Catholic novel so beloved in critical discussion exists definitively in this country only in Greene's work and in a direct imitation such as Read's *The Upstart* (1973). Greene himself derives his specific Catholic mode much more directly from the French writers than from any English predecessors, though there are hints of anticipations in Benson, Rolfe and perhaps Ford Madox Ford.

Introduction

There remains, nevertheless, a wide range of material that shares certain characteristic themes and concerns, both general 'Catholic' ones and ones that seem to relate specifically to the situation of Catholics in this country. It is easy to overestimate the degree to which British Catholics have felt separated from British society and culture. According to the influential view of John Bossy, the main aspiration of the Catholic Church here has in fact been to achieve a respected status akin to one of the bigger nonconformist denominations.[14] Since the novelists have included far more converts and intellectuals than the Catholic community at large, the fiction has clearly been unrepresentative in that it is far more likely to reveal the use of Catholicism as an ideological weapon against the status quo. Yet, despite the truth in Bossy's view, there is no doubt that Catholics in Britain have also been accustomed to being thought of as an alien minority and that, with at least part of their minds, they have thought of themselves in this way too. In this sense, therefore, Catholic fiction is articulating, even if in exaggerated form, something of the experience of the whole community.

Catholicism has certainly opened novelists up to historical and international traditions otherwise closed to the British, and its art and symbolism have had a rich appeal. The popular Catholicism so beautifully described, for example, in Antonia White's *Frost in May* (1933) has itself proved, for all its defects, a mine of devotion, lyricism, humour and folklore. Above all it has come to provide an exotic yet at the same time oddly familiar lexicon of emotional allusion, as in Graham Greene:

> the plaster statues with the swords in the bleeding heart: the whisper behind the confessional curtains: the holy coats and the liquefaction of blood: the dark side chapels and the intricate movements, and somewhere behind it all the love of God.
> (*The Heart of the Matter*, 1948, 1950 reprint: 49)

Adrian Hastings has wryly observed that the British seem to believe that there is only one real religion, Roman Catholicism and that is wrong![15] Some Catholic writers have written purely for the edification of their own community, but those of any degree of aspiration have sought a non-Catholic audience as well, and they often exploit this ambivalent British fascination with the exotic religion that has its own fifth column here. As these novelists work and rework the perennial Catholic themes of suffering and death, sin and expiation, they do so with a special consciousness of writing in a Protestant and then increasingly a secular and materialist country, with its own new 'liturgy of big business, a rosary of abbreviations and percentages' (Beryl Bainbridge, *Another Part of the Wood*, 1968: 36). If their work is sometimes highly reactionary or melodramatic or shows signs of what has been termed a special 'Catholic neurosis', they still combat with vigour the archetypal British heresy of Pelagianism: the view that we are 'saved', so to speak, not so much by God's grace as by our own moral decency. In seeking to shake that complacency these novelists characteristically highlight paradoxes of grace and providence that subvert and transcend ordinary human morality.

The early American Catholic novelist Jedidiah Huntingdon asked rhetorically whether it might not be possible for 'romantic fiction' to be 'imbued with Catholic faith and morality, so as to serve the interests of religion?'[16] In seeking a wide audience to edify and proselytize, Catholic novelists have often thus adopted popular modes on the fringes of the more respectable novel. The use of supernatural material has sometimes led them to fantasy and fable, and the whole belief in providence has well-established implications for literary form. The minority position of Catholics here has itself contributed to a special rhetoric of exaggeration, and traditional Catholic preconceptions may sometimes overlap to a surprising extent with a fashionable modern self-consciousness about fiction. Writing about Muriel Spark, Malcolm Bradbury has commented that Catholics have contributed more than their proportionate share to aesthetic speculation in the English novel. Peter Ackroyd has also claimed recently that one legacy of a Catholic upbringing is a sense of the 'sacramental view of language. Chanting those Latin chants for your formative years is a great help when trying to write English prose. The greatest gift religion can give anybody is the use of language.'[17]

All these generalizations about Catholicism and formal factors in the novel – whether favourable or unfavourable – have to be treated with some caution, however, as we shall see. A variety of pressures have combined to lead many Catholic writers away from classic realism, and modern criticism is prepared to find a much wider range of these fictional modes acceptable and interesting. Yet many other Catholic novelists purport to write realistically but fail to develop convincing characterization and plot. There is no necessary link between this failure and Catholicism, but neither Catholicism nor postmodernist criteria can be used to justify it. At the same time there is no evidence to suggest that Catholics are somehow inherently incapable of writing well in the more realistic kinds. In these and in many other respects it proves illuminating to examine the major Catholic writers in the context of the host of lesser figures.

Part one
A chronological survey

· 1 ·

The nineteenth-century Catholic novel

The 'Second Spring'

The story of nineteenth-century British Catholicism is by any standards an astonishing one. The eighteenth-century Catholic community was small. Though its dormancy has been exaggerated, it was under financial pressure, often rural based, and inevitably quietist in ethos, at least after the end of Jacobitism as a viable option. As the perceptive novelist Josephine Mary Ward, herself the daughter of an 'old Catholic' aristocratic family, later pointed out, there was the danger that the 'enforced seclusion and inaction of penal days' would become ingrained, though a few upper-class laymen were already beginning to fight for legal emancipation.[1]

The first book with any real claims to be regarded as an English Catholic novel, Elizabeth Inchbald's highly readable *A Simple Story* (1791), dates from the latter part of this stage in the history of English Catholicism. Its author was a talented, politically radical actress, a remarkable woman who has recently received more of the critical attention that is her due.[2] Her own liberal views are apparent in the novel, for example, in the careful way she explains that her aristocratic priest hero Dorriforth 'nicely discriminated between the philosophical and the superstitious aspects of his role' (1967 edition: 3). Though Catholic motifs soon cease to be important, they are a source of great piquancy when Dorriforth has to take his young Protestant female ward into his house. When he succeeds unexpectedly to the family title, he is persuaded that it is his duty to marry her in order to keep the line Catholic. It was only such aristocratic and major gentry families that had possessed the wealth to pay the penal fines and provide protection for Catholics of lower status, and this, to modern eyes, extraordinary decision that Dorriforth should marry is a mark of how crucial the role of such families was held to be.

A Simple Story shows that eighteenth-century English Catholicism differed markedly in many other ways as well from what later came to seem the definitive forms of the religion. Dorriforth is always called 'Mr', for example, and does not wear clerical dress. The latter and the title 'Father', now taken for granted, were in fact nineteenth-century innovations into British Catholicism by those who admired Italianate modes. Edward Norman captures the mood of the earlier era well, commenting on the Catholic chapels that began to be built after the mid-eighteenth century:

> There was an absence of statues, votive lights, or almost any other ornament. Incense was rare, and so was reservation of the Blessed Sacrament and devotions to the saints. The atmosphere of the religion within was also peculiarly adapted to the Age of Reason: the emphasis was on benevolence, just as in the eighteenth-century Anglican Church, and the tone was pietistic.[3]

The social provenance of English Catholicism was already beginning to change before the end of the century, however. The middle-class element was still small, but it was increasing, and the focus was becoming more urban. The effects of Irish immigration were beginning to make themselves felt. Clerical influence over the community was also growing. Yet Grace Kennedy can still write in 1823 in her novel *Father Clement*:

> The Roman Catholic traveller would sigh as he remembered that in Britain his Church is almost forgotten, her places of worship in ruins, or stripped of the character they once bore, now dedicated to another faith; her services regarded as unmeaning ceremonies; her doctrines held as too absurd to be professed by rational men.[4]

She overstates the case no doubt, but it is clear that such a religion represents no threat to the prevailing ethos, or at any rate no *corporate* threat.

Cardinal Wiseman wrote with pardonable exaggeration that the Catholic Emancipation Act of 1829 'was to us what the egress from the catacombs was to the early Christians.'[5] The Act was more the result of the pressures of the Irish situation than of increased tolerance in England, and it was not, of course, passed without bitter opposition and controversy. Nor did it cause an immediate revolution in habits. Many pious Catholics, as Josephine Ward indicates, were to continue their isolation from the mainstream of British life for a long time to come. But the increased access of at least some Catholics to the public world had an obvious effect both on British Catholics themselves and on the popular conception of them.[6]

An aesthetic and cultural interest in Catholicism had meanwhile been growing in some circles because of the cult of medievalism, which had been encouraged by the popularity of the novels of Sir Walter Scott. In other respects too Victorian criticism was helping to foster a wider recognition of the Catholic Church's achievements in the arts, and this was bound to generate sympathy, even if many of its symptoms were only superficial. In a marvellous exchange in *Barchester Towers* (1857), for example, the artist Bertie Stanhope shocks the new low-church bishop by announcing that he has always personally been more attracted to Rome.

Medievalism in its profoundest sense was responsible for a trickle of conversions to Catholicism that occurred long before the main wave: the architect Welby Pugin, Sir Kenelm Digby and Ambrose Phillips de Lisle among others. The cultural significance of these conversions far outweighed the actual numbers involved, for the romantic 'Gothic' sentiment that led here into Catholicism was no mere fad of antiquarianism. Especially in its most directly political formulation in the work of Digby, who was influenced by the theories of John Lingard and William Cobbett about the baleful social effects of the Reformation, this movement confronts and challenges the contemporary world in the interests of an aggressive and critical return to the Catholic past.[7] But characteristic ideological traps and dilemmas reveal themselves already in this first of many versions of a self-consciously Catholic critique of modern English society. Broadly speaking, both the conventional 'old Catholic' emphasis of the eighteenth century and the rarer 'liberal' approach that is sometimes found then as well seem to yield too much to the prevailing ethos of contemporary English society, whether by an unchallenging withdrawal or a degree of accommodation. But the nostalgic myth of the past developed by the English Catholic converts who make up this Gothic party raises the question of how to distinguish an authentic Christian condemnation of 'the world' from an ideologically motivated rejection of modern developments as such.

As is well known, three major factors combined to change the whole picture of English Catholicism after the mid-century: the massive scale of the Irish immigrations, the restoration of the hierarchy in 1850 and the influence of the Oxford Movement conversions. The enormous increase in the Catholic population and the expansion in church building were almost entirely the result of the Irish influx. They made up approximately four-fifths of the total number of Catholics in Victorian England. Frederick Faber wrote with alarm in 1849, 'The Irish are swamping us; they are rude and unruly and after many complaints the Catholic tradesmen are leaving us.'[8]

Astonishingly in one way, predictably perhaps in another, this Irish presence was almost completely ignored by the novelists, themselves, of course, upper or middle class in background. The sole exception is the sentimental work *Poverty and the Baronet's Family, A Catholic Novel* (1845) by the early pre-Oxford-Movement convert Henry Digby Beste. When the head of the O'Meara family is drowned saving the life of a baronet's son, the other members are left destitute. But they eventually rise to social acceptance in England through their virtue and innate gentility, proving in the end to be dispossessed members of the native Irish Catholic aristocracy.

The restoration of the hierarchy created a high profile for Catholicism and was the subject of considerable controversy for several years. The presence of a cardinal in the heart of Protestant London had an inevitable impact on consciousness and both Wiseman and his successor Manning were in their different ways extremely formidable men with an enormous sense of the dignity of their position. Both were strong ultramontane supporters of papal authority and admirers of Italianate devotions. Their efforts were assisted by the new religious orders and the popular genius of Faber, an Anglican convert with a gift for writing fervently emotional hymns, and these influences combined to bring about a considerable degree of centralization and uniformity in the religious practices of the Catholic populace.

The extravagant devotions and attire of the new orders at first displeased the old Catholics. The distinguished priest-historian John Lingard asks 'how to send away those swarms of Italian congregationists who introduce their own customs here and by making religion *ridiculous* in the eyes of Protestants *prevent it spreading here*'?[9] Certainly the new modes made it easier for the enemies of Catholicism such as Archbishop Benson of Canterbury to portray it as the 'Italian mission'. The influence of the small Gothic party that had claimed to look back to true English ways was inevitably swamped. But the danger that the Irish, the converts and the old Catholics would remain three totally separate groups was a very real one. Beste complained from his own experience that the old Catholics did not welcome converts: 'These people have been oppressed, and depressed, and compressed together, till they are incapable of sympathy for any who are not of their old coterie and connection.'[10] The imposition of even a superficial degree of uniformity served eventually to bind the community together and to give the Irish immigrants at least elements of a common Catholic culture with the English.

It was important too that both Wiseman and Manning believed in the possibility of and indeed the necessity for the conversion of England. The transfer from Anglicanism to Catholicism may seem to our more secular and ecumenical age a trivial matter of theological minutiae. Many conversions were doubtless for such highly technical reasons. But the attack on the Church of England's liberalism and problems about authority could in some cases have deep ideological significance as a rejection of the Victorian establishment. In Manning in particular doctrinal and devotional ultramontanism combined with a critique of the ethos of modern Protestant England, including its unjust patterns of privilege, though little of this found its way into fiction until the last decades of the century.

Still, the Catholic presence in the land could no longer be ignored now, and the presentation of Catholicism as a powerful alternative set of values was helped by the highlighting of very obvious external differences. Several of the conversion novels indicate, for example, that Anglicans found a special impressiveness about the service of Benediction, a ceremony fostered by the Italian party and quite unlike anything in the contemporary Church of England.[11]

Early fiction: histories and conversion stories

The evangelistic ambitions of the restored hierarchy had a specifically literary impact when Cardinal Wiseman himself wrote the popular historical novel *Fabiola* (1854), a tale of the early Christian martyrs, and commissioned a whole series of Catholic historical novels that included the more distinguished work *Callista* (1856) by John Henry Newman. But the English Catholics had neither been permitted nor had permitted themselves to partake fully in English cultural life. From their ranks had appeared beautiful books of devotion and even distinguished works of scholarship, but the later attacks upon their cultural and intellectual standards by novelists such as Edmund Randolph and Frederick Rolfe were not without foundation. Wiseman's own novel was enormously popular, but the cultural conditions for writing novels or providing much of a readership for them were only just beginning to exist.

It was obviously the mid-century Oxford-Movement conversions that made all the difference to the literary culture of English Catholics. They were accompanied by and generated an enormous degree of heart-searching and heartbreak, and they were soon reflected in a mass of novels dealing with the subject of conversion and the controversies and apologetics associated therewith.[12]

The greatest convert, Newman, of course towers above his contemporaries as a theologian, and his total intellectual importance can hardly be overestimated. His theology provides a model for combining the timeless elements of Christianity with a proper sense of change, and it is scarcely an exaggeration to say that his role in modern Catholicism is analogous to those of St Augustine or St Thomas Aquinas in the medieval Church. Yet his attempt to reconcile major elements of reason and romanticism also gives him a central place in English Victorian thought. As is widely accepted, he is the only British Catholic thinker to provide not only a critique of the central Victorian synthesis but also an intellectual alternative that is neither backward-looking nor modishly liberal.[13]

His own two novels *Loss and Gain* (1848) and *Callista* hardly occupy a major place in his work, but they show something at least of his gifts and his intellectual pre-eminence. *Loss and Gain*, though a fictionalization of his own conversion, succeeds in transcending both autobiography and apologetics and is able to combine a genuine sense of emotional suffering with elements of the Peacockian novel of ideas. Instead of attacking the work by the standards of realism, as some critics have done, it is surely better to recognize its brilliance as a hybrid form.[14] Some of the debate the characters engage in is admittedly so detailed and technical that no one could possibly have spoken like that even in Oxford in the middle of the Oxford Movement, but Newman often manages to make these discussions entertaining and amusing, and some aspects of Anglicanism are treated with masterly satiric wit. At the same time, the novel is a moving demonstration of the personal cost of conversion in terms of career and place in society. Manning is clearer about the political dimension of such a rejection than Newman, but the latter leaves the reader in no doubt that conversion involves the personal but also representative renunciation of a whole comfortable ethos. As his hero Reding is told by a Catholic,

> Do not be offended if I suggest to you that the dearest and closest ties, such as your connexion with the Protestant Church involves, may be on the side of the world in certain cases. It is a sort of martyrdom to have to break such; but they who do so have a martyr's reward. And then, at a University you have so many inducements to fall in with the prevailing tone of thought; prospects, success in life, good opinion of friends – all these things are against you.
>
> (1869 reprint: 105)

Callista also concerns a conversion, though in the very different setting of third-century Africa. It tells the story of a beautiful Greek pagan woman, attracted by Christianity but not convinced that it is anything more than a lovely dream and deeply reluctant to give up the family customs of her old religion. She is arrested for helping to shelter Christians and, although by no means yet a believer herself, refuses to sacrifice to the Emperor. Eventually she is converted and baptized in prison and goes to her martyrdom.

Historical fiction, as Wiseman saw, provided the opportunity of combining apologetics with entertainment. It is fair to say, though, that Newman handles the genre far better than his predecessor. Both writers parallel the persecution of the early Christians with attitudes to Catholicism in Victorian England, but *Fabiola* is much more melodramatic in its treatment of the sufferings of the martyrs. Yet Newman's relative restraint does not preclude emotional interest and suspense. His well-known conviction that religious assent comes from the deeper levels of the mind seems to provide an imaginative aesthetic for a novel of conversion that helps keep intellectual and emotional elements in balance.

Newman, to be sure, is just as concerned as his predecessor with the apologetical purpose of showing the continuity of the Church of Rome with the early Church. The Mass is essentially the same, and he refers to 'the Blessed Sacrament'. Yet he is more nuanced than Wiseman, less purely and directly anachronistic. To take one tiny but revealing example, he explains at one point that priests already wore vestments kept for the special purpose of Mass rather than their normal daily clothing, but he is careful to add the qualification that these garments were not as much '*sui generis*' as they later became.[15] The seeds of the future are present in the past, but what we see is the development of doctrine and practice rather than a completely anti-historical identification of the modern Church with the ancient.

Significant though these details are theologically, they can hardly, of course, be said to add to the liveliness of the novel. But if there are places where Newman sounds like a liturgical and doctrinal textbook, there are other famous passages of high drama such as the description of the locust storm. Overall, Newman is much more successful than Wiseman in incorporating historical learning without sounding pedestrian, but at the same time the historical perspective helps to distance the book from the more obviously autobiographical elements of *Loss and Gain*.

Most of the rest of this first generation of conversion novels concern themselves with arid apologetics and the narrow confessional arguments between Roman Catholics and high Anglicans. The heavy-handed introduction of theological technicalities into fiction is amusingly illustrated in a passage Margaret Maison quotes from a conversion novel by E. C. Agnew, 'When he [the priest] informed her that the same Divine Being, of whose perfections they had discoursed on the preceding evening, would in the three persons of His essential unity descend on her soul in Baptism, Lilia immediately inquired, "By particles, or emanation?"'[16]

Romance and popularization

Such technical details were perhaps to be expected when the converts of this first generation were themselves mainly clergymen or ordinands, but the second generation came from a much wider range of backgrounds that included society ladies and professional men. These converts and the growing middle-class element among the native Catholics together formed the nucleus of a novel-reading public. The new audience sought entertainment as well as edification, and all the issues were increasingly popularized. The fluent novels of Lady Georgiana Fullerton, for example, included stories of conversion like *Mrs Gerald's Niece* (1869) as well as an historical novel of the Elizabethan period, *Constance Sherwood* (1865).

These two main genres began to intertwine themselves more and more with the staples of Victorian romance and sensationalist fiction: foundlings and inheritance struggles, melodramatic villains, emotional reconciliations and death-bed repentances. The Italianate popular piety and eucharistic devotions fostered by Faber and others proved to overlap well with the techniques of sentimental fiction. It is the eucharist and the saintly death of Eulalie in Agnes Stewart's *Eustace, or Self-Devotion* (1860), for example, that finally converts Madame St Aubert, 'an infidel to the heart's core':

> Madame kneels at the foot of the bed, and bends in lowly adoration, and under sacramental veils she acknowledges and feels as in times gone past, that wondrous mystery of the presence of the Lord. I hear that smothered sob, I know that the pride of her infidel heart is shook; that the prayers of the dying girl have been born to heaven by its own bright angel; that the incense of her sweet example hath saved a soul.
>
> (190–1)

A similarly romantic and sentimental piety is cultivated in the works of Cecilia M. Caddell, who writes of Christ and His mother at the crucifixion, for example, as: 'He bleeding away his life for the love of man, she with the sword of sorrow in her bosom, and both so sorrowful, and all for us!' (*Home and the Homeless*, 1858, 1; 138). M. C. Bishop attempts a theological justification for this emotional tone itself. In her *Elizabeth Eden* (1878) the heroine's conversion is encouraged by falling in love with a Catholic millionaire, and he says to her:

> Ah, my Eve, my darling, we have to be thankful for emotional theology. Emotion, love, if you like so to name the main emotion, moves on the face of inanimate creation, and again it is very good. Leave negation and scepticism, and live the full life for which you have faculties.
>
> (III, 213)

As with several of the works already mentioned, the theme of conversion is often linked instead with the renunciation of earthly love and the flesh. In what Margaret Maison calls this 'heroine-lover-faith triangle,' however, pious messages can themselves easily enter into alliance with prurience, sensationalism and masochism. A sub-theme of the complex is adulterous love, a major theme anyway in the English novel, as Tony Tanner has shown, and one highlighted by Catholic motifs such as the sanctity of marriage and the well-known over-concentration on sexual ethics.[17] The usual way that Catholic novelists of this time choose to treat this potentially very explicit topic is, naturally enough, to exclude actual adultery and describe an idealistic, highly romantic love that an unhappily married Catholic still has to renounce. Lady Georgiana Fullerton's *Ladybird* (1853), for example, tells the story of its heroine Gertrude's love for Adrien d'Arberg. When she hears that he has entered a Catholic seminary she marries Maurice in despair, but she has been misinformed. Maurice dies, but by then Adrien has decided to become a Jesuit missionary and Gertrude works among the poor to expiate the sin of her undue attachment to him.

Rather less rigidly proper and pious in tone are the works of the American expatriate, Catholic convert and divorcee Pearl Craigie [John Oliver Hobbes], whose novels were the first by a Catholic to receive much attention in the non-Catholic literary world. George Moore once claimed to have kicked her in Hyde Park in frustration at a rejection, and her own novels obsessively work and rework the theme of the renunciation of earthly love. In the two most ambitious works *The School for Saints* (1897) and *Robert Orange* (1900) Robert, whose father was a renegade priest, falls in love with the beautiful young Brigit, who is married to an evil man. The apparent death of her husband leaves them free to marry, but on their honeymoon before the marriage has been consummated they hear that he is still alive. At a terrible cost of self-sacrifice they renounce each other. Later the husband really dies, but not before Robert has decided to enter the priesthood and Brigit has to renounce him for a second time.

The subtlest Victorian Catholic novel of the renunciation of earthly love is *One Poor Scruple* (1899), by Josephine Mary Ward, whose account of the Riversdale family has already been quoted. The widow Madge Riversdale, a lukewarm Catholic, is finally prevented from breaking the rules of her faith and marrying the immensely rich divorcee, Lord Bellasis, by the influence of her sister-in-law Mary, who herself becomes a nun. No plot summary can do justice to the impressive psychological realism and restraint of this work. As Bernard Bergonzi points out, it also conveys a vivid sense of its period. The Catholic characters have to treat with the *fin de siécle* intellectual Mark Fieldes, modelled on W. H. Mallock and Pater, and the 'new woman' figure of Cecilia Rupert.[18] There is a sense, indeed, in which *One Poor Scruple* enacts, if only in part deliberately, the history of nineteenth-century British Catholicism as a whole. In experiencing a wider social world the Riversdales encounter the new temptations that begin with Catholic Emancipation. They also encounter in Fieldes and Cecilia Rupert the intellectual pressures on belief that became so widespread in the latter part of the century.

New challenges and confrontations

For Catholic fiction throughout the main run of this period had been based on the presupposition that Christianity itself was completely unassailable. What are put forward as the essential issues are the confessional debate about whether Roman Catholicism or Anglicanism is the true faith or the personal dilemmas of sexual ethics. By now, though, it was becoming difficult even for the most pious of conservatives to ignore the fact that the situation had changed. As every account of the period indicates, the work of Darwin, Lyell and the German critics was calling into question the very bases of orthodox biblical faith, and scepticism could be seen to have made clear inroads into sections of British society and culture.[19]

As is also well known, other enormous pressures – social, political and economic – were meanwhile threatening the foundations of Victorian confidence. Violent trade cycles afflicted the British economy from the 1870s and industrial unrest intensified. The influence of socialist and other radical movements spread throughout Europe, and more conventional Victorian ideas about the role of women (which it had been in the interests of some writers to present as a complete consensus on the subject) were much more widely questioned.[20]

A very different symptom of change and unease which was also much remarked upon at the time was the extraordinary growth of interest in psychic phenomena.[21] As Browning memorably shows in 'Mr Sludge the Medium' (*Dramatis Personae*, 1864), the enthusiasm for spiritualism itself was intense, but this was only one aspect of a more general revival of occultism. The Theosophical Society was founded in 1875 and the Society for Psychical Research in 1882, and visionaries such as Madame Blavatsky became fashionable gurus. If all this represents in one sense a movement away from scientism and complacent materialism it is nevertheless a spiritual search to which mainstream Christianity remains largely irrelevant.

Armed with the Church's traditional lore, Catholic novelists obviously feel more prepared to speak on such topics than to deal with the far more fundamental political pressures. The pious Lady Georgiana Fullerton's hero D'Arberg discusses mesmerism as early as 1853 in *Ladybird*:

> that mysterious subject which can no longer be treated with ridicule, but as is still as far as ever from any satisfactory solution; which baffles so many theories, opens a door as it were into another kind of existence; shows glimpses of a mode of being, an agency of the senses, and a whole order of natural laws or supernatural effects which are well calculated to confound man's reason, to humble his presumption, to alarm his scruples, and to suggest the exclamation of Hamlet, 'There are more things in heaven and earth than we dream of in our philosophy.'
>
> (II: 23)

Nevertheless he sternly forbids the experiment. To Catholic writers these interests may be positive in so far as they are the symptoms of a hunger, but they are also dangerous and misguided. Edward Dering's hero says in *The Ban of Mablethorpe* (1894) that 'Human hearts, when they are not frozen by intellectual pride, long for something beyond the perishable: and if you deprive them of the supernatural, they turn to the preternatural' (p. 43).

The more general political and religious crisis was for a long time ignored. It was the message of Edmund Randolph's extraordinary novel *Mostly Fools, A Romance of Civilisation* (1886) that the Church had tragically failed to take its opportunity of providing an authoritative answer amidst the new scepticism and social problems. An eccentric American tells the hero prophetically, 'there ain't more than two religions in the future, belief and disbelief. If belief is to stand, you Christians must join hands' (I: 134). Unfortunately, in an 'age of infidelity the Church did nothing.' 'Brought up in a quaint and dangerous asceticism of thought,' English Catholics were 'turned out upon a world of which they were as ignorant as babes' (I: 70).

In the field of politics likewise the Church, according to Randolph, had fallen under a 'fatal transcendentalism':

Protestantism in all its forms stood painfully disintegrated. You had, side by side, a religious organisation, a Church – the great Church of history; the one human society which shrinks from the solution of no human problem as too difficult, which holds in its laboratory a remedy for every evil to which the social flesh is heir: and yet at this time of crucial moment it came forward with none. Its followers, instead of leading by the extra light in which they were so fortunate as to bask, groped blindly at the tail of events; no matter of state reform, no single item of the national progress has ever owed its initiative to them . . .

(II: 92)

There is much truth in these indictments. Yet, by the time Randolph was writing, some of these issues were being faced, if belatedly and piecemeal. The very specifically confessional topic of the Papal States was the first political matter to receive much attention among Catholic novelists, but it soon became a symbol of the whole confrontation of the old Christian order with modern political forces. Pius IX, at first regarded as a liberal pope, had been forced to flee from Rome in 1848 and a republic was briefly established. The Pope was soon restored, but the Papal States and then Rome itself, apart from the 'prison' of the Vatican, were later to be lost to the royalist forces.

Most Catholics found themselves on the opposite side to the liberal British consensus on the subject. One of E. H. Dering's heroes announces in *The Ban of Mablethorpe* (1894) that 'Christian Rome has been in the hands of worse than vandals, ever since it was taken by the foulest treachery that ever disgraced a crowned head' (I, 70). Another in *Sherborne* (1875) goes to join the papal regiments. A cardinal tells an English socialist in William Barry's *Arden Massiter* (1900) that the Vatican has been robbed by the Italian government and that now it has no more than the 'patrimony of the poor' left to it (p. 17).

J. Richard Beste's *Modern Society in Rome* (1856) on the other hand is a detailed, liberal Catholic novel on the subject, with sympathy both for the Pope and Garibaldi and with the hope that the Pope would reform the papal government and come to accept a lay constitution and democracy. Even on this very specific issue it was possible for Catholics to take different views, but liberal Catholics were obviously in a small minority, and life became more difficult for them after this time because of Pius IX's own reaction.

Yet Dering returns obsessively to the topic, most notably in the portrait of Augustus Twerlby in *The Ban of Mablethorpe*, whose disciple Fetherhed comes fortunately to realize at the eleventh hour 'what a beastly sneaking thing it is to be a liberal Catholic!' (196). All Dering's villains are sceptics, liberals and political radicals, and it is in his novels and in the historical novels of William McCabe that the battle lines for the war between Christianity and all the rising forces of secularism, popularism and socialism are most clearly drawn. It is the central thrust of Dering's whole work that the only hope for a true conservative social order, as the convert hero in *Sherborne* says, lies now in Catholicism, since the Church of England, which once at least contributed to stability, is in disarray. But Twerlby's allies in the conspiracy are Madame Diabloski and the General Foreigner: 'ill-bred manners under an oily surface, greenish grey eyes powerful by force of malice, a black beard closely cut and a fixed expression of evil purpose' (26). The struggle here is only a microcosm of the international one for, horrifyingly, 'The Catholic sovereigns of Europe threw off the fear of God, and let the monster [Revolution] escape them' (55).

Edmund Randolph is absolutely at the opposite end of the political spectrum, and *Mostly Fools* develops from a satire on the inward-looking eccentricities of English Catholicism into a panoramic political novel. The hero becomes an MP for an Irish constituency and the leader of what amounts to a Catholic party. But the appointment of an unsympathetic Archbishop of Westminster makes his position untenable. He disappears into the wilderness, but when he reappears it is, in an extraordinary development, as the leader of a small South American republic. He brings in a radical tax system and his country becomes a vast empire through his inspired leadership. In this period the Church had arisen 'like a phoenix' throughout the world 'in countries where she was of the people' (III: 234). Where 'she had become a fallen thing in the hands of a clique, she was barely able to hold up her head again.'

Despite Randolph's own complaints, these political issues have finally come to the fore. Pearl Craigie's *Robert Orange*, for all its theme of sexual renunciation, has much more ambitious purposes too. It attempts, like Randolph, nothing less than a comprehensive panorama of the politics and ethos of the Victorian age, including a sympathetic portrayal of Disraeli himself, for Orange is an important political figure in his own right with the potential to reach the highest office. When Orange becomes a Catholic Craigie is suggesting that the ultimate solution to the problems of the age will only be found in Catholicism, because, as Disraeli himself is made to say to the hero, 'you will find nowhere out of Rome poetry and the spirit of democracy and a reverence for authority all linked together in one irrefrangible chain' (115).

The late Victorian novels of Canon William Barry confront both the political issues and the crisis of faith with some subtlety of thought, though in a very sensational tone. Although the portrayal of the socialist revolutionaries in *The New Antigone* (1887) is absurd, the English socialist Arden Massiter in the novel of that name is a sympathetic figure who hopes that the Church will follow the precepts of the Sermon on the Mount and come to side with the poor. Though old confessional issues are revived in a heavy satire on Protestantism in *The Two Standards* (1898) the attack spreads out to include the whole of modern materialism and capitalism. By now the existence of free-thinkers and agnostics has finally been recognized and the theme of conversion has therefore itself had to expand.[22] In *The New Antigone* the beautiful feminist Hippolyta is not a religious believer at all, and Barry portrays her as being converted to a realization of the ill consequences of her commitment to free love after she sees the lives of the London poor. In the end she becomes a nun.

The extremism of Barry's solution of Hippolyta, of course, reflects the anxiety that the 'new woman' created. Mark Fields comments on Cecilia Rupert in Ward's *One Poor Scruple*: 'We have not known many women who held nothing to be sacred but their own happiness. We shall get to know them, Lady L. Twenty years hence you and I may have met many other Cecilias' (p. 355). Cecilia herself later commits suicide. The portrait is not without compassion and even sympathy, however, and Barry's Hippolyta is herself a noble and idealistic figure who has to be put on the right track rather than a wicked fallen woman. More predictably M. C. Bishop reminds her readers in *Elizabeth Eden* that it is in the marriage service that the Catholic Church shows 'its recognition of woman's large place in the order of society' (p. 264).

The more interesting of the late Victorian Catholic writers are at least aware of the new issues. The ambitions of Craigie in *Robert Orange*, Randolph, Dering and Barry all show in their very different ways a widening of themes in the Catholic novel and a direct recognition of the scepticism and the new progressive politics of the time. They present Catholicism as the sole solution to modern problems, the only way of preventing the triumph of revolution or, in a rarer emphasis, as the only true route to social justice.

This period also saw the most extreme refraction of Victorian aestheticism and the most exhibitionist way of opposing bourgeois Victorian values, the *fin de siècle* movement. The appeal of the Roman Church in such circles is well known. Lionel Johnson and Ernest Dowson, Aubrey Beardsley, John Gray and eventually Wilde himself were all converts. Despite the extreme moral respectability of Victorian Catholicism the Church was seen as attractively exotic and unpuritanical, and a certain Catholic privileging of suffering had its own masochistic attraction.

In France the decadent movement contributed through the work of Huysmans to the powerful Catholic literary revival, and to what has seemed to critics the definitive mode of the Catholic novel, a violent and romantic reaction against the modern world with a powerfully conservative political bias. In England the influence remains a relatively superficial one, at least in the novel. The earlier works of Pearl Craigie and the sentimental novels of Henry Harland reflect only the lighter side of the 1890s mood in tone, atmosphere and setting. Early in the next century Robert Hugh Benson shows curious signs of decadent interests in the midst of his novels of edification. John Gray, *fin de siècle* poet, once the friend and presumed lover of Wilde, was later, as a Catholic priest, to write the future fantasy *Park* (1932). Only in the work of Benson's former friend Frederick Rolfe are 1890s and decadent impulses taken up into Catholicism but also made part of a confrontation with the culture and ethos of his contemporary world in an analogous way to the French writers.

But Rolfe's work remains totally idiosyncratic. From the late Victorian period on Catholic writers have come to confront the pressures of a more secular age, but they do so in a much less intense and less corporate way than in France.

A final specifically theological reflection of the Church's problematic relationship with the modern age, the new science and biblical criticism, is the so-called modernist crisis at the end of the century. Edward Norman defines 'modernism' as 'the attempt by some Catholic scholars to apply historical and scientific knowledge to Biblical criticism, and to seek to claim for intellectual enquiry, and the methods by which it is conducted, a measure of autonomy from ecclesiastical authority.'[23] Yet Catholicism in many respects found it easier to deal with the new thinking than Protestants did. George Moore's Monsignor Mostyn in *Sister Theresa* (1901) and W. H. Mallock's Father Stanley in *The Old Order Changes* (1886) are presented as admired examples of successful accommodation (though neither author, admittedly, was a Catholic at the time of writing). The papal reaction early this century against such trends was obviously an extreme one. It is by no means easy therefore to define the exact shifts by which liberalism may be said to have shaded over into modernism or to know which figures to categorize as full or partial modernists in England. Mivart and George Tyrrell were among those who had to leave the Church and Lord Acton and von Hügel were regarded with grave suspicion as extreme liberals.

The matter took some of its urgency in this country from the fact that the idea that Anglican liberalism was selling the pass had been the cause of many conversions to Rome, the home of true orthodoxy and authority. Liberal Anglicanism has been a fruitful theme for Catholic satire all the way from the nineteenth century through Ronald Knox and Evelyn Waugh's Mr Prendergast to Alice Thomas Ellis. M. C. Bishop's *Elizabeth Eden* provides a typical example when the Rev. Christopher Harley is described as giving 'gentlemanlike assent to the elaborate and scientific religion which, with whatever mortal power he had, he endeavoured to adapt to the latest currents of thought' (II: 113). The fear that the enemy was also now inside the gates is partly what causes Edward Dering's extraordinary fury at liberal Catholics. Edmund Randolph on the other hand appears to have been the rare genuine article of a full-fledged modernist himself. His hero Roland Tucker explains that:

> The religion of the multitude was a childish thing, sufficient perhaps, and all they were capable of. But he knew that in the Church were many high and holy souls who penetrated these forms, these arcana and symbols, and faced the essential truths unveiled.
> (*Mostly Fools*, III: 203)

In *Out of Due Time* (1906) Josephine Mary Ward provides a relatively sympathetic account of Count Paul d'Estranges who falls into modernism and is condemned by the Church, partly through his own fault and partly through the machinations of the 'ultra party', who accuse Paul of being a freemason.

The narrator-heroine is engaged to marry Paul, but eventually breaks with him when he leaves the Church. The author attempts from this perspective a balance of orthodoxy and compassion:

> I think it must be – it is surely right – that the subtle distinctiveness of the Catholic mind should be easily made anxious as to what is new, or human nature being what it is, it might fall in love with every novelty. But to those whose whole duty is to go forward, and especially to the women who must be with them . . . what subtle tortures may be applied.
>
> (p. 134)

Modernism has a high profile in ecclesiastical history but even those who might be considered its fellow travellers made up no more than a tiny minority. In the debate between the modern world and Catholicism it clearly represents an extreme wing of accommodation, but it is of more significance ultimately for the reaction it provoked than in itself. The encyclical *Pascendi* of 1907 put an apparent end to its influence. As a consequence, as we shall see, a rigidification of doctrine and an increased centralization became so pervasive in Roman Catholicism as to be regarded as its very essence by friends and foes alike. The tendency for Catholic criticism of the modern world to be ultramontane and reactionary in form was strengthened, and the suspicion of modernism delayed the influence of Newman's potentially more fruitful model for a hundred years.

· 2 ·

Catholic fiction 1900–45

The Church and Catholic writers in a new secular era: 1900–18

Ford Madox Ford's fable *Mr Apollo, A Just Possible Story* (1908) vividly castigates the unimaginative secularism of the Edwardian era, portrayed as the logical development of Victorian free-thinking and sociological changes that Ford hated. A manifestation of the god Apollo is ignored and misunderstood, so that a well-known newspaper editor, for example, chooses to run a series on popular occultism instead. At the end the god destroys large numbers of the packed houses of the urban proletariat in order to let in light for his favoured disciples to live.

Ford obviously reflects from his own scathingly élitist perspective here various anxieties that were widespread in the new era, despite its apparent stability – worries about the effects of industrialization, the condition of the urban poor, and the growing influence of the mass press. Clearly though, his central preoccupation is the alarming growth of religious scepticism, and again this concern was widespread. C. F. G. Masterman wrote in his influential *Condition of England* (1909) that 'Belief in religion, as a conception of life dependent upon supernatural sanctions or as a revelation of a purpose and meaning beyond the actual business of the day, is slowly but surely fading from the modern city race.'[1]

Ford comments in *Mr Apollo* that groups of young people came to the Milnes's house to discourse 'of Hygiene, of Aesthetics, a little of music, a great deal of Socialism, hardly at all of Religion.' Yet he makes an exception for Roman Catholicism, adding 'but then with a frenzied animation, for several were Roman Catholics, and charged the deniers of Romish miracles with lack of perception, of logic, and the historic sense' (p. 93).

Ford's own stance in *Mr Apollo* is theistic and supernaturalist rather than specifically Christian, but he was himself a Catholic convert. Though his actual religious allegiance seems to have been no more than nominal, his cultural and socio-political reaction against the modern world was given a particular form by his Catholicism, and his early work presents 'the old feudalism and the old union of Christendom beneath a spiritual headship' as an ideal norm.[2] His historical trilogy *The Fifth Queen* (1906–8) in particular focuses on the clash between an old Catholic order and the new secularism represented by Thomas Cromwell.

Ford is certainly correct in emphasizing in *Mr Apollo* that Catholicism was flourishing despite signs of increasing secularism in society at large.[3] 'Whatever churches were empty in Britain,' thinks Father Smith in a complacent retrospective mood in Bruce Marshall's *All Glorious Within* (1941), 'the Catholic churches were always full' (1945 reprint: 172), and this had been true for many years. Catholic numbers were continuing to rise, and the special English Catholic paradox of an alien quality combined with élite and even establishment favour was very apparent in the Edwardian period with the role of influential Catholic peers and the interest and sympathy of the king himself: ' . . . the bishop asked Father Smith if he had heard the rumour that King Edward VII had been to Lourdes and knelt during the procession of the Blessed Sacrament. Father Smith said that he had heard all sorts of rumours about King Edward VII, but never one quite like that.' (p. 33)

Meanwhile the potential readership for novels had been growing both among Catholics and the public at large. Despite or perhaps because of the increased secularism the popular taste for religiosity remained high, and, as always, it was the trappings of Catholicism that held the greatest appeal in sensationalist popular fiction.

A steamy novel by Robert Hitchens called *The Garden of Allah*, for example, was an enormous best-seller in 1905. It told the story of the love affair and marriage of a beautiful Catholic aristocrat with a man who, unknown to her, is a renegade Trappist monk. Eventually they give each other up and he returns to his monastery. His frustrated yearning for women is sensationally conveyed, but it is the combination of this with the overblown religious emotionalism of the book that created its appeal.[4]

The novels of the priest writer John Ayscough (Monsignor Bickerstaffe-Drew), if certainly not sensational in the same way as *The Garden of Allah*, are also essentially romances: extravagant with gipsy fortune tellers in *Dromina* (1908), gentler in the best-known work *San Celestino* (1909), the story of the medieval hermit who became pope. Escapist in a different manner again is another popular success of the time, *The Cardinal's Snuff Box* (1900) by the American expatriate Henry Harland. Here Italian Catholics seem to consist entirely of aristocrats like the wise old cardinal and his beautiful niece or of pretty peasant children who are the objects of sentimental piety: 'Oh, I am sure, I am sure, it was the Blessed Virgin herself who sent us across their path, in answer to that poor little creature's prayers' (p. 95). The politics are right-wing but with an almost Firbankian feeling of self-parody at times, as in the idea that Marie Antoinette is soon to be canonized. A mild critique of bourgeois

England is suggested on aesthetic grounds, but the 1890s impulses modulate gently into Edwardian sentiment.

The growth of the reading public and the sense of confidence within British Catholicism are both reflected particularly in the popular success of the fluent novels of Monsignor Robert Hugh Benson, star convert son of a notoriously anti-Catholic Archbishop of Canterbury. In these novels too sentimentality and melodrama abound, but they are used to convey a Catholicism that is itself not escapist but fiercely ultramontane and hard-faced. The historical novels are highly romanticized and full of suspense, but make powerful propaganda points. *Come Rack! Come Rope!* (1912), a stirring story of an Edmund Campion figure, remained required reading for Catholic schoolboys up to the sixties. In a startlingly melodramatic conclusion the priest hero on the point of martyrdom on the scaffold gives absolution to his own father who had apostatized from the faith.

Benson's novels of contemporary life are often set in comfortably described country houses and promulgate conventional apologetics. He has undeniable gifts, however, for broadly drawn characterization and dramatic contrasts. What he above all conveys in the midst of otherwise predictable patterns is a sense of the paradox and power of faith. Taking up the note of Francis Thompson's famous 'The Hound of Heaven' Benson makes a character in *Loneliness* (1915) say of faith, 'It is, Frightful. It grips you: and it won't let you go. You can kick and scream and protest; but it's got you. You can think you've lost it; you can laugh at it: but you haven't lost it: you've only covered it up' (342–3).[5] The same motifs fascinate Waugh and Greene. Benson is in fact the first British Catholic novelist to show much interest in the French Catholic decadent strand that begins with Huysmans. He refers to the latter on occasions and is very intrigued by the idea of vicarious suffering.[6] Even the motif of the self-sacrificial vow or bargain with God that so appeals to Greene later is to be found in *A Winnowing* (1910).

The suspicion remains that such elements in Benson are not always strictly controlled by his edifying purposes. His literary sensationalism helps to create exciting stories and convey the dramatic paradoxes of faith and the place of suffering in the Christian life. It is also the expression of his own more idiosyncratic and even bizarre interests, a life-long personal fascination with the occult, for example, that seems, as we shall see, to some extent disguised by the entirely proper warnings provided in *The Necromancers* (1909).

The paired future fantasies, *Lord of the World* (1907) and *The Dawn of All* (1911) are two of Benson's most revealing works. They show the influence of H. G. Wells both in form and content and they seek to confront the rise of scientism, socialism and free-thinking. They portray contrasted apocalyptic situations, with the Church in one case reduced to a tiny remnant, in the other victorious over the whole world. The first facilitates the expression of Benson's interest in suffering and martyrdom, the second the obverse side, his ultramontane triumphalism.

The decadent Cyril Dell in *The Sentimentalists* (1906) has been said to be a portrait of Benson's erstwhile friend Frederick Rolfe. The two had gone on a walking tour together and co-operated for a while on a literary project. But the eminent monsignor was advised against working with the crustaceous failed candidate for the priesthood and incurred, like many others, the latter's hatred for pulling out of it. Rolfe later pilloried Benson in *The Desire and Pursuit of the Whole* (published 1934) as the Rev. Bobugo Bonsen, 'a stuttering little Chrysostom of a priest, with the Cambridge manner of Vaughan's Dove, the face of the mad hatter out of *Alice in Wonderland* . . .'[7]

Fin de siècle and decadent impulses are certainly present in Rolfe's work, as well as the stubborn idiosyncrasy that is a major element in his character. In *Nicholas Crabbe* (published 1958) this latter element is recognized, but the religious conclusion seems to be a compensation rather than a transcendence of personal suffering. As David Lodge has said, this is less the case with *The Desire and Pursuit of the Whole*.[8] But Rolfe's own bitter personal experiences linked up with his 1890s anti-bourgeois attitudes to make him the scourge of British Catholic respectability and bad taste. Even his sense of the exotic, though no doubt part of his initial attraction to Catholicism, has a more cutting edge than in the work of his contemporaries. He uses Renaissance Italy in the historical novels and contemporary rural Italy in *Stories Toto Told Me* (first published 1895–6) as part of a campaign against what he considers the Puritanism with a Catholic face characteristic of English Catholicism.

It is in *Hadrian VII* (1904), the story of the election to the papacy of a failed candidate for the priesthood like himself, that a certain paradoxical quality of greatness in Rolfe is most apparent. It is the most obvious compensation fantasy and yet the richest and in some senses most disinterested of his novels. The specific political solutions, for example, are, like Benson's, monarchist and aristocratic, relating to Rolfe's romantic Jacobitism and themselves part of the elaborate mechanism of personal compensation. Yet the work is excitingly topical in its actual account of political issues and not at all escapist in the way it conveys the pressures of the new socialism.

If Rolfe, moreover, is a man who has fallen foul of the institution, the work combines personal bitterness with genuine faith to present its extraordinary vision of a Church that purifies itself. As with John Gray's *Park* the amazing prose style is thus at its best both the expression of aestheticism and eccentricity and the transcendence of them. This prose is at the same time idiosyncratic and yet impersonal, modern and yet archaic. For all its arrogance and its incidental amusements and felicities it becomes in the last analysis inseparable from a surprisingly balanced theological vision:

He was accused of an anarchistical kind of enthusiasm. When He heard that, He said

> 'We are conservative in all Our instincts, and only contrive to become otherwise by an effort of reason or principle, as We contrive to overcome all Our other vicious propensities.'

That was considered an additional indecorum. . . . His autocratic dogmatism, which really was due to His entire occession by His office, shocked the opportunist, irritated the worldly-prudent . . . At first, a lot of fantastic instabilities prepared to hail Him as a Reformer: but He gave dire offence to them, and to all pious fat-wits, by flatly refusing His countenance to any kind of Scheme or Society. 'The Church suffices for this life,' He said; and His sentence 'Cultivate, and help to cultivate individuality, at your own expense if possible, but never at the expense of your brother,' was highly disapproved of. Where did the Rights of Man come in? But then Hadrian was quite certain that Christians actually had no worldly 'rights' at all.

(1935 reprint: 164–5)

Like Ford Madox Ford both Benson and Rolfe attack what they present as a newly militant secularism and scientism, but Rolfe's works sold little in his lifetime and, though Benson was a popular success, he remains very clearly the spokesman for a Catholic ghetto. The novels of Belloc and Chesterton are only a small part of their total work, and the presence of Catholicism is mainly implicit and oblique. Essentially the two are participants in an age of reformist debate, popular controversy and journalism. Chesterton, for example, had a weekly column on the *Daily News*, and both he and Belloc wrote for various periodicals as well as editing their own. Their public debates with Shaw and Wells were famous, and it was in them that they found their most representative opponents. For the special significance of their whole long campaign is the way that as spokesman for neo-orthodoxy they succeed in taking the war to the enemy.

Inescapably linked together in their own time as doughty allies, they have come to be linked together subsequently by many critics as total reactionaries. If this is understandable in the light of their anti-Semitism and Belloc's later extreme rightwards shift, it is still a considerable oversimplification, and there are differences between the two anyway in tone, outlook and temperament. It was politics that first brought them together, and their original allegiances were radical ones. They begin in fact as classic figures of an age of reform, but their version of liberalism makes them oppose Fabian-style state solutions. This links up with a characteristic late Victorian reaction against urbanization and industrialism. As time goes on, it gradually becomes more difficult to disentangle their politics from their religion. They come to put at the heart of their whole system Lingard's and Cobbett's argument that things went wrong at the Reformation and that it was only the medieval order that enshrined true democracy. Their polemics turn eventually into a war against the whole modern secular age.[9]

Belloc's novels are primarily satires on the corruption of the modern political and financial system. *Mr Clutterbuck's Election* (1908), for example, portrays modern parliamentary democracy as an elaborate con-trick, since both parties are in reality dominated by the financial interest. Though these novels make little specific reference to Catholicism, Catholic preconceptions about usury, for example, lie behind them. In *Emmanuel Burden* (1904), the most impressive, an exporter of hardware in the City of London is caught up through his son's influence in the network of an elaborate financial fraud. The tragic inevitability with which the story moves acts out the deep-rootedness of the corruption; the satire on politicians, bankers, peers and clergymen portrays the complicity of a whole establishment. When Burden dies, Belloc, unusually for him, invokes the presence of another dimension: 'Then it was dark; and the

Infinite wherein he sank was filled with that primeval Fear which has no name among men; for the moment of his passage had come.'[10]

Belloc's is essentially a Church and culture-orientated Catholicism, obsessed by what went wrong in the past. Chesterton's novels also contain satiric elements and strong political themes. But his optimism and *joie de vivre* give his work a very different tone to Belloc's, and this relates to his very real genius for grasping and expressing certain essentials of the Christian vision. That vision, he believes, imposes technical choices on the Christian writer, in particular a decision against any narrowly defined realism. The way he works out the implications of this has given his novels more lasting significance than Belloc's, and they have been widely praised again in an era of post-modernist criticism.[11]

For the whole thrust of Chesterton's aesthetic is towards affirming the centrality of the imaginative, fictive faculty: 'The simple need for some kind of ideal world in which fictitious persons play an ideal part is infinitely deeper and older than the rules of good art, and much more important.'[12] He finds that faculty more properly embodied in popular literature than in the highbrow fiction of his time, and his own work exploits and embodies the conventions of detective stories, spy fiction and romance. The celebration of the childlike tastes of the common man itself connects up with Chesterton's political distributism, the desire to devolve power back to the individual on the model of an idealized medieval social order. His whole approach thus fuses style with content and ideology and turns literary mode itself into a religious and political statement. If the realist fiction of his contemporaries is associated with a materialist, bourgeois and secular ethos, the kind of prose romance which he offers as an alternative has analogues that are meant to evoke a whole cultural context without necessarily falling into any simple imitative 'medievalism'.

The prolific work and polemical fluency of Chesterton and Belloc gave them a position of considerable and long-standing pre-eminence in the British Catholic cultural world. They helped to cure the sense of intellectual inferiority experienced by British Catholics who ventured out of their own community, and for several decades to be a Catholic intellectual in England meant almost inevitably to be one of their disciples.[13]

For Belloc and Chesterton constantly contrive to suggest that they speak with the weight of an age-old international order and the true Englishness of the past against the parochialism of British Protestantism and modern secularism. Obviously enough, their influence was baleful in some respects, but they did at least present Catholic Christianity as a critique of and confrontation with the present order in Britain. In retrospect, moreover, Chesterton's testimony to the essential paradoxes of Christianity can be seen to have been an indispensable one for its time.

The novels of Belloc's and Chesterton's friend Maurice Baring are more conventionally realistic, though not without specifically technical interest themselves in their exploitation of narrative techniques. Written between 1922 and 1935, the series is extremely narrow in social range. Baring's father was an Edwardian merchant banker who had received a title. His novels reflect his background in that they deal exclusively with the small, immensely rich élite of the Edwardian plutocracy, and his scene switches between London houses, country estates and fashionable continental watering places.[14]

The plot and theme of each novel is in a sense the same too: the story of love affairs and marriages that go terribly wrong and of true love thwarted by social pressures or moral dilemmas. In brief quotations an Edwardian purple-passage element in Baring is clear. But immersion in the whole world of these novels, the complex slow-moving plots in which idealistic characters are involved in elaborate love triangles and terribly ironic long-lasting emotional frustration, creates a powerful, if oppressive sense, a 'tragic Shakespearian realisation of the pity and waste of things' (*C.*, 1924; 1926 reprint: 725). *C.* itself, for example, tells at great length the life story of its eponymous hero who seems doomed to tragic frustration and unrequited love. Even as a child he accidentally breaks the head of his sister's favourite doll. The central motif of his adult life is the fact that he falls in love with the beautiful but empty Leila and thus misses his chance of true love with Beatrice.

As in all Baring's novels romanticism and pessimism take a special colour from his religion. Catholicism is presented not as the solution to the political problems of the day but to the dilemmas of personal suffering and frustration. What it offers is the capacity to make the inevitable suffering redemptive. In some of the early novels apologetics are allowed to get out of hand, but *C.* is impressive apart from anything else in that its hero is not finally converted, despite his attraction to Catholicism. This enables Baring to balance apologetics and pessimism, avoiding direct proselytizing while in another sense fulfilling that purpose more effectively by offering C. as a warning of the futility of life without God and the dangers of neglecting the opportunity of grace.

The whole series shows Baring obsessively working and reworking in retrospect his ambivalent attitudes of nostalgia for and criticism of the doomed upper-class world of pre-war English society. It comes to assume a wider, more representative significance in the special sense he conveys of the power of what Christians call 'the world', in this case the enormous weight of the pressure of Edwardian 'society' and its conventions:

> 'You see, you don't think religion matters one way or the other. We think religion matters more than anything else in the world. And people like your father and mother . . .' she stopped.
>
> 'Call something else religion,' said C. 'I have always known that. I know *that* isn't religion at all, only it's just as strong. I mean, they think going to church is like leaving cards, only that doesn't prevent them thinking it tremendously important.'
>
> (*C.*: 302)

Compton Mackenzie's *Sinister Street* (1913) is a novel of disappointed pre-war youthful idealism rather than Baring's retrospective world-weariness, but it too has a massively representative quality, as was widely recognized even at the time. Michael Fane comes to see his civilization as a 'great complication of machinery fed by gold and directed by fear',[15] but, significantly, he rejects not only the old order but also the popular secular reformism of the time:

Man for man standing in his own might is a blind and arrogant leader. The reason why the modern world is so critical of the fruits of Christianity after nineteen hundred years is because they have expected it from the beginning to be a social panacea. God has only offered to the individual the chance to perfect himself, but the individual is much more anxious about his neighbour. How in a moment our little herds are destroyed, whether in ships or on the sea or in towns by earthquake, or by the great illusions of political experiment! Soon will come a great war . . .

(1916, reprint, II: 1131)

The clear implication at the end of the book is that in the face of the crisis Michael will decide to become a Catholic priest, an echo of the author's own conversion in April 1914.

The products of Ford Madox Ford's greatest creative period, *The Good Soldier* (1915) and the four novels that comprise *Parade's End* (1924–8) can hardly be considered 'Catholic' works in any full sense, but they explore in passing certain sociological and ethical dilemmas of English Catholicism with some evidence of inwardness on the subject. *The Good Soldier* is especially famous in literary history as a brilliant example of the formal device of the unreliable narrator. This device has nothing to do with Catholicism as such, of course, but it is worth noting that Catholic writers have often found it especially useful and that Ford's version has its own – admittedly low-key and ambivalent – Catholic aspect. The technique of using a neutral or sceptical narrator has helped the more sophisticated Catholic novelists to display the triumph of faith and grace over an apparently objective or even prejudiced observer, as in *C.*, *Brideshead Revisited* and *The End of the Affair*, whilst at the same time enabling them to distance themselves from propaganda. The fact that the wife of Ford's 'Good Soldier' is a Catholic is shown to be crucial to the way she responds to her husband's adulteries, but the events are seen through the eyes of a narrator hostile to the religion. This is one of the ways in which his story has to be read between the lines and, though the implications as a whole remain hardly favourable, he is made to pay tribute despite himself to a certain wisdom in the 'queer shifty ways of Roman Catholics' who are said to be 'always right' perhaps 'in dealing with the queer shifty thing called human nature' (1962 reprint: 213).

The massively panoramic *Parade's End* has come to be seen as the definitive portrayal of the First World War as the terrible final symptom of the death of British civilization. Though Ford was far from alone in this conservative pessimism, his nostalgic cultural Catholicism has a special, if subordinate, contribution to make here. As various critics have emphasized, Tietjens is the 'last Christian gentleman', the whole war the revelation of an 'Armageddon for a Christian civilization'.[16] The judgement on England is connected in Ford's mind with its treatment of Ireland and the judicial murder of the saintly Father Consett. Tietjens is left at the end with a life of peaceful withdrawal, having given up his hopes for society itself. In the fact that his heir will be a Catholic Ford makes pointed reference to Tietjens's sense of personal expiation for the crime of the seizure of Catholic lands at the Reformation.

Post-war reaction

The widely attested trauma of disillusionment that the post-war generation experienced was as much with religion as with patriotism and secular ideals. An old Benedictine monk refers in Compton Mackenzie's *The Heavenly Ladder* (1924) to 'that resentment against almighty God which some of the intellectual humanitarians I know seem to feel most strongly' (p. 323). The process of secularization had been continuing rapidly since the mid-Victorian period, but the war had shown up the early jingoism and empty conventional quality of much English religion, and the social upheaval itself loosened the restraints on expressions of unbelief. Father Smith in Marshall's *All Glorious Within* (1941) remarks 'In the old days a man said that he went to church on Sundays even if he didn't but now he says he plays golf and would be very distressed if his men friends found out that he really went to church' (p. 98). Lady Cresset in Antonia White's *The Sugar House* (1952) has a similar story to tell of the new era: 'The whole atmosphere seems to have changed since the war. It's no longer just a question of Catholic or Protestant. One hears more and more of people who believe in nothing' (1982 reprint: 98).

For at least the first decade and a half after the war secularism and agnosticism certainly seemed to hold the intellectual high ground. Belloc and Chesterton had less influence on the public at large than before the war, though they remained central to the intellectual life of the Catholic community. With the defence of Christianity left otherwise to Platonists and Anglican modernists it is fair to say that Chesterton was almost the sole intellectually challenging defender of Christian orthodoxy of the time.[17]

Post-war hedonism and the overthrow of traditional moral standards are conveyed in brilliantly exaggerated fashion in the early novels of Evelyn Waugh. Waugh learnt much from Ronald Firbank, whose novels themselves combine an amoral twenties atmosphere with decadent Catholicism in a remarkable blend. Firbank's works can hardly be taken as Catholic novels in any obvious sense, of course, and neither can these early works of Waugh's, though he wrote later that ten years of his own experience of the life reflected in them (Mayfair between the wars) was enough to convince him of the need for God.[18] In a famous passage from *Vile Bodies* (1930) Father Rothschild also presents the hedonism of the Bright Young Things as the product of a disillusionment that is itself perhaps a symptom and prelude to the recognition of a deeper religious need:

> 'Don't you think,' said Father Rothschild gently, 'that perhaps it is all in some way historical? I don't think people ever *want* to lose their faith either in religion or anything else. I know very few young people, but it seems to me that they are all possessed with an almost fatal hunger for permanence. I think all these divorces show that. People aren't content just to muddle along nowadays . . . And this word "bogus" they all use . . . They won't make the best of a bad job nowadays. My private schoolmaster used to say, "If a thing's worth doing at all, it's worth doing well." My Church has taught that in different words for several centuries. But these young

people have got hold of another end of the stick, and for all we know it may be the right one. They say, "If a thing's not worth doing well, it's not worth doing at all."'

(p.143)

For deeper reflection on the traumatic shock to secular optimism and to liberal or conventional religion that the war represented made it apparent that the strong sense of the Fall and the need for salvation in orthodox Christianity might actually have something to say. Philip Gibbs's *An Age of Reason* (1921), for example, uses the realities of the war to pour scorn on the hopes of scientism. The scientist Hesketh Jerningham believes in 'the religion of Reason'. His son calls his speech at the British Academy 'H. G. Wells stuff'. But Hesketh's father has a Steinach glands rejuvenation operation that goes horribly wrong. His whole family undergo experiences that show the inadequacy of Hesketh's creed. Later events serve thus to confirm the view that it was his 'material philosophy of life that brought about the Great War' (p. 260).

An intellectual revival of orthodox Christianity was in fact on the way, its luminaries Karl Barth, Reinhold Niebuhr and Jacques Maritain. Roman Catholicism, apparently free by this time from any hint of modernism, was itself well placed to be a beneficiary of these new trends. Robert Keable's *Simon Called Peter* (1921), another of the rather daring popular religious novels that use Catholicism more readily than other forms of Christianity, is significantly prophetic in this respect beneath the sentimentalism and sensationalism of the story. The hero, an Anglican clergyman, had believed, like Napoleon, that 'Christianity meant more . . . as the secret of social order than as the mystery of the Incarnation' (p. 67). He loses his faith through his experiences as a chaplain in the war. He decides that Christ is more likely to be found among publicans and sinners and has a passionate affair with the near-pagan Julie. An experience in Westminster Cathedral prepares him for conversion to Catholicism, and Julie nobly relinquishes him.

The intensifying economic and political pressures of the late twenties and early thirties – the rise of fascism above all – polarized political opinion among intellectuals, but also contributed to a significant minority revival of orthodox religion. More drastic solutions than liberalism could proffer seemed to be called for, and this was as true in the theological realm as in the political. As Adrian Hastings says, the thirties began to see a 'breakdown of the agnostic consensus of the enlightened and . . . the growing sense that a belief in supernatural religion really was an intellectual option for modern man.' The radical Protestantism of Barth takes the cross, revelation and the supernatural seriously, and the neo-Thomism of Maritain, highly influential outside his own communion, was in some ways a Catholic equivalent. There were a series of well-known conversions to high Anglicanism and Roman Catholicism at this time and, as in the Victorian period, it was the sense of final authority that these converts seemed to value most highly.[19]

Catholicism and the routinism of certainty

To be a Roman Catholic had come to mean espousing a very clearly defined set of doctrines and way of worship, centralized and ultramontane, markedly set apart from contemporary English ways in certain respects and powerful in its sense of certainty. Attractive though this absolute doctrinal assurance was to many converts, Edward Norman in a magisterial summary registers the overall impression, however, of 'a Church which had become confident and routinized; splendid in its pastoral machinery, but lacking the genius of inventiveness'.[20]

Antonia White's *Frost in May* (1933), based on her own convent school life in Roehampton, is a brilliant and painfully sensitive account of one representative aspect of this community. The paradoxical combination of strangeness and yet utterly taken-for-granted routine in the day-to-day life of Catholicism in this country is conveyed through the viewpoint of the new girl Nanda, a recent convert:

> On Saturdays every child in the school went to confession and, in the evening, after 'Exemptions', there were special devotions in the vestibule of Our Lady of Good Success. Here stood a silver-crowned statue of Our Lady, a replica of the one which had miraculously arrived at Aberdeen in a stone boat without sail or rudder, which was honoured as the special help of students. There were always little red lamps burning before it on behalf of brothers with imminent exams. On Sundays all the children heard two masses and a sermon in the morning and went to Benediction in the afternoon.
>
> . . . Both Our Lady and the Holy Child she spoke as naturally to as to her friends. She learnt to smooth a place on her pillow for her Guardian Angel to sit during the night, to promise St Anthony a creed or some pennies for his poor in return for finding her lost property, to jump out of bed at the first beat of the bell to help the Holy Souls in purgatory.
>
> (1982 reprint: 38)

There is a beauty in these observances that are so strange to Nanda, but in sensing her bewilderment we also become aware of elements that are absurd. The novel deliberately makes the life of the school emblematic of the life of the Church as a whole, and the absolute self-confidence of this regime, its complete certainty of being right in every particular, comes close to destroying Nanda in the end.

Various commentators, most of them Catholics themselves, have argued for the existence of a distinctive 'Catholic neurosis' compounded out of authoritarianism, superstition and the peculiarities of Catholic moral teaching. In a controversial article in 1959 the Benedictine theologian Sebastian Moore suggested in particular that to give children prefabricated and final answers to all the mysteries of the universe was to run the risk of stunting intellectual exploration and emotional growth.[21] These are difficult matters, and it will be necessary to return to them, but *Frost in May* is the most poignant of a variety of fictional accounts of Catholic education that show the potential roots of such a neurosis. What White especially succeeds in conveying is the presence of very genuine beauty, devotion and love here too, and it is precisely this that makes the whole complex so heartrendingly hard to disentangle.

It is only an apparent paradox that this religion should appeal to so many writers and artists and foster so much creativity, even if the greatest work occurs mainly, it seems, on the margins. Converts could easily ignore the more stifling aspects of day-to-day Catholic life in an appreciation of timeless liturgy and authority. Colour and ritual have their own superficial appeal, but the deeper levels of traditional symbolism are a rich mine of the work of David Jones. For occasional individuals such as Eric Gill and Graham Greene there is a stimulus in the very tension with the immense authoritarianism of the institution. The great majority, however, are attracted precisely by that sense of authority, and their Catholicism continues to reinforce the deep conservatism that drew them to it in the first place.

The fiction of the brilliant convert Ronald Knox, for example, is only a sideline in his career and remains limitingly donnish, but even his biting controversy is almost as ultramontane in its preconceptions as Robert Hugh Benson's work had been. Knox is a wonderful scourge of the kind of Anglican modernism that with 'suave politeness, temp'ring bigot Zeal, / Corrected "I believe" to "One does feel",' but it is as if he feels compelled to go to completely the opposite extreme.[22]

Most Catholic fiction until the late thirties indeed gives the same impression of refusing to engage with contemporary realities. The conventions of love-and-religion romances such as Isabel Clarke's have changed little since the Victorian period. Enid Dinnis cultivates whimsical, quasi-mystical fairy tales as in *The Road to Somewhere* (1927). At a more exalted level Sheila Kaye-Smith's once highly praised historical novels explore the Catholic past of England. Compton Mackenzie's lengthy trilogy *The Altar Steps* (1922–4) is the last major tale of conversion from Anglicanism.

John Gray's only novel, the remarkable *Park* (1932), reflects Spenglerian pessimism about the future of Western civilization. Its hero, a priest like Gray himself, awakes to find himself in a world where black people are the dominant race, but the fact that they are Catholics provides a certain sense of perspective in the strange new world. The novel has a chiselled austerity of tone and diction, but this keeps its relationship to contemporary concerns oblique and its main impulse is to present the Church as the only lasting source of beauty.

The sharpening crisis: Waugh and Greene

If the sharpening sense of political and ideological conflict encouraged conversion to a conservative, almost escapist 'fortress' Catholicism, the crisis was eventually, of course, to reach a point that made escapism virtually impossible. John Strachey wrote in *The Coming Struggle for Power* (1932) that after his early novels Evelyn Waugh 'had clearly only three alternatives open to him. He could either commit suicide, become a communist, or immure himself within the Roman Catholic Church. He chose this last and easiest alternative.'[23] As a matter of fact this exaggerates the appeal of Catholicism as an alternative to communism among intellectuals at this time. Nevertheless the growing feeling that the ideological choices were becoming starker was in the end to bring the Catholic novel out of the backwaters. Both Waugh and Greene eventually come to write directly about Catholic themes in a contemporary context and Compton Mackenzie moves, for example, from *The Altar Steps* to *The Four Winds of Love*, an ambitious intellectual and political chronicle of the ideological options in the third and fourth decade of the century:

> Communism or Fascism – they may be mutually destructive, but they are both expressions of distrust in the individualism which has made such a mess of the world. We are watching now, I fancy, the beginning of the end of an epoch which started with the Renaissance and the Protestant Reformation and the discovery of America and the conception of England as an extra-European state.
>
> (*West to North*, 1942 reprint: 297)

Despite Mackenzie's comment the anti-communist emphasis meant that there was likely to be much more sympathy with fascism among British Catholics, though there was never much active involvement. But apart from Graham Greene and Eric Gill most Catholic artists and writers were hardly of leftish sympathies. The influence of Belloc was by now entirely in a reactionary direction. The concordat between Mussolini and the Vatican created sympathy for the Italian dictator. Belloc and Waugh both express pro-Mussolini sentiments and even the more liberal Josephine Mary Ward is revealingly ambivalent in her novel *In the Shadow of Mussolini* (1927) and appears to accept large aspects of the Duce myth. No reservations of any kind trouble Douglas Jerrold in *Storm over Europe* (1930), an impassioned and blatant pro-fascist fantasy in which the Church allies itself absolutely with the right. Naturally enough the Spanish Civil War drove Catholics further in this direction because of republican attacks on priests and nuns. The position of the small minority of British Catholics who did not side with Franco was a very difficult one, as Bernard Bergonzi shows movingly in *The Roman Persuasion* (1981).

Both Graham Greene and Evelyn Waugh begin their careers reflecting similar moods and preconceptions to their non-Catholic contemporaries. Like Waugh's novels of the world of the twenties Greene's early- and mid-thirties novels make only passing reference to Catholicism. They portray their characters as the victims of vast impersonal forces, economic and ideological, and create an atmosphere of rootlessness and edgy international tension that has been compared to Auden.[24]

With *Brighton Rock* (1938) and *Brideshead Revisited* (1945) Greene and Waugh both move towards specifically Catholic themes. It is their fate thereafter to be classed together as 'Catholic novelists', but they could hardly be more different in some ways. As Greene was later to say, 'We were deeply divided politically, were divided even in our conception of the same Church.'[25] Waugh is clearly right wing; Greene, unusually for a Catholic of the time, as Orwell points out, a man of the left whose sympathy with communism stops short of identification because he believes it does not pay enough attention to the individual.

Yet their strategies are in some senses parallel ones all the same. Both are in reaction against the complacencies of bourgeois liberalism. Waugh's early ambiguous response to the Bright Young Things turns into a romantic celebration of a Catholic aristocracy, whose amoral behaviour is legitimized by association with the paradoxes of faith. Greene's exploration of Catholic paradoxes is more elaborate and constant than Waugh's, but clearly also presents an anti-bourgeois drama, though with a cast of characters from the opposite end of the spectrum – criminals, outlaws and exiles. It is the sense of crisis in the period itself, of course, that creates this attraction to an extremist mode of Catholic writing, but if the sharpening of the ideological choices lies behind Waugh's and Greene's choice of specifically Catholic subject matter this is true in no simple or direct sense. Notoriously, of course, their Catholicism generalizes and intensifies a thirties world-weariness and cynicism rather than transforming it. 'Point me out the happy man and I will point you out either egotism, selfishness, evil – or else an absolute evil,' thinks Scobie to himself in a very characteristic reflection from the later *Heart of the Matter* (p. 125).[26] If both *Brideshead Revisited* and *The Power and the Glory* propose Catholicism as an alternative to communism and secular egalitarianism, then they do so in very different and rather oblique ways.

What is undoubtedly true is that, in coming to be recognized as among the country's leading novelists, Waugh and Greene altered the whole status of Catholic literature in England. It was only from this time, as David Lodge remarks, that 'The Catholic Novel' became a recognizable entity with the informed public. Yet Catholicism remains to a remarkable degree exotic and almost alien in atmosphere in their work despite their contemporary focus. Neither has much relationship with or interest in portraying the daily routine of ordinary British Catholicism, 'Rosary and Benediction on a Sunday evening at the parish church of an industrial suburb, followed by a meeting of the Legion of Mary and a whist drive organized by the Union of Catholic Mothers', as Lodge puts it.[27]

Bruce Marshall is one Catholic novelist of the time who does attempt this, perhaps because as a Scots cradle Catholic he avoids the class and other difficulties of English converts. Marshall purports to write with deliberate realism about humble Catholic life, but in *Father Malachy's Miracle* (1931), for example, he juxtaposes this with direct supernaturalism. Here the prayers of a saintly priest transport a dance hall to a remote rock in response to an Anglican vicar who does not believe in miracles. But the book veers uneasily between mild satire and pious sentimentality, and the uncertainty of tone signifies a deeper contradiction. On the one hand there is criticism of the Church as well as of Anglican modernists and the secular world for refusing to accept the miracle and not knowing how to deal with it. Yet at the end the dance hall is transported back again and Father Malachy has therefore had to learn the lesson that remarkable signs may achieve nothing and that God's ordinary ways are best. In other words Marshall criticizes the routinism of the Church from a prophetic perspective and yet at the same time affirms it. This is a split found elsewhere in Marshall and it is a central dilemma for British Catholicism as a whole.

· 3 ·
Consolidation and change 1945–present

Consolidation and opposition

In contrast to the situation after the First World War, there is evidence to suggest that the Second World War actually strengthened traditional religious belief and practice in Britain.[1] Instead of a Christian patriotic ideology being implicated as a cause of the war, it was clearly secular pseudo-religions and ideologies that this time stood condemned.

Some important conversions and reconversions occurred. Muriel Spark's Nicholas Faringdon in *The Girls of Slender Means* (1963) is obviously intended to be a representative figure in having become a Catholic in 1945 after being divided for some time between 'two equally drastic courses of action, suicide and Fr. Martin D'Arcy, S. J.' Antonia White became a troubled but committed Catholic again in 1941 and wrote three more novels continuing the story of Nanda. A. J. Cronin wrote *The Keys of the Kingdom* the next year to mark the renewal of his faith, and its author's own years away from Catholic practice and a concentration on essentials in wartime conditions both obviously contribute to the radicalism of this portrait of an unusually open-minded and tolerant priest who sees the good in Protestants and atheists. Another example is Pamela Frankeau, who became a Catholic in 1942, and went on to write a prolific series of novels about sophisticated characters, fond like herself of gambling and the South of France, who encounter supernatural realities.

The more lasting and widespread feeling of fighting which was seen in the last analysis as a just war meant that there was less of the sense of pure nihilism that had followed the First World War. For Lodge's group of young Catholics in *How Far Can You Go?* (1980) the war had been imbued by their religious education with 'a mythic simplicity, the forces of good contending with the power of evil, Hitler being identified with Satan, and Churchill, more tentatively, with the archangel Michael' (1982:49). Of course uneasiness about the actual prosecution of the war as well as its social consequences remained. Bruce Marshall's *Vespers in Vienna* (1947) confronts moral dilemmas about the position of the Church and particularly the papacy in the conflict. Evelyn Waugh writes in the trilogy *Sword of Honour* (1952–62, revised edition 1965) the greatest British novel about the Second World War, and he is very unusual in reaching the conclusion that it cannot be regarded as a fully just war in Catholic terms. His hero Guy Crouchbank rejoices in the pact between Germany and Soviet Russia. Now at last the enemy is clear. He is in arms against the 'modern age' itself. He is therefore deeply disillusioned by the later alliance between Britain and Russia. His fight against the modern world ends, like Tietjens's in *Parade's End*, with defeat. Like Ford's hero he has had to give up public causes, though he wins a purely private victory at the close.

Waugh's earlier *Brideshead Revisited*, published in 1945, spans in tone and theme the whole of his career from the Bright Young Things of the Oxford chapters to the chastened post-war mood. In nostalgically attempting to counteract wartime bureaucracy and egalitarianism, it also anticipates the post-war 'world for Hoopers', a world of secularism, democracy and bureaucracy that means the destruction of all the social ideals Waugh held dear.[2] Only the preservation of Catholicism and Ryder's own conversion to it have given a providential significance to events Waugh bitterly regrets from a purely social perspective.

Waugh's hatred of the post-war government and the secular reformist spirit is spelt out clearly in *Sword of Honour* and in the short future fantasy *Love Among the Ruins* (1953). In the latter Britain has become a totally secular state in which Christmas has been finally replaced by Santa Claus day and sex education and penal reform have gone to absurd extremes. Miles the hero was the creation of the State: 'He was the Modern Man . . . His history, as it appeared in multiplet in the filing cabinets of numberless State departments was typical of a thousand others' (p. 5). Placed in an orphanage by the indigence of his parents, who had been ruined by the machinations of the politicians, Miles has huge sums spent on him, 'sums which fifty years earlier would have sent whole quiverfuls of boys to Winchester and New College' (p. 6).

Anthony Burgess is not a Christian believer but he has a strong sense of having been brought up as part of a Catholic sub-culture. He uses traditional British Catholic motifs – the idea of the Reformation as a social as well as a religious disaster, the feeling of being an exile in a Protestant and secular land – as rhetorical myths or distancing devices. The whole complex of sentiment is used to reinforce and express a political dislike of the drab uniformity, utilitarianism and reformism of post-war Britain very similar to Waugh's. In *A Vision of Battlements* (written 1949, first published 1961) the character Julian says memorably:

> A new world, I believe. Wide boys, drones, a cult of young hooliganism. State art. Free ill-health for all. Lots and lots of forms to fill in. The *Daily Mirror's* increasing circulation. Nostalgia among ex-flying types, sick for the lost mess games. Returning corporals killing their wives. Bureaucracy growing like a cancer.
>
> (1965 reprint: 236)

It is an Augustinian sense of sin and the Fall that ultimately makes the nostrums of liberal reformism futile and this sense of the realities of evil was obviously intensified by the revelations about the concentration camps. Burgess quotes Sartre's statement that it is because of the war that 'we have been taught to take evil seriously'.[3] In a scene from the later *Earthly Powers* (1980) the novelist Toomey's visit to a concentration camp confirms in him a sense of evil and original sin in which, ironically as a non-believer, he is opposed to a Pelagian Pope, Carlo Camponati, Pope Gregory, his relation by marriage. He says after his visit, 'I wanted to have Carlo with me there to smell the ripe gorgonzola of innate human evil and to dare to say that mankind was God's creation and hence good' (p. 458).

In Burgess's own work this sense leads into a semi-serious Manichaeism, though with a Catholic bias. More usually the sense of evil strengthens an orthodox Christian world view. Catholic writers obviously have a considerable amount of traditional lore to contribute on this subject, and they do so in the widest possible variety of modes. The power and popularity of Tolkien's *Lord of the Rings* (1954–5), for example, derive in part from its mythic reenactment of the struggle between good and evil, which is at the same time an escape from the drabness of post-war society. Tolkien himself wrote in a letter in 1953 that *The Lord of the Rings* is a 'fundamentally religious and Catholic work'.[4] Religious preconceptions underlie his whole attitude to fantasy, and the world he creates embodies Christian values, though it would be wrong to take it as direct Christian allegory. But Tolkien's 'shire' has many of the features of Chesterton's ideal society, and his hobbits relate to Chesterton's vision of the common man, a potential hero by God's grace. There is a potential contradiction, however, between this emphasis and the elaborate hierarchies of Middle-earth, which once again seem to be deliberately set against post-war values.

Gabriel Fielding's *The Birthday King* (1962) on the other hand is a direct account of the Nazi era in Germany that in a sense demythologizes evil by revealing it to be the consequence of a series of apparently trivial compromises. It tells the story of a Jewish-Catholic family of armaments manufacturers. One brother co-operates with the regime and the other, a kind of scapegoat, goes to the camps, though he survives at the end. The final recognitions that this impressive novel suggest are the age-old truths about the realities of a fallen world. Life in the camps is like ordinary life, only 'speeded up' (p. 297), and all bear some guilt for the evil.

In her own highly idiosyncratic way Muriel Spark also rejects the secular complacencies and reformism of the time and reveals a strong sense of the pervasiveness of original sin. At the end of *The Girls of Slender Means* (1963), for example, a soldier surreptitiously stabs a girl in the crowd during the VJ night celebrations and we are reminded that there is no armistice for the war between good and evil and that the recent General Election will not bring about utopia either. It is an unexploded bomb from the blitz that has shown up the realities of evil beneath the charm of the hostel which had seemed a genuinely utopian community to Nicholas at first. It is the vision of evil in a selfish and greedy act by the glamorous Selina that is responsible for his conversion.

Spark's sense of these realities takes the form of an arch and fastidious detachment from the pretensions of the fallen world. She offers a special combination of social satire and an awareness of the supernatural forces that work themselves out in the post-war bohemian sub-culture of *The Comforters* (1957) and *The Bachelors* (1960a), and in the apparently mundane London setting of *The Ballad of Peckham Rye* (1960b):

> the children playing there and the women coming home from work with their shopping-bags, the Rye for an instant looking like a cloud of green and gold, the people seeming to ride upon, as you might say there was another world than this.[5]

The fifties were once commonly held to have represented a period of social realism in English fiction, a reaction against experimentalism. This view has increasingly come to seem an oversimplification, but Spark herself has often been accorded a major role in counteracting the supposed trend. The heroine of her first novel *The Comforters*, for example, is writing a thesis on form in the modern novel, and the book self-consciously considers the relationship between form and theological issues such as free will, thus beginning a strong tendency in her work to link religious vision and a degree of technical experiment. Spark belonged to an intellectual Catholic circle at Aylesford Priory that included Gabriel Fielding and Christine Brooke-Rose, whose own early novels are Catholic satires with a not dissimilar tone to Spark's.

Spark's own innovativeness must not be exaggerated, however. What the early novels especially illustrate is the degree to which traditional Catholic preconceptions may sometimes overlap with experimental or fashionable post-modernist interests. This applies above all to a special self-consciousness about fiction. The 'Puritanical' rejection of fiction as a lie is more commonly regarded as characteristic of Protestant culture, but there are versions of this rigorism, especially associated with St Augustine, in Catholic tradition too, and it combines interestingly there with a more general respect for the arts. Spark herself has said self-deprecatingly and ironically that the novelist's art is 'very much like the practice of deception' and called her own books 'a pack of lies'.[6] She is more accurately regarded not as a theoretical post-modernist as such but as a writer whose quirky Catholic stylishness and supernaturalist feeling of the limitations of normal reality contribute to an especially arch sense of the novelist's problems with truth.

Social change in an 'unchanging' Church

As the examples of Greene, Waugh and Spark show, the distinctively 'Catholic novelist' has remained cut off not only from the mainstream of British values but also to a considerable degree from the life of the main body of the Catholic community. David Lodge has amusingly explained how it was paradoxically the very remoteness of the 'Catholic novel' of Greene and others that helped him to deal with his own situation as a Catholic schoolboy:

by presenting authentic religious belief as something equally opposed to the materialism of the secular world and to the superficial pieties of parochial Catholicism. The idea of the sinner as a representative Christian was appealing to the adolescent mind, suggesting (in a wholly theoretical way, for I was as timid as I was innocent) that being a Catholic need not entail a life of dull, petty-bourgeois respectability. The extreme situations and exotic settings on which these writers thrived were, however, very remote from my experience . . .[7]

Yet in many ways the institutional Church was actually flourishing in the post-war world that so horrified Waugh and Burgess. The anti-democratic sentiments of Belloc, associated with a by now unthinkable anti-Semitism, had gone out of favour. Catholic schools thrived after the Butler Education Act gave them greater state funding. Far more Catholics began to go to university, and there was a steady drift to the South-east and an accelerating increase in the middle-class proportion of the Catholic population. Despite the continued sense of apartness and the critique of the new order expressed by the most important novelists, Catholics in general were coming to fit in more comfortably from a sociological perspective with the centralist consensus of English society.[8]

As he well recognizes himself, David Lodge is a clear example of these trends: lower middle class in background, grammar school and university educated. His class origins and the fact that he was a cradle Catholic rather than a convert meant that he was not cut off from ordinary Catholic life either. *The Picturegoers* (1960) provides a rare fictional portrait of Catholic parish life, satiric in places indeed but basically affirmative, since it is contact with it that leads to the conversion of Mark Underdown and his decision to enter the priesthood. As Lodge says of Greene's and Mauriac's work, 'When I came to try and write fiction for myself I domesticated their themes to the humdrum suburban-parochial milieu that I knew best.'[9]

The so-called 'angry young men' of the late fifties were represented at the time as working-class writers who had been to grammar school and university but found themselves afterwards at odds with a complacent establishment.[10] One of the best known of them, John Braine, was himself a Catholic by birth like Lodge. The famous first novel *Room at the Top* (1957) may show signs of this in the strong affirmation of the personal and moral significance of sex that Joe Lampton tries to his cost to deny. Braine's later *The Jealous God* (1964) portrays or purports to portray ordinary parochial Catholicism in Yorkshire, though the work is more obsessive and Greene-like in tone than Lodge's in its analysis of a guilt-ridden schoolteacher.

Neither *The Picturegoers* nor *The Jealous God* conveys any sense that British Catholicism was about to enter into its greatest crisis since the Reformation. Despite important shifts in the sociological attitudes of British Catholics in the post-war period there was little sense of change in the externals of Catholic life. As Adrian Hastings describes in an eloquent passage worth quoting at length:

> . . . the Catholic Church functioned and flourished as it had done, apparently almost unchanged, for many centuries. The Latin Mass . . . had been

altered only marginally since the Middle Ages . . . All seemed still as it had been when Henry VIII ascended the throne or when, in a seventeenth-century manor house, Catholics gathered behind barred doors to hear the mass of Gerard, Garnet or Henry Morse. Nuns still wore their antique habits, their strange distinctive head-veils. Minor seminaries were still filled with hundreds of small boys from working-class homes trained in their teens in Latin and celibacy. Benediction and rosary, the nine First Fridays, plenary indulgences . . . the pattern of popular and even clerical piety remained utterly remote from that of most other Christians in Britain. At the end of every Latin mass, kneeling at the foot of the altar priests switched to English to pray for the conversion of Russia: three Hail Marys and an appeal addressed to St Michael. 'Do thou, Prince of the heavenly host, thrust down to Hell Satan and all wicked spirits who wander through the world for the ruin of souls.' The Catholic Church remained indeed a law unto itself.

(p. 490)

All this in itself both signalled and contributed to the preservation of a certain sense of apartness. When the Orkneys writer George Mackay Brown became a convert to Catholicism in 1961, he did so far from what seemed the mainstream of British culture. His reaction was against 'the new religion, Progress, in which we all devoutly believe', and his novels and short stories have continued to privilege an agricultural society.[11] They oppose themselves in a remarkable way at the same time against what are very specifically seen as the individualistic, 'Protestant' and secular norms of the modern realist novel. *Greenvoe* (1972) and *Magnus* (1973), are, in the words of one critic, an attempt to see how far the novel can 'transcend its conventional restrictions – written prose, private experience and social realism – in the direction of communal ritual, dramatic presentation, and a poetic orchestration of styles'. *Magnus*, the story of the Orkney Saint Magnus Martyr, in particular depends on an astonishing blend of Norse saga and saint's legend, and Brown makes clear that 'to celebrate the mystery properly the story-teller must give way to a ritual voice.'[12]

Brown's reaction against the modern world obviously comes from his own very particular cultural context, but it drew immense strength, as for many others, from the apparently unchanging nature of Catholicism and its rituals. His sense of the eternal symbolism of the Mass, very much at the heart of his work, must have been reinforced by the fact that the liturgy and language had in practice remained virtually the same for so many centuries.

'Gusts, damaging storms?'

All this was to change soon; too swiftly, indeed, and traumatically for many. What amounted to a cultural revolution in the sixties in British society at large went along with massive changes in the general pattern of national religious practice. At the same time a great renewal and destruction of benchmarks occurred in national and international Roman Catholicism as such through the work of the Second Vatican Council.

Though many aspects of the sixties are seen in retrospect to have been transient and superficial and others have gone into reverse with the Thatcher years, in two very relevant respects at least the cultural changes seem to have been more permanent. It is hard to believe that the increased permissiveness in general attitudes to sexuality and in the treatment of sex by the media will ever be completely reversed, whatever constraints are put on actual behaviour by the AIDS threat. The huge leap in the secularization process also seems to have had lasting effects. Put bluntly, the average Englishman and woman had until this period been at least an occasional churchgoer. Now churchgoing is no longer any kind of norm. The spiritual search of young people in the sixties was often an enthusiastic one but it had very little link with the established churches. England was ceasing to be even nominally a Christian country.

Because of the Sunday Mass obligation congregations in Roman Catholic churches dropped off less than in other denominations, and so the relative position of English Catholicism was in many respects strengthened. But, far from preparing for an important new centrality of Christian witness in Britain, the process of renewal in the Church produced a devastating internal crisis instead. In the words of Rumer Godden in *In This House of Brede* (1969) the changes came not as 'a fresh breeze as perhaps Pope John had intended, but in gusts, damaging storms' (p. 388).

The Second Vatican Council, the greatest ecclesiastical event of the century for Protestants as well as Catholics according to Adrian Hastings, began to meet in 1962.[13] For many years a theological renewal had been taking place on the continent, though its impact among British Catholics had so far been tiny. A greater sense of the way God worked in the ordinary secular world and in basic human experience had developed at the same time as a growing recognition that some aspects of the Church since the Council of Trent were more provisional and time-bound than had once seemed the case.

To summarize a complex process, the influence of the theological experts at the Council broadly speaking worked in these directions. The whole image of the Church began to alter. In a careful shift of emphasis that has far-reaching implications, the Roman Catholic Church was presented no longer as the one and exclusive true Church but rather as the central body in which that true Church subsists.[14] A degree at least of participation in that one true Church is no longer denied to other churches, so that an enormous boost was given to ecumenism. With remarkable speed the situation changes from one in which it is a mortal sin for a Catholic to attend a service in a non-Catholic church to one in which Pope John Paul himself worships with the Archbishop of Canterbury in Canterbury Cathedral (1982).

Another striking consequence of the new ecclesiology was that the clearer recognition that God works in the world as well as in the Church created a sense of legitimate interest in the struggle for political justice. Pope John XXIII had in mind, according to Piers Paul Read in his brilliant novel *Monk Dawson* (1969), nothing less than 'a total reversal of the Catholic Church's traditional attitude on social questions. No longer were the pious permitted to believe that the material plight of their fellow men was irrelevant to the quest for eternal salvation' (p. 43). This combines with the influence of the ever-increasing Third World proportion of the Church to create the so-called liberation theology, the belief that the search for social justice is part of the very essence of the gospel. At the Medellin conference of bishops in Colombia in 1968 a 'preferential option to the poor' was firmly asserted.

Despite the Church's traditional anti-communism and the history of communist persecution of Catholics, the new social thinking led to a more sympathetic approach to Marxism. By a previously unthinkable transformation an initial *rapprochement* sometimes became, indeed, a virtual identification. A general support for just revolution was even translated into action in some cases, and the story of the most famous 'guerilla priest' Camillo Torres caused a considerable stir. In Italy several priests stood as Communist Party candidates and even in England a Catholic Marxist group developed based around the Cambridge magazine *Slant*.

The implications of all this took a long time to work their way through, if indeed they ever have. An immediate furore occurred about what might have seemed the relatively superficial change from the use of Latin in the Mass to the vernacular language. Yet in a sense the symbolic significance of this was immense. In this one shift the image of the Church as changeless, of which the continued use of Latin was a visible sign, was dented, and the universality of the international Church was to some degree downgraded in comparison with the needs of the local community. Evelyn Waugh, for example, was heartbroken. He comments in a revised preface to the *Sword of Honour* trilogy that he finds himself unexpectedly to have written an 'obituary of the Roman Catholic Church in England as it had existed for many centuries . . . All the rites and most of the opinions here described are already obsolete . . . It never occurred to me, writing *Sword of Honour*, that the Church was susceptible to change.' Like Gilbert Pinfold he made a point of avoiding the new liturgy whenever possible.[15]

Rumer Godden's *In This House of Brede* describes the turmoil created in an aristocratic English convent:

> 'Vernacular.' The word, to Dame Agnes, was flaming red as hell fire. 'I'm glad they call it "vernacular". It's not even English,' and, 'Where is our universal Church?' she demanded. 'Once upon a time, from the north pole to the south, in either hemisphere, you would have found the Mass the same, and could join in and worship in it; now we are split into divisions . . .'
>
> 'Muddled thinking, muddled thinking,' said Dame Agnes, as one cherished tradition after another was felled by popular vote. Soon many of the nuns were asking in anguish, 'Does any good ever come out of a Council?'
>
> 'So much,' said some, 'is slipping away – being lost.' 'So much,' said others, 'is coming in.'
>
> (389–90)

Many of the changes were greeted with similar incomprehension and hostility, but the sense of disturbance was not limited to the reactionary elements. The new theology of marriage and the laity and the revised view of the Church made many progressive priests wonder if their sacrifices were worth while. The newspapers were predictably fascinated. As Piers Paul Read says in *Monk Dawson* 'any priest who ran off and got married was sure of a big spread' (p. 45). But it was dissatisfaction with the slowness and in the end with the very notion of an institutional Church as much as problems with celibacy that caused so many priests to leave. When one of the most distinguished English Catholic theologians, Charles Davis, left not only the priesthood but also the Church, the shockwaves were enormous.[16]

John Cornwell's *The Spoiled Priest* (1969) is a vivid account of the departure of several young Benedictines. Sex is an issue for them certainly, and the frustration leading to Father Gilbert's affair with Sandra is described as well as the resulting disappointment. But Gilbert in a rebellious lecture to his clerical students before his own departure says priests have been leaving 'to save themselves from the death of institutionalism' (p. 149). In a bitter reunion of three 'spoiled priests' at the end, only Malachy has been able to retain any hope in the future of the Church, and that a vague one. Mark has remained completely cynical and Gilbert, it appears, amidst the debris of domesticity, says, secretly every night, a Latin Mass in his room.

Monk Dawson, the best novel of a 'spoiled priest' from this period, becomes, like Lodge's *How Far Can You Go?*, a trajectory through the whole experience of the changes in the Church as they affect the life of the eponymous hero. As a naïve and idealistic monk at a Benedictine public school Dawson is carried away by the new ideas. His failure to bring about change at a sufficiently rapid pace within his own institution disillusions him, and he has a breakdown and leaves the order to take up a position at Westminster Cathedral. Here his contact with the problems of London causes him to lose his faith, though he retains his idealism. He leaves the priesthood and becomes a crusading journalist for a time, but in a pointed reversal of the usual failed-priest story he grows disgusted with the world and decides to become a Trappist monk at the end.

Much of the controversy of the time focused on birth control, an issue which raised central questions about the relationship between individual conscience and church authority and tradition and which presented the clearest possible clash between the pressures of a hedonistic and permissive society and a conservative asceticism. Progressive priests had in fact for some time refused to condemn 'artificial' birth control, and the hope grew that Rome would officially permit it. When Pope Paul VI reaffirmed the traditional teaching in *Humanae Vitae* in 1968 there was considerable disappointment, and since many Catholic couples continued to ignore the teaching older ideas of authority were further weakened.

Bruce Marshall's *The Bishop* (1970) reflects this in the story of a conservative bishop's attempts to impose the dogma on a reluctant diocese. If Lodge's *The Picturegoers* is basically affectionate and affirmative, his *The British Museum Is Falling Down* (1965) is a much more farcical and bitter satire in tone, showing the influence of the controversy in this respect. It tells the story of a single day in the life of Adam Appleby, a young Catholic graduate student, who is frustrated by the constant prohibition against birth control and afraid that his wife might be pregnant for the fourth time.

The general movement towards secularization and permissiveness was obviously parallel to and related to some of the new movements in the Church:

> The spirit of protest was abroad, but Michael had not yet been able to find a cause he could plausibly identify with. He was too old for the student movement, too apolitical for the New Left (*Slant* had finally bored him), too moral (or too timid) for the Counter Culture of drugs, rock and casual sex. He was finding himself pushed to the margins of the decade, forced into a posture of conservatism which made him feel as if his youth were disappearing at an ever-increasing speed, like the earth beneath an astronaut. The idea of challenging ecclesiastical authority in the cause of sexual fulfilment for married couples and freedom of speech for priests seemed an opportunity to hitch his wagon to the *Zeitgeist* in good faith. Michael did not, of course, analyse his motives as explicitly as this, and did not understand (he accounted for it purely as impulse buying) why, shortly after sending off his subscription to Catholics for an Open Church, he bought a pair of the new-style trousers with flared bottoms and a copy of the Beatles 'white' double album, his first non-classical record. He had joined the sixties, in the nick of time.
>
> (*How Far Can You Go?*: 122)

Such an overlap, nicely treated by Lodge, enables conservative Catholic novelists to portray the whole renewal movement as a simple phenomenon of trendiness. In *The Takeover* (1976) Muriel Spark satirizes what she regards as the new modishness of the Church in the person of two American Jesuits. In *The Abbess of Crewe* (1974) she shows markedly less sympathy for the progressive nun Felicity than for her heroine the Abbess. Rose, Alice Thomas Ellis's heroine in *The Sin Eater* (1977), says,

> 'The last time I went to Mass – and it *was* the last time – there was the P. P. facing the congregation, standing behind his table, and joining in the singing of the negro spirituals and the pop songs and Shall-we-gather-at-the-river ... They want you to kiss the person next to you ... We've already got Moody and Sankey, and soon it'll be snake-handling.'
>
> (pp. 97, 96)

For her the Church has simply 'lost its head':

> 'It is as though,' she went on, 'one's revered, dignified and darling old mother had slapped on a mini-skirt and fishnet tights and started ogling strangers. A kind of menopausal madness, a sudden yearning to be attractive to all. It is tragic and hilarious and awfully embarrassing. And, of course, those who knew her before feel a great sense of betrayal and can't bring themselves to go and see her any more.
>
> (1986 reprint: 98–9)

In John Braine's *The Pious Agent* (1975) the hero's confessor, who turns out to have been a communist spy all along, says that the Church has been intent on destroying itself, and no wonder with 'such a drivelling idiot as Pope John in charge of it.' In *Earthly Powers* Anthony Burgess satirizes a Pope John figure for his misguided Pelagian optimism which has brought about havoc by ignoring the realities of original sin. The introduction of the vernacular indirectly causes the death of the Pope's and the author's niece and nephew, since they are eaten in an act of cannibalism as part of an Africanized Mass.

One of the clearest signs of Pope Gregory's misguidedness for Burgess is his sympathy for Marxism. As might be expected, Graham Greene is much more sympathetic to the new enthusiasm in the Church for social justice, and his are the first British Catholic novels to pick up on the subject of liberation theology. *The Comedians* (1966) contains a sermon on those lines, and *The Honorary Consul* (1973) is a sympathetic portrait of a revolutionary priest Father Rivas. Greene has always had a remarkably strong sense of tension with the institution. This combines with his political sympathies to give the new theology a particular fascination for him, especially as he comes to think of himself personally as more and more on the margins of the Church anyway. *A Burnt-out Case* (1961) and *The Honorary Consul* both make powerful use of the new ideas and in particular explore the motif of the 'anonymous' Christian outside the Church.[17]

In his first novel *Game in Heaven with Tussy Marx* (1966) Piers Paul Read shows a specific interest in Catholic Marxism. Later novels such as *Polonaise* (1976) and *The Free Frenchman* (1986) impressively explore the complexities of European politics but reach the conclusion that any purely political solution is futile and ethics impossible without God. The same idea is urged in an English context in *A Married Man* (1979). *The Upstart* (1973) meanwhile reveals a special self-consciousness about writing a 'Catholic novel', deliberately combining Evelyn Waugh and Graham Greene in the story of a middle-class young man taken up and then dropped by an upper-class family. He takes a terrible revenge but loses his appetite for it, becoming one of those sinners so popular in Catholic fiction whose very sins lead him to God.

David Lodge's *How Far Can You Go?*, already quoted from several times in this chapter, is the most central, amusing and compassionate account of the changes in Catholicism throughout this period. It follows the lives of a group of young people at the London Catholic University Chaplaincy through the fifties to the seventies. Their experiences are both vivid and representative. The young priest chaplain leaves the priesthood. The majority of the students marry and go through all the problems of the birth-control dilemma and, in several cases, adultery and divorce as well. Ruth becomes a nun and a fervent member of the charismatic movement that tries to renew Catholicism by the introduction of Pentecostal ways of worship. Miles decides to accept he is gay. Lodge is highly adept at intertwining the stories of all of them with the events of ecclesiastical, political and cultural history of the era: the Vatican Council, the Beatles, the assassination of Kennedy.

But his central theme becomes the gradual collapse of the whole elaborate, slowly built-up metaphysical system which Catholics were brought up in and converts expected to conform to, a system in which the fundamentals of Christianity were combined with a wide range of traditions, philosophy, ethical theories, disciplines and devotions in one apparent whole:

that marvellously complex and ingenious synthesis of theology and cosmology and casuistry, which situated individual souls on a kind of spiritual Snakes and Ladders board, motivated them with equal doses of hope and fear and promised them, if they persevered in the game, an eternal reward. The board was marked out very clearly, decorated with all kinds of picturesque motifs, and governed by intricate rules and provisos. Heaven, hell, purgatory, limbo. Mortal, venial and original sin. Angels, devils, saints, and Our Lady Queen of Heaven, Grace, penance, relics, indulgences and all the rest of it. Millions of Catholics no doubt still believe in all that literally. But belief is gradually fading. That metaphysic is no longer taught in schools and seminaries in the more advanced countries, and Catholic children are growing up knowing little or nothing about it. Within another generation or two it will have disappeared, superseded by something less vivid but more tolerant.

(p. 239)

This system had also depended upon elaborate sociological supports, and its collapse is indistinguishable from the collapse of those supports, the decline in Catholic 'apartness' through increased social mobility, the influence of the media and so on. The comments in *How Far Can You Go?* are confirmed by sociologists and theologians. Karl Rahner wrote that throughout the whole world Catholics were moving into a period of 'diaspora', separated from communal and institutional supports. Eamonn Bredein has spoken of the decline of the Christian 'commonwealth' and Anthony Archer has spoken of a decline of corporate pressure and identity, so that Catholics have moved into a more individual and 'Protestant' way of doing things.[18] Both Bernard Bergonzi and David Lodge have argued that these new emphases and the decline in the sociological 'apartness' of the British Catholic are, for better or worse, destroying the distinctive perspective that produced the 'Catholic novel'.[19]

All this must not be exaggerated. The impact has been far greater among middle-class graduates such as those described in *How Far Can You Go?* than in the wider community, where inertia has often reigned. As Piers Paul Read writes in *Monk Dawson*:

The Catholic Church in England was protected from these harsh changes by its easy and insular situation. There was no competition for righteousness as there was, say, in Holland with its vital Protestantism and moral Socialism. There were no Mormons or Baptists hunting for wavering souls, as in the United States. A handful of Dominican friars did their best to ferment discussion and reform, but the large part of the clergy still looked to Dublin rather than to the Continent for inspiration and example . . .

(pp. 44–5)

British Catholics certainly did not avoid the turmoil, but they often gave the impression of trying to do so. In some quarters the Council has simply been ignored and people have continued, though diminished in number, almost as before. They have felt encouraged in such a position in recent years, if only in part legitimately, by the example of Pope John Paul II who himself seems unenthusiastic about certain aspects of the Council and in some ways represents and has enforced a new conservatism.

As this survey has shown, Catholic attitudes to art and a firm sense of traditional Catholic identity have provided the cultural base from which certain Catholic writers have made a distinctive contribution to British fiction and a distinctive critique of the British status quo. Their rhetoric has exaggerated the general Catholic alienation from British society, but their strategy clearly could not have succeeded if they had not in this reflected what has been at least an *element* in British Catholic experience.

The relative decline of the Church of England and mainstream Protestantism in recent years has given Catholic writers an even more central role in expressing a Christian viewpoint in the novel. At the same time the change in the sense of Catholic identity since the Second Vatican Council has made that contribution more problematic, especially since novelists come from the social grouping that has been most affected by the new trends. Despite continued resistence to these influences it is difficult to believe that the old certainties can ever be restored. When Anthony Archer argues, however, that the typical modern English Catholic has become more liberal and individualistic in outlook, he is very clear that this also implies that the Church has completely given up its critique of secular society now and the hope of suggesting an alternative. Such a critique had been no more than a partial one, it is true, and had often come from a reactionary direction. But if such an important segment of the Christian Church has really ceased to be able to offer an alternative vision at all here, then the loss of a distinctive voice in the novel would be only one symptom of a much more far-reaching and tragic failure.

Part two

The Catholic 'difference'

· 4 ·
'This alien land'

The 'difference' of English Catholics

In Waugh's *Brideshead Revisited*, Sebastian says to Charles Ryder:

'. . . I wish I liked Catholics more.'
'They seem just like other people.'
'My dear Charles, that's exactly what they're not – particularly in this country, where they are so few. It's not just that they're a clique – as a matter of fact they're at least four cliques, all blackguarding each other half the time – but they've got an entirely different outlook on life: everything they think important is different from other people.'
(Reprint 1949: 80)

The New Testament presents the Christian likewise as one marked off from non-Christians and the world by an essential difference. Christians are 'aliens and strangers in the world', according to St Peter's First Epistle (2:11); the 'bearers', in the words of a modern theologian, 'of essentially different needs, goals and satisfactions' to those of the society that surrounds them.[1]

The 'world' to which St Paul says Christians must not be conformed is not, of course, to be confused with this physical earth as such but consists rather of the whole complex of the structures of worldly power and status organized without reference to God. It has both a political and a social dimension. When a character in Josephine Mary Ward's *One Poor Scruple* says that people sell their soul to the world now, not the devil, she has in mind all the pressures of 'society' in the upper-class county sense, and she is speaking in a particular historical context in which Catholics were moving in such circles more openly than ever before (p. 201). But her comment may be seen as a particular example of the pressures of social convention and environment in a non-Christian world or one that pays no more than lip-service to Christian ideals. It is a significant part of the process of salvation to be freed from the delusive values, dominion and oppression of that 'world' in all its different dimensions. The individual and communal Christian lifestyle is meant to represent a challenge to it, and the coming of God's kingdom signifies its ultimate overthrow.

A rather difficult balance is suggested all the same in the idea of being 'in the world but not of it'. Complete withdrawal is not an option. Christians clearly have a responsibility for those in the world and, whether they want to or not, may have to live the main body of their lives there. Their task is the difficult one of being detached from 'the world' and presenting an ideological challenge to it, whilst at the same time remaining active in it.

As Piers Paul Read's *Monk Dawson* finely shows, unworldliness is itself after all rather an ambiguous concept. The young Dawson is presented from the beginning as hypersensitive, a 'friend somehow too precious for ordinary use'. At the age of seven he is heavily punished for refusing to eat meat after seeing the school's herd of cows. A naïve idealism underlies both his decision to become a priest and his decision to leave. By the time he decides to return to a stricter order at the close, the whole book has come to pivot on the question of whether 'Monk Dawson' is 'unworldly' in the sense of being withdrawn, eccentric, naïvely idealistic or in the sense that he has seen the worthlessness of this passing world and become the bearer of a supernatural critique of its values. Read's own view is clearly that Dawson has learnt something and moved from one kind of unworldliness to another, but the clever use of the third-person narrator, Dawson's sceptical childhood friend, preserves the possibility of ambiguity.

In a well-known passage an early Christian writer says that Christians 'dwell in their own countries but only as sojourners. . . . Every foreign country is a fatherland to them, and every fatherland is a foreign country.'[2] If Monk Dawson represents the 'unworldliness' of the Christian he also represents English Catholics. For the minority status and 'alien' quality of Catholics in England can itself be presented as a special, concentrated instance of this essential Christian 'difference'. There is no doubt that Waugh wants Sebastian's comment, a central theme of *Brideshead Revisited*, to be read in this way. Disarming the reader by his criticism, Waugh still wants to intimate that Catholics are 'different' because they are in possession of supernatural truth and therefore display, as Compton Mackenzie's John Ogilvie also comes to believe, 'an assurance and security which [makes] them curiously independent of this world' (*The East Wind of Love*, 1937; 1973 reprint: 233).

This assertion that Catholics are different is a constant refrain in the British Catholic novel. Gabrielle Donnolly, for example, writes in *Holy Mother* (1987) that 'To be Catholic in England was to be subtly outside the rest of the community.' England was a Protestant country and in order to live in it at all Catholics had been forced to adopt

> more or less slowly and with more or less success, the protective colouring of this alien land that was the land of their birth. They had hidden their plaster statues in drawers and their Leonardo Madonnas in the backs of

cupboards; had forced themselves not to mention if it was St Joseph's day or the feast of the Assumption; had disciplined themselves not to cross themselves when lightning flashed or to bow their heads at the name of Jesus, or ask St Anthony to help find lost keys, and never ever, if humanly possible, to let slip the fact that they went regularly to Mass. For the most part, they succeeded; for the most part those around them, friends and colleagues, were aware of their Catholicism dimly if at all, certainly had no idea of the breadth of the chasm that lay between the way they seemed to be and the way they were.

(pp. 11–12)

But Donnolly's selection of detail and diction is deliberately arch. Her alternation between 'plaster statues' and 'Leonardo Madonnas' and between crossing 'themselves when lightning flashed' and bowing their 'heads at the name of Jesus' suggests that the strange difference of Catholicism as a whole is an ambiguous one, encompassing both high art and bad taste, both piety and superstition.

The special history and sociology of the English Catholic community have served both to focus and further complicate these ambiguities. The genuine religious difference has become entangled with secondary and even negative peculiarities that Catholic writers are themselves often eager to point out. Are English Catholics in the same position as the early Christians, the 'bearers of essentially different needs, goals and satisfactions' to the values of the world around them? Or are they unworldly in a pejorative sense and purely for reasons of persecution, inbreeding, and characteristic neurosis? The hero of Edmund Randolph's *Mostly Fools* is greeted on his first arrival at St Augustine's school by a 'small boy only four feet high, dressed in a scarlet cassock and biretta' (I: 33), and the eccentricity of the school becomes for Randolph an apt emblem of the absurdity of the whole of English Catholic life.

Ford Madox Ford's unsympathetic non-Catholic narrator in *The Good Soldier* takes a very long historical perspective to describe Leonara's distinctively English Catholic conscience. He says it has been

> driven in on the English Catholics. The centuries they have gone through – centuries of blind and malignant oppression, of ostracism from public employment, of being, as it were, a small beleaguered garrison in a hostile country, and therefore having to act with great formality – all these things have combined to perform that conjuring trick.
>
> (*The Bodley Head Madox Ford*, vol. 1: 61)

Josephine Mary Ward comments in similar fashion, as quoted before, on the way that the 'persecuted had come, in many cases, to idealise the enforced seclusion and inaction of penal days' (*One Poor Scruple*: 100). Rolfe in *Hadrian VII* is openly contemptuous. The Pope explains in an epistle to his fellow countrymen that the penal laws, 'which from 1534–1829 had deprived them of "that culture which contact with a wider world alone can give," had rendered the Catholic aborigines corporeally effete and intellectually inferior to the rest of the nation' (p. 187). Yet the whole matter is bound up with complex ideological issues, as we shall see, and the same Catholic writers who analyse, passionately or dispassionately, the more negative aspects of the English Catholic difference also often seem to wish to highlight that difference as a special mystique.

Foreignness

The most obvious way for its enemies to interpret the difference of Catholicism is, of course, to present it as literally a foreign influence. To the Victorian Anglican Archbishop Benson Roman Catholicism was 'the Italian Mission'. The anti-Catholic Victorian novelist Catharine Sinclair wrote in a splendid phrase that 'Romish principles are as out of place in an English drawing room as an Italian organ grinder in a palace.'[3]

As we have seen though, this emphasis on the foreign aspects of Catholicism is developed by Catholics themselves as part of the mystique of difference as well as by the Church's opponents. For a few Catholic writers indeed – Henry Harland, Ronald Firbank perhaps – it is quite literally the foreign associations of Catholicism that make up its appeal. Superficial though such an attraction may be, it can assume ideological dimensions as an attack on or an escape from a stuffy British bourgeois ethos. Even Henry Harland cultivates the sentimental charms of Italy to some extent at least in deliberate contrast to the contemporary English scene, and Frederick Rolfe uses Italy much more aggressively as a critique of English – including English Catholic – Puritanism.

Graham Greene and Anthony Burgess both use a foreign Catholic environment to contrast with and criticize the secular trivialities of England. In Burgess's first novel *A Vision of Battlements* the Catholic Gibraltar setting is shown to have more sin and evil in it than England, but to be for that very reason more real, and the whole presentation is obviously influenced by such motifs in Greene.[4] The latter's trip to Mexico as a journalist reporting on the government's persecution of the Church showed him a place in which the true issues were no longer concealed: 'Here were idolatry and oppression, starvation and casual violence, but you lived under the shadow of religion, of God or the devil.'[5] This is later, of course, to provide the backcloth for the great drama of *The Power and the Glory*.

The Africa of *The Heart of the Matter* is more murky and confused, but it still entangles the very English and 'decent' Scobie in a conflict of damnation and salvation that would not have occurred if he had stayed in his own country:

> Why, he wondered, swerving the car to avoid a dead pye-dog, do I love this place so much? Is it because here human nature hasn't had time to disguise itself?. . . . Here you could love human beings nearly as God loved them, knowing the worst: you didn't love a pose, a pretty dress, a sentiment artificially assumed.
>
> (Reprint 1950: 30)

Naturally it is Greene's intention to suggest that it is Catholicism as such rather than the foreign environment that is the core of this drama. He asserts the essential identity between Scobie and the Portuguese captain in an intense passage already quoted to show the special emotional imagery of Catholicism:

> He had discovered suddenly how much they had in common: the plaster statues with the swords in the bleeding heart: the whisper behind the confessional curtains: the holy coats and the liquefaction of blood: the dark side chapels and the intricate movements, and somewhere behind it all the love of God.
>
> (p. 49)

Yet when Greene transposes the drama to England, he is forced – revealingly – to look for situations themselves already extreme: criminal Brighton, London in the blitz, for example.

A handful of writers indeed prefer to highlight the *contrast* between British and continental Catholicism as a way of attacking the spiritual and cultural deadness of their own co-religionists here. Rolfe in particular turns such a strategy into a systematic satire on the insularity and pallor of British Catholicism, woundingly calling Westminster Cathedral, for example, an 'ugly veneered pretentious monstrosity . . . a futile monument to one man's vain desire for notoriety' (*Hadrian VII*: reprint 129). Aesthetic snobbery is also involved in Pope Hadrian's differentiation between continental and British Catholic liturgy:

> I can hear Mass with devotion as well as with aesthetic pleasure in a church which has dark corners and no pews. I've never seen one in this country where I can be unconscious of the hideous persons and outrageous costumes of the congregation, the appalling substitute for ecclesiastical music, the tawdry insolence of the place, the pretentious demeanour of the ministers.
>
> (p. 48)

In a more purely religious critique Margaret, the heroine of Alice Thomas Ellis's *The Clothes in the Wardrobe* (1987), experiences through her contact with a Catholic convent in Egypt, 'what seemed like a different religion, a thing of unimaginable heights and depths, of light and shadow' (p. 48). Her mother on the other hand, a 'very English Catholic', thinks a nun's life a terrible waste.

More commonly, the cultural identification of British Catholics with a wider world is emphasized instead as a self-congratulatory piece of apologetics. Father Smith in Marshall's *All Glorious Within* expresses the most usual form of this, saying that Catholics here should be proud that they 'alone among their fellow countrymen are in step with European tradition' (p. 16). Hilaire Belloc had his own caustic remarks to make about the native British Catholics, but it is he who develops the commonplace about the 'European' aspects of Catholicism into the most ambitious of all attempts to use Catholicism as an ideological control on the British people. The basic aim, in which the actual novels have only a marginal part to play, was to enlist the British in what he presents as the defence of European civilization itself against barbarism and secularism. He attempts, in other words, to highlight and strengthen those elements in

Britain's identity that he regarded as part of its European Catholic heritage, while at the same time castigating its provincial Protestant deviancies.[6]

The dangerous political implications of such a strategy are the subject of Bernard Bergonzi's *The Roman Persuasion*, where it leads the publisher Martin Tollybeare into fascism. When he takes over a Catholic journal despite the reservations of the more English party, the first sign of deterioration is his determination to change the name of the *English and Overseas Review* to *Res Latina*:

> Mr Belloc has used it, certainly, but it's a much older idea than that. It's meant to recall the origins of Christian civilization in the Roman world, and the essentially Latin nature of that civilization. As Catholics we are inevitably also Romans.
>
> (p. 36)

The treason that the end of this novel points towards is obviously an extreme instance, but the idea of the foreign allegiances of Catholicism has often raised the whole question of loyalty. For several centuries the belief specifically that Catholics owed allegiance to 'the Pope of Rome' was the justification for persecution and the penal laws. Once genuinely matters of life and death, these have by now been largely transformed into ideological and rhetorical strategies in fiction. In *Urgent Copy: Literary Studies* (1968), for example, Burgess writes with a flourish, 'I remain as an English Catholic the subject of an alien *raj*'[7] and goes on to insist that 'Catholic patriotism must necessarily be of a qualified kind' (p. 14). When his hero decides to emigrate to Italy at the end of *The Worm and the Ring* (1961) rather than remain in the secular, chromium-plated society of post-war Britain, the point is made that:

> They were going to seek the other side of themselves in an exile which was not wholly exile, for England had not been completely a home for them and their kind for nearly four centuries.

In *Tremor of Intent* (1966) these motifs are flamboyantly developed into the idea of Catholics as a fifth column. The early pages memorably evoke the alien, oppositional quality of the Catholic college of Bradcaster, which 'did not, sir, smell of Rupert Brooke's or your England. The school smelt of Catholicism, meaning the thick black cloth of clerical habits, stale incense, holy water, fasting breaths, stockfish, the tensions of celibacy' (p. 5). It is this sense of an alien background that provides the psychological preparation for Hillier's career as a spy. Later though, his liquidation is ordered by his own side, because as a Catholic the British authorities can never afford to trust him fully. The novel ends with Hillier's decision to enter into a more profound war and become a deeper kind of subversive as a priest:

> 'What they call a late vocation,' said Hillier. 'I had to go to Rome for a kind of crash-course. But one of these days we'll meet again on a voyage, and I'll be a real imposter. Another typewriter technician or a computer salesman.

'This alien land'

I think, though, I'll be travelling tourist. Otherwise, it'll just be like old times – sneaking into the Iron Curtain countries, spying, being subversive. . . .

'Like the Jesuits in Elizabeth's time,' said Alan.

(p. 239)

In the much wider context Terry Eagleton has argued in an influential study that most of the greatest British writers of this century have been exiles and emigrés.[8] It is clear that being a Roman Catholic may have its own contribution to make to this sense of opposition to the dominant culture, and the Catholic internal 'exiles' in England have the advantage of having the authority of Catholic tradition behind them. As Eagleton comments, such major writers as Waugh and Greene in their very different ways use their Catholicism as a 'point of transcendence' from which their culture can be criticized and placed (p. 137).

Englishness

All these emphases on the 'foreign' and oppositional quality of Catholicism are much more intensely represented in Catholic fiction, of course, than they are in the Catholic community at large because of the higher proportion of converts and intellectuals among the novelists. What has struck most recent commentators and historians on the contrary is the essentially home-grown quality to Catholicism here. Edward Norman writes, for example, 'Despite the insistence on Roman authority, it is a notable feature of English Catholic history that it has remained very English.'[9]

It seems only proper therefore that Wilfred Cartwright should pointedly reply to his nephew's assertion of the Roman aspects of Catholicism in Bergonzi's novel, 'I like to think of myself as an Englishman first. I don't find that irreconcilable with being a Catholic' (p. 36). What soon becomes clear, however, is that the whole debate is more of an ideological than a factual one. The strategy of highlighting the 'alien' character of Catholicism which Catholic writers cultivate as a weapon against the status quo clashes with the Church's more general aim of being accepted here. It is essential for the purposes of self-defence, apologetics and proselytizing to show that there is nothing inherently unEnglish about the religion.

Naturally enough therefore Catholic novelists often parody the accusation that Catholics are unEnglish and attribute it to Protestants as a mark of their ignorance or bigotry. In M. C. Bishop's *Elizabeth Eden*, for example, the heroine, later herself to be a convert, says 'You will never get the Romish plant to thrive in British soil.' In Robert Hugh Benson's *An Average Man* it is said of Catholicism by a very unsympathetic character that 'It isn't English', and elsewhere to become a Catholic is compared to marrying an actress in that both are out of harmony with English country life. Claude Batchelor's father in Antonia White's *The Lost Traveller* is particularly shocked by his son's conversion because he thinks that 'All Roman Catholics are foreigners. I can't see why the

Church of England isn't good enough for you. I don't hold with these foreign religions and never shall' (p. 204). The insistence with which the charge is referred to obviously suggests how much it rankles.

What Claude Batchelor tries in vain to get his father to see is that, far from being a foreign import, Catholicism had been the religion of England up to the time of Henry VIII (p. 204). Waugh describes Lord Marchmain as saying to his wife on his conversion, 'You have brought back my family to the faith of their ancestors' (p. 194). This idea of Catholicism as 'the faith of our fathers' is a deeply felt one among British Catholics, and from very early on in the fiction such an essential Englishness is often asserted. Elizabeth Inchbald's Mr Dorriforth, for example, is an English gentleman of the classic mould as well as a Catholic priest, and he is the first of a long line of Catholic priests strategically portrayed as very English – Waugh's Father Phipps, for example, 'a bland, bun-faced man with an interest in county cricket which he obstinately believed us to share' (*Brideshead Revisited*, reprint: 76). The whole motif of 'Englishness' is especially central in the novels of Edward Dering, Robert Hugh Benson (despite his ultramontane bias), Sheila Kaye-Smith and Evelyn Waugh.

The accusation of disloyalty is above all, of course, denied with great indignation. The hero in Benson's *Come Rack, Come Rope* is shown as refusing absolution to Babington because of the latter's intention of assassinating Elizabeth. Wilfred Cartwright in *The Roman Persuasion* reminds himself after a discussion about the Armada with a Spanish priest that 'Even the Elizabethan Catholics, persecuted as they were, were patriotic men who wanted to resist invasion. One of Queen Elizabeth's admirals in the defence against the Armada, Lord Howard of Effingham, was a Catholic' (p. 69).

Instead of emphasizing how European British Catholicism is or alternatively castigating it for its lack of colour, culture and fervour in comparison with the continent, such writers seek to highlight the differences between British and foreign Catholicism in an ostensibly more neutral or objective way that often shades over into celebrating its distinctiveness here. Pearl Craigie maintains in *The Dream and the Business* (1906) that England will never be cosmopolitan and that 'Catholicism–Protestantism itself – takes peculiar characteristics in this nation' (p. 113). Very much the same point is made in Sheila Kaye-Smith's *Gallybird* (1934) when the Frenchwoman Louise returns with some relief to her own country. French Catholicism, she feels, is 'remote from normal English religion, whether Protestant or Catholic' (p. 409). In a fine moment in Rachel Billington's *Occasion of Sin* (1982) the heroine Laura, on an adulterous trip to Italy with her lover Martin, passes

> heavy church doors open for the evening, candles flickering. For a second Laura is stabbed with the memory of her own Catholicism. But this ornate darkness is so different from her quiet English experience that she quickly discounts it.
>
> (1983 reprint: 177)

In *The Roman Persuasion* the urbane, sympathetic but somewhat worldly Monsignor Whitmarsh remarks to Wilfred of the dangers represented by

'This alien land'

Belloc's kind of ideological takeover-bid: 'I think it a pity that someone like your highly intelligent and well-read nephew tries to tell us that we can only be good Catholics by picking up a lot of unsuitable Continental notions and trying to imitate Italians and Spaniards' (p. 137). The model he recommends instead is a very different one, and one with deep roots in the history and ethos of the English Catholic community:

> The English Catholics have never gone in for ideas very much, so they've avoided extremes, despite their admiration for Mr Belloc. They've kept up a decent tradition of piety and devotion in their own way, and they've always had a proper loyalty and respect for the Holy Father without being extravagantly Roman.
>
> (p. 136)

What would seem on the face of it to present a much more intractable problem is bluntly summarized by a character in Lodge's *How Far Can You Go?* in the remark that 'English Catholicism is largely Irish Catholicism' (p. 40). The numerical preponderance of Catholics of Irish origins and the influence of Irish priests can be hardly be denied. Father Finbar from Tipperary in the same author's *The British Museum Is Falling Down* is clearly meant to be a representative figure as one of those priests who 'seemed to regard the London parish in which he worked as a piece of the old Country, which had broken off in a storm and floated across the sea until it lodged in the Thames Basin' (1983 reprint: 29).

In a famous nineteenth-century comment one Catholic writer wrote, however, 'The average Englishman despises the Irishman. . . . I am sorry to say I cannot make any exception amongst the Protestants and Catholics of England in this feeling.'[10] Whatever the domination at normal parish level, the Irish exercised only a small influence on the ideologies of English Catholic writers. Enclaves of almost purely English Catholicism have always existed anyway for intellectuals and the upper classes. This is nicely caught by Piers Paul Read in the comments by Monk Dawson's mother: 'There are so many Irish among Catholics, aren't there? That's what's so nice about Kirkham – they're all English priests, aren't they? Here we only get Irish ones' (*Monk Dawson*: 36).

In so far as the Irish presence could present a class or political threat to English Catholics or a problem for them in their desire to prove their faith indigenous it is one that is solved to a considerable extent by simply ignoring it. After the early, unusually sympathetic and sentimental treatment in Beste's *Poverty and the Baronet's Family* described in chapter 1, the Irish Catholics in England receive little attention in fiction until the late fifties and early sixties of this century.

Even the political issue of Home Rule is largely ignored. The radical Edmund Randolph's hero in *Mostly Fools* is an MP in the Irish Nationalist interest. Ford Madox Ford's Catholicism is obviously one reason for his sympathetic treatment of the saintly Father Consett in *Parade's End* who is unjustly shot by the British after the Casement trials. The Scots Nationalist Compton Mackenzie provides the only major treatment as part of the vast panorama of *The Four Winds of Love*. The English government is described as sending the Black and

Tans to put down the Irish whilst preaching self-determination of nations at Versailles. The hero's IRA friend Fitzgerald is shot by the British in a death of which he has had a dramatic premonition.

In the late fifties and early sixties the situation changes with novelists such as David Lodge and John Braine who had been brought up in ordinary parochial Catholicism. Lodge's *The Picturegoers*, for example, is almost a parable from one perspective: the first Catholic novel for a long time to deal with the lives of Irish Catholics in England is also precisely *about* the encounter between a young, alienated, English intellectual Mark Underwood and the Irish family, the Mallorys. At first he finds the trappings of their faith distasteful: 'the plastic holy water stoup askew on the wall, the withered holy Palm, stuck behind a picture of the Sacred Heart which resembled an illustration in a medical textbook and the statue of St Patrick enthroned upon the dresser' (p. 40). Gradually, though, his attitude changes:

> . . . retrospectively he envied the Mallory children their hardships – the shared beds, the shoes that pinched, the heaps of washing, the inconvenience of too many babies in too short a time, the lack of privacy, the meagre pocket money, the quarrels and tears, because with these things went other things infinitely precious, laughter and love, tenderness and the joy of living, things signally missing from his own childhood.
>
> (p. 106)[11]

He is reconverted through his contact with them and decides by the end to become a priest.

All this has its elements of sentimentality, though Lodge shows more negative aspects of Irish influence in the character of Damien O'Brien. But his basic point is that the English Catholic rejection of the Irish is not just a class one, part of the 'pervasive snobbery' identified by Piers Paul Read, not just a blind disclaimer of any responsibility for the political situation in Ireland, but also a deep-rooted psychological manifestation. The English need what Lodge portrays as Irish warmth, and the snobbish refusal to allow themselves to learn from and receive from their co-religionists is a refusal to allow certain wounds in the national psyche to be healed.

In an ironic and witty passage in *Unconditional Surrender* Evelyn Waugh describes a non-Catholic praising Cardinal Hinsley's war speeches for their patriotism and saying approvingly that they show him to be 'an Englishman first and a Christian second' (1983 reprint: 62). In the last analysis it seems to have been this danger of remaining too English rather than of not being English enough that has proved the greater temptation for English Catholics. The British Catholic sense of separateness, itself a deeply ambiguous one as we have seen, has not usually in practice prevented Catholics from conforming to most of the norms of British society. Upper-class Catholics, despite their religion, have always in a sense been part of the British establishment, and the majority of Catholics have been by no means as cut off from the mainstream of British life and values as is often thought.

As several novels show, the English Catholic public school provides a special focus for this question. In the fine first paragraph of Read's *Monk Dawson* hints of those Gothic conventions of mysterious country houses and sinister monks so popular with nineteenth-century Protestant writers are invoked to portray the strangeness of the first impressions of a Catholic preparatory school:

> Acting on mistaken principles of piety and snobbery, my parents sent me to a boarding-school in the English country-side which was run by Benedictine monks. On the first day of the first term they drove me there themselves, to the country house surrounded by woods which smelt of wild garlic and dead crows. I was then seven years old. We were given tea by the headmaster, Father Francis Ashe, in a part of the school that was afterwards out of bounds to the boys, and then they drove away, leaving me alone for the first time in my life – alone with this priest in his black habit and hood.

But the strangeness of Kirkham proves to be relatively superficial and eccentric. What we really see is a basic accommodation to upper-class English norms, as Dawson himself later comes to recognize. There is a paradox after all in the whole idea of monks running expensive schools and training the children of the upper classes. In the traditional Officers' Training Corps, for example, 'On Mondays and Fridays the monks themselves would change out of their black habits into military uniforms, and then teach us how best to use bayonets and Bren guns' (p. 13). The Second Vatican Council causes considerable self-questioning among the monks. How can they reconcile their founder's intentions of providing a charitable education for the poor with their present position? But the view that the Abbot comes to accept

> was that the nature of the school at Kirkham must be related to English society, not to the Roman Church. Their religion might be as pure and modern as you like, but the businessmen of Birmingham and the aristocracy of Scotland would not send their sons to an academy for saints. Thus the monks continued to teach the boys how to kill, and one or two of the more fanatical reformers were found parishes in South Wales.
>
> (p. 48)

The faith of our fathers

Yet it is precisely in reaction against this modern English status quo that many writers have chosen Catholicism and developed its ideological implications, as we have seen. In exaggerating the alien aspects of the religion for that purpose, however, they have laid themselves open to the charge of lack of patriotism. Another group cleverly avoids this danger by fashioning the popular idea of 'the faith of our fathers' into a potent ideological weapon against the contemporary ethos and reinterpreting *true* Englishness as a long-lost quality which needs Catholicism for its fulfilment. The death of the old faith in Ford Maddox Ford's *The Fifth Queen* is shown to usher in the terrible new age of secularism in which we still live. In Baring's *C.* the convert Bede says to the hero, 'The English had gone wrong because they had fallen into a rut from the straight road of their true inheritance: Catholic England, Chaucer's England, to which the whole of Shakespeare's work was the dirge' (p. 389).

G. K. Chesterton's Hearne seeks to demonstrate in *The Return of Don Quixote* that the modern aristocracy are interlopers:

> I have found very few people possessing any pedigrees that would be recognised in the heraldic or feudal sense of medieval aristocracy . . . in all the three counties coming under my consideration, the men who seem to have no claim whatever to noble blood are the noblemen.
>
> (p. 280)

Similar strategies make it possible to mount a critique of the modern establishment from the perspective of an older truer establishment, and to combine a characteristic snobbery about Catholic aristocratic connections with a certain radicalism in a nostalgic quasi-feudal emphasis. A powerful feeling of dispossession is voiced – a quite literal dispossession in some writers, in whose work the modern Catholic exile and alien proves to be the original owner, the true heir. At the end of Ford's *Parade's End*, as noted in chapter 2, for example, there is a special sense of expiation in the fact that Tietjens's heir is to be a Catholic:

> 'Spelden on sacrilege,' he said, 'may be right after all. You'd say so from the Tietjenses. There's not been a Tietjens since the first Lord Justice cheated the Papist Loundeses out of Groby, but died of a broken neck or of a broken heart . . .
>
> (1963 reprint: 222)

Edward Dering and his family always wore seventeenth-century dress in his manor house at Baddesley Clinton, and his novels obsessively emphasize this idea of the Catholic gentry as the true and original possessors. Catholicism in his works is the essence of 'the English home-life that was – the life which modern radicalism is seeking to destroy by the help of modern principles and modern habits' (*The Ban of Mablethorpe*: 74). These novels are full of complaints at the despoliation of the Catholic gentry under the penal laws, and his good non-Catholics try, like Tietjens, to make restitution. The previously anti-Catholic owner of Mablethorpe is himself converted on his deathbed and leaves the estate to his nearest Catholic heir. Providence defeats various complicated conspiracies by apostates and evil foreigners and ensures that Catholics finally come back into their own.

Evelyn Waugh's critique of modern England also contains elements of the myth of the true Catholic past and is obviously bound up, like Dering's, with the Catholic aristocracy and gentry. In *Brideshead Revisited* Charles Ryder reads Mr Samgrass's history of the Marchmain family, which was 'typical of the Catholic squires of England'. Their long generations of suffering under the penal laws had taught them lessons of courage and self-sacrifice that had contributed to the heroic deaths of Lady Marchmain's three brothers, and so the family is to die out with Bridey:

These men must die to make a world for Hooper; they were the aborigines, vermin by right of law, to be shot off at leisure so that things might be safe for the travelling salesman, with his polygonal pince-nez, his fat wet handshake, his grinning dentures.

(1949 reprint: 123–4)

Scots Catholic writers are not subject to the special class pressures of English Catholicism. In Scotland, according to Bruce Marshall's Father Smith, 'the Church is the Church of the poor . . . and on the whole I'm not sorry, since it tends to keep both clergy and people in the invigorating spiritual and material conditions of primitive Christianity' (*All Glorious Within*, 1945 reprint: 71). But the strong Calvinist presence and the greater degree of open hostility towards Catholics make them even more prone to the glorification of a pre-Reformation past. Father Smith goes every St Andrew's day to say a prayer in the High Kirk for the conversion of Scotland:

As he knelt there, with the sun falling in through the stained glass windows upon the sheen of his old black coat, Father Smith thought away down the centuries back to the days when there had been a high altar in the chancel. There the Augustinian monks had sung their daily high mass and the passing of the hours had been rhymed on God's wise good clock of matins, lauds, prime, terce, sext and none. The Salve Regina had been sung among the shadows of the pillars, because the monks had thought that it was only fit to make the same sort of noise in time as they would hear throughout eternity.

These days had gone from Scotland now and Father Smith prayed that they would soon return, because he knew that only in the poetry of faith could men find happiness and purpose.

(*All Glorious Within*: 49–50)

The usefulness of this as a strategy is shown by its popularity with several Scots writers. The most extreme example is the work of Fionn MacColla, a convert both to Catholicism and Gaelic, who presents Calvinism as the cause of 'every Scottish ill' in several novels and works of polemic.[12] In the introduction to *The Albannach* (1932), written before his conversion, he goes so far as to say that 'Reformation Protestantism was not Christianity, or even a form of Christianity, but its almost complete antithesis' (1971 reprint, III) which matches the most extreme Protestant attacks in its virulence. The novel gives an account of the hero Murdo's own gradual reaction against Calvinism. An Irish priest Father O'Reilly is an impressive quasi-symbolic figure and he and Murdo read Irish and Scots lyrics to each other. When Murdo says at one point, 'O Ree, what have we lost!', the priest exhorts him 'Say rather what we shall recover!' (p. 97). The work reaches its symbolic climax in a contrast between the infernal circle of those frantically seeking progress in Glasgow and 'a long column of men marching with rhythmic pace, slowly, over the shoulder of Carn Ban, the wind piping a coronach among the trees' (p. 287).

The other full-length novel, *And the Cock Crew* (1945), is a powerful account of the Highland Clearances. In a debate between the Presbyterian minister who is misled into supporting them and a Gaelic poet, the latter says it would be better for the people to be pagan or papist 'if as you say they would thereby strike more deeply with their roots and be more firmly set to preserve our race in its variety and potency on earth' (1977 reprint: 134).

For George Mackay Brown the assertion that true Scottishness is pre-Reformation Scottishness is also a central one. Reaction against the 'Knox-ridden Nation' is especially clear in *Greenvoe*, which contrasts Mrs McKee's frightened dreams of her guilt-ridden inquisitions by the Kirk with Brown's praise of pre-Reformation Scotland for its aesthetic sense and carefree mores. Both *Greenvoe* and *Magnus* assimilate the eucharistic imagery of Catholicism to celebration of an agricultural pre-industrial society, for Brown's whole value system, like MacColla's, depends upon the vital organic link between such a society, true art and Catholicism. It was this living organism that the Reformation destroyed, 'the word was imprisoned between black boards, and chained and padlocked, in the pulpit of the kirk – impossible for it to get free among the ploughs and the nets, that season of famine.'[13] Seeing fundamentalism as the enemy of all the true allegories and analogies of the word, Brown nicely reverses the usual Protestant accusation that the chained bibles of the medieval church meant that the word of God was not read.

Greenvoe, the chronicle of an imaginary Orkney fishing village which is all but destroyed by the demands of a sinister 'defence' project, owes something to the comic novel, *Rockets Galore* (1957), by the most famous Catholic Scots Nationalist writer, Compton Mackenzie. The source of the fictional island in Mackenzie's popular novels is Barra where he lived for some years and which had itself been untouched by the Reformation. Anti-Calvinism is virulent in Mackenzie's own non-fictional *Catholicism and Scotland* (1936). Even at its most sophisticated, as will be explored later, Mackenzie's nationalism reveals itself to be similar to all these other versions of true Englishness and Scottishness in that it propounds a particular cultural mediation of Catholicism as definitive and cultivates the image of a golden age long ago.

The wide variety of responses in British Catholic fiction to the question of how 'foreign' or 'English' Catholicism is obviously reflects a wide range of ideological strategies. What lies at the heart of it all is how much challenge Catholicism is to be allowed to pose to established values, and this applies to British Catholics themselves as well as to those enemies of Catholicism who self-protectingly present it as no more than a foreign virus. A legitimate Christian critique has easily become confused with the various vested interests described here as well as the more general political purposes to be analysed in chapter 7. Catholicism has often proved a powerful ideological weapon, but those who have used it in this way have naturally enough been less ready to let their own values be put to the question.

· 5 ·

Catholic chic

'A poetical and aristocratic religion'

Christianity is presented in the New Testament as a religion that undercuts all forms of worldly dominion and worldliness, including the attractions of status. St Paul writes to the Corinthians:

> Take yourselves for instance, brothers, at the time you were called: how many of you were wise in the ordinary sense of the word, how many were influential people, or came from noble families? No, it was to shame the wise that God chose what is foolish by human reckoning; those whom the world thinks common and contemptible are the ones that God has chosen – those who are nothing at all to show up those who are everything.
> (I Cor.I, *Jerusalem Bible*:26–9)

If to be or to become a Catholic is to become 'different' in the sense in which the early Christians were definitively different – if it is to stand against and renounce the values of the world, its status and glory, then it would seem a humble, unglamorous road. For Newman's hero in *Loss and Gain* it meant the lacerating loss of Oxford and the end of worldly hopes. Charles Reding is warned in particular that 'An English clergyman is a gentleman; you may have more to bear than you reckon for, when you find yourself with men of rude minds and vulgar manners' (p. 328). Monk Dawson in Read's novel of that name becomes for a time part of the trendy sixties world of permissiveness and the media and lives glamorously with the beautiful and wealthy Jenny, but he leaves that world in disgust at the end, as we have seen.

The whole movement of Robert Hugh Benson's *An Average Man* (1913) is towards just such a moment of full recognition – the pointed contrast at the end between the glittering county marriage of Percy Brandreth-Smith, which has only come about because he has decided not to convert to Catholicism, and a scene in which the ex-Anglican curate Mr Main loses his new job as a commercial traveller. Main has sacrificed the whole world to become a Catholic, and his unprepossessing personality and manner are the emblems of the genuine and proper unworldliness of 'this failure of an Anglican curate, an uncomfortably angular man, who was proud and pleased to be a traveller in cocoa' (p. 364).

In the traditional imagery of theological apologetics, frequently repeated in the fiction, the Church stands secure in timeless truth, looking down on all the modish fads and follies of the day. According to MacIan in Chesterton's *The Ball and the Cross* (1909), 'Christianity is always out of fashion because it is always sane; and all fashions are mild insanities. When Italy is mad on art the Church seems too puritanical; when England is mad on Puritanism the Church seems too artistic' (p. 148).

Yet when Claude Batchelor's wife, Isabel, in Antonia White's *The Lost Traveller* follows her husband into the faith, 'Catholicism seemed to her a poetical and aristocratic religion. Nothing would have induced her to wrestle with historical or doctrinal problems but she had already gone so far as to buy herself a crystal rosary and a black lace mantilla' (1982 reprint, vol. I: 202). When Miriam in Lodge's *How Far Can You Go?* is introduced to Catholicism by her future husband Michael, she too finds it 'just what she was looking for: it was subtle, it was urbane, it had history, learning, art (especially music) on its side' (p. 58), and she compares it most favourably with the 'gloomy Sabbatarianism' and 'charmless liturgy' of the Protestantism in which she had been brought up.

A wide variety of factors combine, it seems, to give Catholicism a certain glamour. It is hard, for example, to imagine *The Tatler* devoting a special article to Methodist or United Reform chic.[1] The very word 'chic' is the one chosen by Belloc in suggesting that the Church must use the world's own weapons: 'we *can* spread the mood that we are the bosses and the *chic* and that a man who does not accept the Faith writes himself down as suburban. Upon these amiable lines do I proceed.'[2]

The word 'chic', of course, seems to imply superficiality and an over-concentration on purely social factors. To emphasize the intellectual, aesthetic and cultural appeal of Catholicism is by no means in itself to fall into such temptations. After all the Church's own belief that grace builds on nature lies behind its immense contribution to Western culture, the traditions of 'history, learning, art' to which Lodge's Miriam refers. Fionn MacColla pointedly contrasts this with the tragically misguided view of the Calvinist minister Maighstir Sachairi who believes that in God's eyes 'the beauty of earthly forms is by Sin turned into a loathing' (*And the Cock Crew*, 1977 reprint: 36).

On the other hand, as Hans Küng points out, the Church would still be the Church if all its great cultural achievements had never been, and some who have most strongly felt the appeal of Catholicism in this regard have never become Catholics themselves. He writes that this 'admiration, which can be found both inside and outside the Catholic Church, is in no way decisive for a person's relationship to the Church' and that it is 'without any essential relevance to the Christian faith . . .'[3] It is very easy moreover to see how such an admiration may begin to shade over into various forms of aesthetic and intellectual snobbery.

The very fact that the historical Church is a vast institution tends to create in its more sophisticated members a certain detachment or tension, a sense of irony, knowingness or even double standards that some find appealing. The minority situation of Catholicism in this country itself leads to the evangelical desire to make the faith seem attractive – the point, after all, of Belloc's remarks – but also creates special temptations to Catholic chic. What can be seen as antibourgeois strands in Catholicism also have their contribution to make here: the exotic associations described in the last chapter and the sense of Catholicism as an aristocratic religion.

The native Catholic aristocracy and the aristocratic converts, the connections with conservative continental aristocracy, and the status of the Catholic public schools have all contributed to this sense of Catholicism as fashionably upper class. In contradiction to the warning that Catholics are ill-educated and low bred, Charles Reding is also warned in *Loss and Gain* of the example of young Dalton, who is said to have been told by a smooth priest that Catholicism is 'the only religion for a gentleman; he is introduced to a Count this, and a Marchioness that, and returns a Catholic' (1869 reprint: 371). Edmund Randolph in *Mostly Fools* goes so far as to say that the Church in England had become an 'aristocratic clique'. Perfectly understandable historical and sociological pressures can easily blend in, it is clear, with the 'pervasive snobbery' that Piers Paul Read identifies as a distinguishing mark of English Catholicism.

An interest in the Catholic aristocracy and gentry is at the heart of Evelyn Waugh's version of true Catholic Englishness, as we have seen. He is attracted from the very beginning of his career by the aristocratic amorality of characters such as Margot Beste-Chetwynde, in part, according to Anthony Burgess, because of a desire to escape his own 'decently bourgeois' background.[4] But, whatever its roots, this is no simple snobbery. The anti-bourgeois emphasis is pervasive among many Catholic intellectuals until the Second World War and it has pronounced ethical, political and religious dimensions.

Waugh's own fictional aristocrats transcend respectable bourgeois codes and conventions and in some sense at least win his approval for living as a law unto themselves. There is a recognition here, as Ian Littlewood writes in *The Novels of Evelyn Waugh*,

> that members of the aristocracy . . . have developed a hierarchy of values different from that accepted by the mass of people, and that one aspect of this hierarchy is the inversion, in certain areas, of what is taken seriously and what is not; trifling matters of form can be treated with deadly seriousness, matters of life and death with frivolity.[5]

The Jesuit Father Rothschild in *Vile Bodies* is obviously in some respects a figure of fun. Yet he is genuinely an insider politically and socially and given to oracular statements that can by no means all be dismissed. During the storm in the sea voyage he remains calm, for, 'To Father Rothschild no passage was worse than any other. He thought of the sufferings of the saints, the mutability of human nature, the Four Last Things, and between whiles repeated snatches of the penitential psalms (p. 8).' There is a certain overlap between this traditional Christian insouciance about life and death and the things of this world and the quasi-aristocratic 'refusal to be shocked, disoriented, embarrassed or involved' Littlewood refers to. Waugh recognizes that the two are not the same, and in a sense the movement of his work is from one to the other. But if insouciance is socially chic, then religious insouciance cannot easily be purified of all social appeal. It is partly Waugh's attraction to the social quality that prepares the ground for the religious attitude.

Brideshead Revisited is the most famous and beguiling conflation of aristocratic chic and Catholicism in English literature. The charm of Sebastian, nostalgia for Oxford, the great house ethos – all these are the essence of the book's popularity. Waugh, as we have seen, wants to suggest that the Marchmain-Flytes are 'different' ultimately because they are Catholics rather than because they are aristocrats. There is nevertheless an overlap between the two differences in that both are an implicit critique of the values of the modern age of bourgeois moralism, to which insouciance is the bravest, most stylish but also, from a religious perspective, most accurate response. Even the self-indulgence of Sebastian can be said to be better than bourgeois pharisaism, for 'God prefers drunkards to a lot of respectable people' (1949 reprint: 128). It is in fact the very 'charm' of the Marchmain-Flytes that creates the first tiny opening in Charles to the love of God, for all our loves are shadows, it is said, that prefigure the ultimate love (p. 265).

Even in this book there is some attempt to transcend purely social values and show their partial quality. Julia has to give up Charles and Charles's dream of possessing the house cannot come to be. Bridey himself is devout but decidedly un-chic, yet he is also right on occasions. But the tone of nostalgia, the romanticism of loss that Littlewood finely analyses, to a large degree contradicts the attempt at chastening.

It is not until the *Sword of Honour* trilogy that Waugh demonstrates, in Littlewood's words, that 'religious faith may sometimes have to be expressed in the least stylish of gestures' (p. 165). The figure of Ivor Claire is revealed to be specious, and Guy Crouchbank's knight errantry corrected. When he is accused of being over-romantic in his proposal to remarry Virginia he says:

> 'Knights errant' . . . used to go out looking for noble deeds. I don't think I've ever in my life done a single, positively unselfish action. I certainly haven't gone out of my way to find opportunities. Here was something most unwelcome, put into my hands; something which I believe the Americans describe as 'beyond the call of duty'; not the normal behaviour of an officer and a gentleman; something they'll laugh about in Bellamy's.
> (*Unconditional Surrender*, 1961: 151; cited Littlewood: 103)

The whole thrust of the trilogy is to confirm this recognition. Crouchbank's achievements, such as they are, come only on the other side of a kind of humiliation, a purging of any sense of social stylishness and of what is fitting in the eyes of the world. He helps a group of Jewish refugees to escape, but hardly plays the heroic role in events that he had imagined for himself. He decides to

Catholic chic

remarry Virginia and adopts as his own her son by the odious Trimmer. After she is killed by a bomb he remarries and his second wife Domenica, when she 'isn't having babies . . . manages the home farm'. His final position is a happy one from a purely personal perspective, but he has been purged of false heroism and ideas of romance.

Yet the book still has the destiny of an aristocratic family at its heart. In the first volume Guy had asked Mr Goodall, an expert in the history of aristocratic recusant families, 'Do you seriously believe that God's Providence concerns itself with the perpetuation of the English Catholic aristocracy?' The answer he receives is, 'But of course. And with sparrows too we are taught' (*Men at Arms*, 1988 reprint: 120). But this is obviously disingenuous on Waugh's part. The implications of the parable of the sparrows are for all Christians, but in using it, through Mr Goodall, to justify the concern with the aristocracy Waugh is, of course, masking the fact that it has been his own, very revealing, choice to deal with this kind of family rather than another.

As Anthony Burgess points out, the whole of Waugh's own later self-presentation itself involves a cult of style, if one of a deliberately unmodish kind. 'The good man retires from the world, cherishing fragments from an incorrupt past', but he does so 'cultivating style, assuming stoical poses that are not without a certain discreet self-mockery.'[6] Burgess's formulation finely suggests a problematic overlap between a traditional Christian stance and a certain worldliness here, like that of a wealthy retired Roman senator of the late empire, half Christian, half epicurean. *The Ordeal of Gilbert Pinfold* (1957) itself seems to confront such recognitions with a very real anxiety.

It would be wrong to present the social appeal of British Catholicism as simply a matter of its aristocratic connections. Catholicism was also the religion of the Irish immigrants and of the rural poor who lived in the protection of the great Catholic houses. There is a certain sense in which it can thus be presented as an anti-bourgeois religion of the high born and low born, despite the fact that the proportion of middle-class Catholics grew steadily. In Rumer Godden's *In This House of Brede* it is said that, 'to find a tramp in the Cathedral was most likely. One of the good things about a Catholic church is that it isn't respectable . . . You can find anyone in it, from duchesses to whores, from tramps to kings' (p. 22). M. E. Blundell portrays Lancashire mill hands worshipping in their poor chapel in *Tyler's Lass* (1926). Compton Mackenzie sentimentalizes the working-class Catholic dancer Cissie Oliver in *The East Wind of Love*. In Bruce Marshall's work the emphasis on the Church in Scotland as the 'Church of the poor' is constant and again very sentimentally expressed, though accurate enough from a sociological perspective all the same:

> As they stood on the top of the steps at the entrance to the presbytery a surge of ragged scruffy children came screeching and scampering up the street from the parish school. Some of them were bare-footed and some were dirty and some of them had jammy rings round their mouths but those of the boys who had caps on took them off as they passed the church because they knew that Jesus was there in the tabernacle. . . .
>
> (*All Glorious Within*: 1945 reprint: 71)

In Anne Redmon's *Emily Stone* (1974) the unsympathetic narrator comments on the heroine Sasha:

> she was delighted by the aristocracy; indeed, whatever political sympathies she had were royalist. She had a picture of the queen, and stood up rigidly in the theatre for the national anthem . . . She would have kissed the feet of a Hapsburg, but she would have washed the feet of a beggar with equal enthusiasm.
>
> (1980 reprint: 14)

An interest in the Catholic poor combines with royalist sentiments and aristocratic sympathies in various quasi-feudal and Jacobite emphases. Frederick Rolfe, for example, was a member of a Jacobite order, and in *Lord of the World* Robert Hugh Benson shows all the royal families of Europe finding protection and solace in Rome after socialism has taken over the rest of the world.

Many artists and writers are attracted to Catholicism through romantic nostalgia, a love of the Gothic and the 'flower of chivalry' (Chesterton, *The Return of Don Quixote*). They have come to associate the religion, like Oxford, with 'all the last enchantments of the Middle Ages'. Ford Madox Ford, like the great Victorian convert Sir Kenelm Digby, invokes all the romance and idealism of chivalry in Katharine Howard's appeal to fight for the old faith and the old order in *The Fifth Queen*:

> Sir, I have read it in books of chivalry, the province of a knight is to succour the Church of God, to defend the body of God, to set his lance in rest for the Mother of God; to defend noble men cast down, and noble women; to aid holy priests and blessed nuns; to succour the despoiled poor.
>
> (1962 reprint: 283)

Anthony Burgess's Catholic hero Howarth in *The Worm and the Ring* feels his heart lift when he sees the village church spire, because it reminds him of the Middle Ages, the 'solid comfortable bed' (p. 21). It is the special emotional tone of such associations that is relevant here, but it will have already become apparent that they also encourage specific ideological and political tendencies and are used to confer legitimacy and romance upon them.

'A beautiful, solemn, dignified, aesthetic religion'

Miriam's comments in *How Far Can You Go?* about the rich traditions of art, music and liturgy in Catholicism are also commonplaces. One of the notorious opinions for which Christopher Marlowe was to be investigated by the Privy Council was: 'That if there be any God or any true religion, then it is in the Papists, because the service of God is performed with more ceremonies, as elevation of the Mass, organs, singing men, shaven crowns, etc. That all Protestants are hypocritical asses.' The Church's appeal to those of an artistic temperament is well known, according to A. J. A. Symons, author of *The Quest for Corvo*.[7]

Such emphases themselves often involve an anti-bourgeois, anti-Puritan bias, as with the 1890s converts and fellow travellers of Catholicism. The superficial attraction of these associations for the *fin de siècle* is caught with a nice touch of parody in Antonia White's account of Claude Batchelor in *The Lost Traveller* (1950) who has been interested in Catholicism since university: 'It had fascinated him then by the very things which gave it such a sinister aura in the eyes of his family. Intoxicated with Wilde and Pater, it had glittered for him with decadent splendours' (1982 reprint: 201). The more innocuous 1890s aesthetic appeal comes across in Henry Harland's novels, where religion itself is described as 'the belief in something that is beautiful and good and significant' (*The Cardinal's Snuff Box*: 97).

The extraordinary novels of Ronald Firbank take aestheticism and decadence with a Catholic colouring to the point of rich and beautiful absurdity. Whether he was a practising or believing Catholic for long is doubtful. He said once, 'The Church of Rome wouldn't have me and so I mock at her', which appears to be a reference to his failure to become a member of the Papal Guard, a function for which he spoke of preparing by going into retreat 'as much for my looks as for the welfare of my soul'.[8] But the elaborate parody of Catholicism and its practices in Firbank has a curious tone of lyricism, affection and inwardness, even an idiosyncratic and by no means totally ironic religious devotion.

In *Valmouth* (1919) the sense of absurdity is foremost and the ecclesiastical sexual decadence relatively unsubtle:

> All these priests in the house I find myself a strain. The old Cardinal, with his monstrous triple-mitre, one goes in terror of. He was in the passage just now as I came through waiting for someone. And last night – there's only a panel door between our rooms – I heard him try the handle.
>
> Their last chaplain – Pere Ernest – I remember was a danger. A perfect danger! He could have done anything with me, Arabella, had he willed. I was plastic wax with him.

The attraction to this religion is purely aesthetic and exotic, a wonderful sense of outlandish names and extravagant liturgy:

> 'Monsignor Vanhove, Father O'Donoghue, Frater Galfrith, Brother Drithelm, Pere Porfirio' – ffines insistently continued in his office until, in sweeping purple and scarlet biretta, Cardinal Doppio-Mignoni himself passed valedictionally through the rooms.
>
> (1961 reprint: 113)

What makes this 'camp' is the deliberate element of exaggeration that moves over into parody certainly, but which also includes enjoyment and inwardness.

In the later works the spirit of aestheticism continues to be enjoyed, but it becomes occasionally less ironic and associated with a devotional sentimentality like Henry Harland's with its own touch of genuineness, as in the lovely cadences of the church names in the following passage:

> Above him great spikes of blossom were stirring in the idle wind, while birds were chanting voluntaries among the palms. And in thanksgiving,

too, arose the matin bells. From Our Lady of the Pillar, from the church of
La Favavoa in the West, from Saint Sebastian, from Our Lady of the Sea,
from Our Lady of Mount Carmel, from Santa Theresa, from St Francis of
the Poor.

(*Prancing Nigger*, 1961 reprint: 163)

In *Concerning the Eccentricities of Cardinal Pirelli* (1926) these more serious elements come to the fore, though the book, of course, remains full of parody and absurdity that verges on the blasphemous: the baptism of dogs, the dancing choirboys of the cathedral and so on. But the sense of the relative sexual tolerance of Catholicism, its anti-Puritan acceptance of the good things of life and its aestheticism create a feeling of admiration and inwardness as well. The book makes a deliberate blur of hedonism and natural mysticism that is also combined with genuine religious respect:

> Some day, Father Felicitas did not doubt, Our Lady would have an organ, an organ with pipes. He had prayed for it so often; oh, so often; and once, quite in the late of twilight while coming through the church, he had seen her, it seemed, standing just where it should be. It had been as through a blinding whiteness.
> 'A blinding whiteness,' he murmured, trembling a little at the recollection of the radiant vision.
> Across the tranquil court a rose-red butterfly pursued a blue.
> 'I believe the world is all love, only no one understands,' he meditated, contemplating the resplendent harvest plains steeped in the warm sweet sunlight.
>
> (1961 reprint: 227)

This too is a deliberately purple passage, but it has a different feel to it than those in *Valmouth*, an element of genuine semi-religious celebration mingled in with the parodic over-writing. Firbank also speaks respectfully here of St Theresa of Avila, though it is only after seven or eight glasses of wine and with a touch of *double entendre* that the Cardinal has his vision of her,

> Long had her radiant spirit 'walked' the Desierto. . . . Worn and ill, though sublime in laughter, exquisite in tenderness she came towards him.
> '. . . Child?'
> 'Teach me, oh, teach me, dear Mother, the Way of Perfection.'
>
> (p. 235)

Firbank's admiration for his central figure of the Cardinal is not in doubt, although it is combined with affectionate mockery. But it is worth noting that Cardinal Pirelli is far from being a totally profane figure, even if his interpretation of Catholicism is indeed an eccentric one. There is the suggestion that Catholicism is a humane and tolerant religion, satisfying to the human spirit, even though the Cardinal has finally gone too far for Rome, and the 'love' with which he is associated, secular and hedonistic though it is, is not without its elements of the love of God,

Catholic chic

Now that the ache of life, with its fevers, passions, doubts, its routine, vulgarity and boredom, was over, his serene, unclouded face was a marvelment to behold. Very great distinction and sweetness was visible there, together with much nobility and love, all magnified and commingled.

(p. 251)

John Gray's mysterious novel *Park* on the other hand takes the aestheticism with which its author had been associated in entirely the opposite direction to Firbank, seeking a purification from all traces of the purely personal and chic. The austere dignity of diction and tone enacts the need for a disciplined and impersonal devotion to the Church as the only lasting source of beauty amidst all the transmutations of history. Liturgy is both the means to this and in a sense the end, the perfectly transcended and successful art-form, and the hieratic timelessness of diction in Gray's liturgical descriptions is thus no accidental adornment but at the very heart of his purposes:

This was the sanctuary, for the procession of the mass moved towards it. It was cut by the unbroken ascending line of some great element of the building and in another direction by a traverse as austere. He could see the bishop at the faldstool however, his ministers moving in ample space & with utmost solemnity & precision, as they vested him.

This was all, at the distance, which could edify or gratify him, until two deacons passed the chasuble over the bishop's head, and Park was certain, beyond any contention, that it was close-sewn with diamonds.

(1966 reprint: 18)

The point is clarified by a later discussion. Park is told by Dlar that

it was right to use in worship the rare things of the creation. It would not be so becoming to make use of such choice substances, nor decent to covet them, for personal ornament, and it would be futile as well; for carrion (one of his synonyms for men and women) could be sufficiently adorned with imitations of diamonds.

Park remembers that in the old world women had worn pearls and that he had not disapproved of this, but now he knows better (p. 77).

The polemics of Scots Catholic writers such as Fionn MacColla and George Mackay Brown naturally enough put a special focus on the anti-Puritan aspects of Catholic aestheticism. In Brown's *Greenvoe*, for example, the accusers of Mrs McKee say:

Think how the Church of pre-Reformation Scotland was – to use a rather vulgar but descriptive phrase – tarted up with all manner of destructive tinsel: the statues and the stained glass, the fuming censers swung by acolytes at gilded altars, the grove of candles about the plaster feet of some saint. The wretched and the ignorant of the earth have always gone down on their knees before this mumbo-jumbo.

I do not need to tell you that Rome still flaunts these gauds and baubles in the face of mankind. And many there are who still hanker after these things, though nominally they are members of our kirk; not only the superstitious either, but people who are supposed to be clever, artistic, cultured. I say it with sorrow; year after year we lose a flock of such people to Rome.

(1975 reprint: 131–2)

Yet if Catholic religious art has a populist appeal to the 'wretched and the ignorant of the earth', then it is obvious that in practice it must often offend the sensibilities of the 'clever, artistic' and 'cultured'. When Sarah in Greene's *The End of the Affair* wanders into a Catholic church, she finds it 'full of plaster statues and bad art, realistic art. I hated the statues, the crucifix, all the emphasis on the human body' (1971 reprint: 107). For Frederick Rolfe this lack of taste is a characteristic of British Catholicism compared with the continent. Evelyn Waugh agrees that the advantages as far as art and taste go in this country at least are entirely on the side of Anglicanism, but he speaks of this not with disapproval like Rolfe but with an inverted kind of satisfaction.[9] For Greene's Sarah indeed it is precisely the bad, over literal and over physical art that prepares the way for her conversion, and a similar point is made in Anne Redmon's *Emily Stone*.

David Lodge shows with a nice touch of parody in *The Picturegoers* how much of a commonplace this inverted aestheticism has itself become. His self-conscious hero Mark Underwood reflects during Mass on:

. . . the common mistake of outsiders, that Catholicism was a beautiful, solemn, dignified, aesthetic religion. But when you got inside you found it was ugly, crude, bourgeois. Typical Catholicism wasn't to be found in St Peter's, or Chartres, but in some mean, low-roofed parish church, where hideous plaster saints simpered along the wall, and the bored congregation, pressed perspiration tight along the wall, rested their fat arses on the seats, rattled their beads, fumbled for their smallest change, and scolded their children. Yet in their presence God was made and eaten all day long, and for that reason those people could never be quite like other people, and that was Catholicism.

(1970 reprint: 150)

Yet the final sentence reasserts a unity. Lodge shows well here one way that sophisticated Catholics try to get the best of both worlds. They retain themselves a strong sense of the Catholic high-art tradition and of their own superiority to the popular forms, but in accepting the latter they at the same time defend themselves against the charge that aestheticism has anything to do with their own allegiance. Lodge captures brilliantly the element of inverted snobbery in Mark, the delights of slumming it, and the contempt combined with paradoxical romanticism (the Browning quotation, 'God is made and eaten all day long') in this approach. In some versions these tendencies may even shade over into Catholic kitsch, to be distinguished from 'camp' in that it is the enjoyment of bad art for its own sake rather than an exaggeration of the aesthetic element of something not meant to be primarily aesthetic. Andy

Warhol, major cultist of kitsch, was himself a practising Catholic with a huge collection of popular Catholic art.

Wit, double consciousness, intellectual chic

Caroline, the heroine of Muriel Spark's *The Comforters*, makes the famous comment that 'the Catholic Church was awful, but unfortunately true'. Tensions of various kinds between a large, authoritative institutional church and its more sensitive and intelligent individual members are obviously inevitable. Lodge's Mark Underwood illustrates above a specialized form of the sense of detachment and ambiguity, the double consciousness that may result, but they may equally well take the more appealing form of wit and irony like Caroline's. It is a special aspect of Catholic chic that Catholics can not only criticize their Church with what seems at times a daring freedom but laugh both at it and themselves. There are almost as many Catholic jokes as Jewish ones. Margaret in L. P. Hartley's *My Fellow Devils* (1951), married to a bad Catholic but later to be a convert herself, complains 'I shall never get used to the familiar, joking way some Catholics speak of their religion' (p. 122).

A self-conscious reaction against Puritan or bourgeois seriousness and solemnity may also be invoked. Fionn MacColla's Father O'Reilly in *The Albanach* plays the chanter, having 'savoured the essence of life and found it good' (p. 95). Burgess's hero in *The Worm and the Ring* delights to remind his prudish wife that Rabelais was a Catholic. Indeed, 'Was not respectability', Father Smith asks himself in *All Glorious Within*, 'the greatest sin of all, since it mistook semblance for sincerity?' (p. 101).

As the next chapter will explore, it is often the most dedicated Catholics, highly conscious of institutional excesses and the faults of the hierarchy, who need this safety valve of wit and irony. Madame de Normandin in A. N. Wilson's *Incline Our Hearts* (1988) 'like many pious people, regarded the clergy of her Church with a distant sort of derision' (p. 170). This is both deeply personalized and taken very much further in the comment by the hero of Frederick Rolfe's *Desire and Pursuit of the Whole*: 'He had seen so many priests comporting themselves usuriously or venally that (although it excruciated his sense of decency) it only strengthened his faith; for he never permitted himself to forget there was a Judas among the apostles' (p. 137). Clearly the careful diction and the reference to 'decency' here are meant to make the contempt sound controlled and dignified, but the author's own bitterness breaks through.

Graham Greene's heroes and heroines, of course, embody the most extreme form of double consciousness and tension with the institution, and their predicaments are far too agonized to create an attractive detachment, wit and poise. Yet the seediness of 'Greeneland' obviously has a special inverted romanticism of its own which has contributed to the remarkable popularity of these novels. Greene exploits the appeal of living on 'the dangerous edge of things', the edge of the respectable Church, the edge of damnation, the special double consciousness and *angst* of the borderlands between faith and scepticism, despair and hope. His tone could hardly be more different from the high camp Catholicism of Firbank, yet it too is anti-bourgeois and arises out of an idiosyncratic development of the decadent movement, though in Greene's case filtered through the novelists of the French Catholic Revival.

Scobie in *The Heart of the Matter* is perhaps the most typical of Greene's heroes, and his suffering has given him the special insight of a privileged explorer. In seeing through all the pretensions of happiness he has reached the very 'heart of the matter':

> The lights were showing in the temporary hospital, and the weight of all that misery lay on his shoulders. It was as if he had shed one responsibility only to take on another. This was a responsibility he shared with all human beings, but there was no comfort in that, for it sometimes seemed to him that he was the only one who recognised it. In the Cities of the Plain a single soul might have changed the mind of God.
>
> (1950 reprint: 123)

To his wife he is one who does not take his religion seriously, but Greene wants his special vision and predicament to be seen on the contrary as essentially Catholic, and Father Rank confirms this at the end by refusing to accept that Scobie is a 'bad Catholic'.

In Sarah Miles in *The End of the Affair* these paradoxes of sin and suffering overlap for once in Greene with more obvious forms of glamour. The agonised, sophisticated and beautiful Catholic adulteress is the epitome of Catholic chic, and versions of her are found in works by Maurice Baring, Piers Paul Read and others. Waugh's Julia Marchmain is another famous example, but Greene's Sarah is perhaps the most stunning of all in her early sexual abandon that turns into the saint's abandonment of sacrifice and compassion and love of God.

When Compton Mackenzie's hero says in *The Four Winds of Love* that most of the humorists in England are Catholics, he has in mind not the wit and irony that the tension with the institution may produce but the special perspective he sees Catholicism as giving on the world and its follies. Authoritative condemnation combines with a sense of detachment and irony that views this world *sub specie aeternitatis* and can laugh at its self-important solemnities. The 'water beneath them is so deep . . . that they can afford to gambol on the surface . . .' (*The North Wind*, 1944; 1968 reprint: 53).

This is the vast reservoir of the age-old Catholic traditions of wisdom and learning to which Lodge's Miriam refers in *How Far Can You Go?* Despite the determined anti-intellectualism of many British Catholics it is a major part of Belloc's strategy to highlight not only the social but also the intellectual lure of Catholicism:

> It is essential for us to impress it upon our contemporaries that the Catholic is intellectually the superior of everyone except the sceptic in all that region cognate to and attached to that which may be called 'Intellectual appreciation' – pure intelligence.[10]

To join the Church of St Thomas Aquinas and Dante, as they are interpreted (say) by Maritain and the great medievalist Étienne Gilson and praised in influential essays by T. S. Eliot, had obvious attractions for a certain type of convert. To stand with such a Church against all the fads and fashions of the present era has a special paradoxical chic of its own, like that cultivated by the so-called 'young fogies' of the eighties, and Chesterton, Belloc, Waugh and others are certainly not immune from it.

At the same time intellectuals often found it satisfying to belong to a Church that also contained large numbers of the poor and uncultivated and that offered as well as philosophy and theology a touching and childlike populism and sentimentality. As with Mark Underwood in *The Picturegoers*, the cultured intellectual convert in England is peculiarly prone to that form of worldly status that C. S. Lewis in a brilliant essay calls the temptation of the inner ring, and to the especially refined version that consists of playing off one inner circle against another.[11] He or she can feel superior to non-believing friends because of a greater degree of spiritual insight and the sense of having overcome the characteristic intellectual's alienation by the very fact of belonging to this large, warm mass of the common people. On the other hand, the convert's superior sophistication, culture and intelligence creates an obvious superiority to the main body of the faithful.

David Lodge comments that, if Joyce had to leave the Church to escape a cultural stranglehold, he himself found that to be a Catholic in the entirely different context of a university in the secular England of the fifties 'was to strike a rather interesting, almost exotic pose before one's peers.' He writes elsewhere that if Catholicism gave him a sense of superiority to the 'materialism of the secular world' his explorations in the Catholic novel of Greene and Mauriac also made him feel at the same time above the 'superficial pieties of parochial Catholicism.'[12] The most extreme variant of this latter sense is found in modernism, and it is expressed in some of the reflections of Edmund Randolph's hero in *Mostly Fools*, for example, where the title has its own resonance in this regard.

At least her parish priest, thinks Rose in Ellis's *The Sin Eater* (1977), little as she likes him, 'hasn't taken to going round in jeans and a T-shirt and a little cross on a chain round his neck imploring people to call him Roger' (1986 reprint: 98). Like self-consciously reactionary Catholicism progressive Catholicism creates its own form of double consciousness and the temptations to intellectual snobbery and an inner circle. The Dominican chaplain of the Dollinger Society discussion group in Lodge's *The British Museum Is Falling Down* is described as being prepared to question the dogma of the Assumption after three drinks and as having such liberal views about the wearing of clerical dress that, if he were unfrocked, as seemed likely, no one would ever know! The narrator comments that it seemed that 'the liberal conscience had a more thrilling existence inside the Church than without' (1983 reprint: 67). Michael and Miriam in *How Far Can You Go?* attend an avant-garde liturgy at a college 'that would have lifted the back hairs on the red necks of the local parish priests had they known what was going on in their midst' (1982 reprint: 133). In vacations, however, they have to go back to the old-style liturgy in the parish churches: 'Moving between these two places of worship, and impersonating the two very different styles of deportment that went with them, Michael sometimes felt like a liturgical double agent' (p. 134).

Spark and Ellis

Intellectual Catholic chic is present to a marked degree in Muriel Spark's work. The popular perception of Catholicism is certainly not that it is a religion of intellectual irony and avid truth-seeking. Spark's Catholic heroines, with whom there is obviously considerable authorial identification, are quirky, painfully honest intellectuals. Caroline in *The Comforters* 'was an odd sort of Catholic, very little heart for it, all mind'. Barbara Vaughan in *The Mandelbaum Gate* is a 'private-judging Catholic'. They cultivate a special double consciousness, aware, unlike their secular friends, of the supernatural, but carefully distinguishing themselves from the majority of their co-religionists. Laurence specifically warns Spark's Caroline in *The Comforters* that 'you have to pick and choose amongst Catholic society in England, the wrong sort can drive you nuts' (p. 24).[13] The suffocating narrow-mindedness, complacency and superstition of the latter is memorably embodied in Georgiana Hogg in the same novel.

Spark herself says that she experienced 'a great sense of release, of psychic release when I became a Catholic'. Catholic dogma became to her 'a norm from which to depart intellectually, north on the compass'. It has given her a special poise and confidence for her perspectives on a fallen world, casting an ironic light on its follies and even its sins and evils, out of which God may bring good. As she mentions in the same interview, 'I don't like to describe serious things too seriously.'[14] This includes a stylishly modest detachment, even from her own art which, with a traditional sense of the deceptiveness of fiction, she refuses to take too seriously either.

Of course there is far more to Spark's work than Catholic chic, and she is careful herself to indicate the limitations of charm. The poise of Selina in *The Girls of Slender Means* is epitomized in her foolish auto-suggestion mantra, 'Poise is perfect balance, an equanimity of body and mind, complete composure whatever the social scene. Elegant dress, immaculate grooming, and perfect deportment all contribute to the attainment of self-confidence.' It conceals a moral emptiness that is actually the heart of evil, as she reveals when she snatches up the Schiaparelli dress in the midst of the fire. She is contrasted with the deeper poise of the vicar's daughter, Joanna, who recites poetry and psalms, and preserves composure, courage and unselfishness in the fire.

More complexly, the charisma of Jean Brodie brings great evil in its wake, but Spark suggests that she could have flourished under Catholicism instead of Calvinism: 'she was by temperament suited only to the Roman Catholic Church; possibly it could have embraced even while it disciplined, her soaring and driving spirit, it might even have normalised her' (1965 reprint: 105).

Yet the detached mockery of the world and its values in Spark is paradoxically the source of an appealing poise that cannot itself be entirely divorced from more purely social factors. It is in this respect closely analogous to Waugh's 'refusal to be shocked, disoriented, embarrassed or involved' as described by Littlewood, which begins as the admiring imitation of upper-class insouciance and modulates into a religious detachment without completely losing touch with its social roots. Spark's deliberate understatement and detached wit comes from an attitude of religious irony at a fallen world, but they are also a personal and social response: 'I think it's bad manners to inflict a lot of emotional involvement on the reader – much nicer to make them laugh and keep it short.'[15] In *The Comforters* in particular, the identification between the author and the fastidious Caroline is close, a weakness to which first novels are prone:

> Caroline realised that she had been staring at Mrs Hogg's breasts for some time, and was aware at the same moment that the woman's nipples were showing dark and prominent through her cotton blouse. The woman was apparently wearing nothing underneath. Caroline looked swiftly away, sickened at the sight, for she was prim; her sins of the flesh had been fastidious always.
> (p. 29)

Style in the later novels has become, it has been said, a moral virtue in itself. It is largely severed from religious values. The test-case is *The Abbess of Crewe*, where again the question of the relationship between author and heroine becomes crucial. So brilliantly light and ironic is the tone that it would obviously be heavy-handed to take the joke seriously. It would be foolish to say that the heroine is entirely endorsed and vindicated within the book as a whole, since it obviously does not work in that literal kind of way. But she is granted a considerable degree of Spark's indulgence and even admiration:

> The Abbess of Crewe, soaring in her slender height, a very Lombardy poplar herself.... Her face is a white-skinned English skull, beautiful in the frame of her white nun's coif. She is forty-two in her own age with fourteen generations of pale and ruling ancestors of England and ten before them of France, curved also into the bones of her wonderful head.
> (p. 10)

The Abbess's view of the mischief-making Felicity seems to overlap to a considerable degree with Spark's own. It is revealing that Felicity's offences are portrayed as matters of style and that they are linked both with the liberal tendencies of Vatican II and with being irredeemably bourgeois. Her sexual activities offend against decorum and so does her way of looking at the world: 'A Lady has style; but a Bourgeoise does things under the poplars and in the orchard' (p. 89). It is 'with that certain wonder of the aristocrat at the treasured toys of the bourgeoisie' (p. 71) that the Abbess looks on Felicity's work-box.

The whole book appears to be set up indeed by a special strategy to permit the expression of sympathy and even identification with the Abbess. Precisely because the fiction is too outrageous to be taken seriously, she is allowed to get away with things that could not otherwise be legitimized. Social and aesthetic stylishness is privileged by religious allusions and substitutes itself for religious values. The Abbess's practice of blending the divine office with English poetry is presented without overt comment, though the beautifully chosen cadences of both are repeated. Comparison with Joanna in *Girls of Slender Means* is illuminating, for the latter is a teacher of elocution, not a professed religious like Alexandra, and the Abbess's own comments deliberately blur aesthetic and religious grace rather than making one an analogy for the other, as in the earlier work:

> 'To the practitioner of courage there is no anxiety that will not melt away under the effect of grace, however that may be obtained. You recite the Psalms of the Hours, and so do I, frequently giving over, also, to English poetry, my passion. Sisters, be still; to each her own source of grace.'
> (p. 98)

Anne Duchêne has commented in the *Times Literary Supplement* on a late revival of Catholic chic in the work of Alice Thomas Ellis.[16] For Lydia in *Unexplained Laughter* (1985) 'there was a definite elegance, a chic in sanctity' (1986 reprint: 109). Such a chic is epitomized in the nun Valentine in *The Twenty-seventh Kingdom* (1982), who is black and beautiful and has the mystical gift of levitation.

Ellis's other Catholic heroines certainly have no claims to sanctity themselves, but they do have a special awareness of spiritual realities, an almost blasé way of taking them for granted that distinguishes them with a kind of glamour from the boringly secular characters that are all around them. Both the novelist herself and her heroines have the distinction, it seems, of being visited from time to time, like the Reverend Mother in *The Twenty-seventh Kingdom*, by 'those undeniable convictions which seldom trouble the non-religious' (1982 reprint: 12). Mary in *The Birds of the Air* (1980), Lydia in *Unexplained Laughter* and Rose in *The Sin Eater* display this special sense of the supernatural, of portents and miracles, though they are far from saints.

Mary, for example, has had her spiritual senses sharpened by bereavement and knows about God's 'extraordinary trick', death. Rose and Lydia are scatty, sexy, unconventional and outspoken. But their form of Catholicism gives them a special sense of supernatural good and evil. It is Lydia, for example, who is aware of the activities of the devil, whom she calls 'Stan', in the follies and lusts and 'unexplained laughter' of the Welsh valley. Rose 'could hardly wait for the Day of Judgement', though she creates a characteristically dramatic pose for it: 'She would stand with her children on the mountain top, waving her black scarf' (p. 181). Mary drinks a toast on Christmas morning:

> 'Well, here's to God,' said Mary, creating a diversion and pouring herself a whisky.
> They stared at her, uncomprehendingly.
> 'It's his birthday,' she said.
> Nearly everyone was shocked.
> (*The Birds of the Air*, 1983 reprint: 138)

At times the contrast between these characters and the secular or Protestant characters who lack such insights shades over into delight in the special chic and modishness of being shockingly unmodish. In their wildness and outrageousness Ellis is not identified with these characters, yet as with Spark and the Abbess of Crewe there is a sense in which she is. She is able to make them her mouthpieces at the same time as disclaiming responsibility for them, and as well as the very genuine *frisson* of the supernatural they convey there are times when the actual content of their views is alarmingly young fogeyish, as with Rose's comments on progressive Catholicism since the Second Vatican Council.

For the changing attitudes of the ecumenical era and the decline in Catholic separateness do not prevent Ellis's characters from delighting to attack Protestantism:

> The door was open. Inside, the church was as clean and clear as a blown egg.
> 'It's so peaceful,' said Ermyn.
> 'You needn't whisper,' said Rose contemptuously. 'There's no one here.'
> She detested protestantism, from the pneumatic sterility of Milton to the ankle socks and hairy calves of Peggy *parchedig*, the vicar's wife. She had been given this appellation, which meant 'reverend', because the village considered her to be minimally more of a man than her husband.
> (*The Sin Eater*, 1986 reprint: 77)

What seems especially characteristic of Catholic chic here is the way that the supposed Protestant lack of the numinous is paralleled, even identified with a lack of glamour.

Part three

The Church and the world

· 6 ·

Images of the Church and the world

The 'sacralization' of the institution

Maureen, the rebellious Catholic, after a series of dramatic incidents that include the appearance of an angel to her old teacher in Hyde Park and a priest's assault on a young girl, finds herself, in a powerful conclusion to Gabrielle Donnolly's *Holy Mother*, stumping 'wearily towards the train that would take her to the terrible, joyful, inevitable, outstretched arms of Holy Mother Church' (1987: 252). The earlier ambivalence is swallowed up in a deeper affirmation, an assertion of mystery and of loyalty to that mystery. Nanda in *Frost in May* comes likewise to realize that

> she was part of the Church now. She could never, she knew, break away now without a sense of mutilation. . . . She rejoiced in it and rebelled against it. . . . Wherever she looked, it loomed in the background, like Fuji Yama in a Japanese print, massive, terrifying, beautiful and inescapable; the fortress of God, the house on the rock.
>
> (1982 reprint: 108)

Both the corporate sense of Catholic 'difference' in Britain described in chapter 4 and the cultivation of Catholic chic described in chapter 5 obviously depend on a firm sense of Catholic identity, the feeling of belonging to a Church itself mysterious and transcendent in its utter 'difference'. Using the popular apologetical technique of creating a fictional non-Catholic whose supposedly unbiased testimony is made to carry the same weight as it would in real life, Maurice Baring has his central character in *C.* write in a letter that 'If I could believe in anything, I think I should believe in your Church. I feel it is a solid fact, a reality, something different from all the others' (p. 636).

For the Catholic Church is unique, the One, True Church, the very Kingdom of God on earth. It is fervently addressed by Newman's Willis in *Loss and Gain* as 'the courts of the true Jerusalem, the Queen of Saints, the Holy Roman Church, the Mother of us all!' (p. 294). Already in a very real sense perfect, this Church stands in its eternal truth far above the mutable realm of secular affairs. The young curate Halliday in Philip Gibbs's *The Age of Reason* leaves a Church of England tainted with modernism to join 'the Unchanging Church' (p. 274). In Baring's *Cat's Cradle* (1925) Mrs Geach tells the hero that the 'old Church' is the one thing that does not change.

What these novelists so earnestly reflect is the process that has been termed the 'sacralization of the institution'. If it is a Protestant bias to speak as if the gospel could transcend all cultural and institutional mediation, it is a Catholic bias to speak thus as if the Church has already fully realized itself.[1] A heavy, ultramontane emphasis on Roman authority, the idea of doctrine as imposed from above rather than proceeding from the whole body of the faithful, a 'triumphalist' celebration of the visible glories of the Church – these are the usual consequences of such a tendency. Catholic tradition is more pluralist, to be sure, than commonly supposed, and these have never been the only options. Baron von Hügel writes refreshingly to his niece, 'Do not, Dear, dwell much upon or worry about the Pope.'[2] But the prevailing official self-definitions and popular images especially throughout the whole period from the Council of Trent to the Second Vatican Council were strongly in the opposite direction. The twentieth-century ecclesiologist Sebastian Tromp, for example, proposes essentially the same view as the Counter-Reformation theologian St Robert Bellarmine. The Church, a visible organization defined by communion with the Bishop of Rome, is unequivocally regarded as the earthly manifestation of the Kingdom of God and it carries all the authority of that Kingdom with it.[3]

It is much more clearly seen today that an unchanging Church is one that has been caught in a time warp. The definitions of Trent themselves naturally have to be seen in the light of their defensive role against the depradations of Protestantism. What has appeared or been presented as the unchanging post-Tridentine Church is really the fixing on and idealization of one stage of the Church's development. The process serves obvious ideological functions and clearly cannot be understood in isolation from them. It has given Catholics an enormous feeling of doctrinal assurance and belonging: 'The sense of discipline and uniformity, the satisfaction that came from unquestioning belief – all those millions upon millions of the faithful, all certain in the one true body of doctrine', as a defecting priest puts it nostalgically in Cornwell's *The Spoiled Priest* (1969: 178). But the authoritarian element in the whole approach has played its part in the so-called 'Catholic neurosis', and in emphasizing loyalty to the institution to such a degree there has even been the risk of underplaying the need for individual conversion to Christ.

The latter accusation, of course, is familiar in exaggerated form from old-fashioned Protestant polemic, but Pope Paul VI himself commented on the need for the evangelization *of Catholics*. The point is splendidly caricatured in the baroque context of Hilary Mantel's *Fludd* (1989), where the eccentric Father Angwin tells the reformist bishop who is trying to encourage Christian witness, 'These people aren't Christians. These people are heathens and

Images of the Church and the world

Catholics.'[4] It carries much greater weight in Dominica's measured comment in Bernard Bergonzi's *Roman Persuasion* that Martin Tolleybeare is 'one of those Catholics who find it easier and more interesting to be Catholic than to be Christian' (p. 99). Her ally, Father Giles Matlock, confirms the view that 'It's possible for orthodoxy itself to become an idol if it's not infused with a living faith' (p. 120).

Yet, as noted in the last chapter, it paradoxically remains at the heart of the experience of being a Catholic, even a conservative Catholic, to be able to preserve a certain freedom or at least a tension with the institution and an awareness of its imperfections. An amusing recent version of Muriel Spark's famous sentiment that the Catholic Church is 'awful but unfortunately true' occurs in the American Catholic novelist J. F. Powers's *Wheat that Springeth Green* (1988). Father Joe Hackett, the hero, is given the wonderful comment that the Church is a 'big old ship, she creaks, she rolls and at times she makes you want to throw up', though, ironically, he means the remark as apologetics.[5]

It may come as more of a surprise to hear that most loyal and dogmatic of Catholics Belloc say that 'The Catholic Church is an institution I am bound to hold divine – but for unbelievers a proof of its divinity might be found in the fact that no merely human institution conducted with such knavish imbecility would have lasted a fortnight.'[6] As with his anti-Semitism the violence with which this sentiment is expressed reflects Belloc's continental background, where such anti-clericalism and cynicism are by no means incompatible with faith.

A more organized and self-conscious tradition of loyal criticism and internal satire is also apparent, though sometimes only with the utmost caution and citing of precedents. J. Richard Beste in *Modern Society in Rome* (1856) explains carefully, for example, that 'there may be abuses in every system, which make no part of it' (I: 114) and invokes the example of those in medieval Catholic England who mocked the clergy and the secondary ordinances of religion without having the least intention of abandoning it (III: 29–30). Internal Catholic satire of the Church may become far more outspoken than this without actually threatening fundamental loyalties. Auberon Waugh's *Foxglove Saga* (1960), for example, is a strong satire on the petty-minded malice of the monastic public school of Cleeve, but Brother Thomas remains the spokesman for a genuine sanctity and wisdom. Touchingly he wonders: 'what heaven can really be like? When all is said and done, I think it must be very much like Cleeve' (p. 28).

What often seems to be going on, however, is that the sacredness of the Church is protected by admitting the facts that any degree of historical sense and empirical observation make it impossible to ignore anyway. Father Smith comments in a classic example in Bruce Marshall's *All Glorious Within* that despite the apparently depressing evidence, 'the Church of God has not failed, because God had promised that even the gates of hell should not prevail against her, and, besides, her mission was set in eternity and not in time' (1945 reprint: 193). A further stage is to make such admissions, as with Belloc's formulation above, apologetical in themselves: the human inadequacies of the Church become, cleverly, an argument that it must have providential protection. Even the famous comment by Spark's Caroline has this apologetical dimension. If someone is clear-sighted enough to see the awfulness of the Church and still believe in it then Catholicism must be true!

The theological implications of the sense of a gap between the institution as institution and as Church of God have thus until recently remained, with very rare exceptions, largely inchoate and on the borders of consciousness. Taken for granted to the extent of being completely unexamined in certain contexts and transformed into apologetics in others, they are in more threatening perspectives faced only with the greatest reluctance and anxiety.

As noted before, Bruce Marshall's novels seem to indicate an awareness of the conflict between the routinism of the church and its prophetic function, but it is one which he is quite unable to resolve. *Vespers in Vienna* (1947) is a particularly revealing, almost painful example of the way that the gap between ideal and institution seems conceded only with the greatest of reluctance and evaded in the interests of apologetics at the same time. The non-Catholic Colonel Nicobar has been billeted after the war in an Austrian convent. In a series of conversations with its superior he convinces her that the Church has failed to preach moral absolutes and the very gospel itself amidst the confusions of war. He and others, including a Russian Communist colonel who is treated with some respect, raise issues that must have occurred to any thoughtful person. How could German bishops praise the German armies and allied bishops their own? Why were there no unequivocal condemnations of the bombing of civilians? What had happened to the imperatives of the gospel and the idea of loving your enemies?

Disturbed by these questions the nun resolves to go to Rome and ask the Pope to do something about it all. In their interview he succeeds in reassuring her that the job of the Church is to continue to preserve and preach the old truths to those who will listen to them rather than to take a new evangelical initiative. On her return she tries to persuade the colonel to the same effect:

> And the purpose of the Church, Herr Oberst, the function of prelates, is to be guarding these old truths a long time ago revealed by God, so that they may still be the same truths to point the way to men in their trouble.
> ....
> No, Herr Oberst, churchmen have often been weak and vain and ambitious and cowardly, but never has the Church of God allowed the lamp of God quite to go out.
>
> (pp. 267, 268)

But if she is convinced by the Pope's words, Nicobar is not, and the split seems to lie within Marshall himself. Both here and in other works a deep unease about the functioning of the Church is revealed and suppressed at the same time in a way that is very representative of the problems sensitive and idealistic Catholics find when they try to work within a basic model of the 'sacralization' of the institution.

'The Ark, the one and only refuge'

Such anxieties in particular have to be repressed in the need to find an eternal and infallible source of truth amidst the maze of modern errors, 'the Ark, the one and only refuge' in the words of Baring's Beatrice in *C*. (p. 519). The desire to feel 'secure', as Belloc put it, 'within the walls of the Church'[7] is obviously an urgent one when authority seems under threat from Anglican liberalism or faith itself under attack by the new science, and it has continued to make a powerful appeal to converts amidst the growing secularism and moral confusion of this century. Compton Mackenzie's John Ogilvie has his daughter baptized a Catholic: 'She might easily live right through this century, and I don't feel its going to be a very easy century to live through without a fortress of the mind to which one can retire and from which one can re-enter the fight re-invigorated' (*West to North* 1942 reprint: 297).

Any distortion in the image of the Church inevitably both results from and contributes to an over-simplification of the Church's relationship with the world. If the Church has to stand against what the New Testament calls 'the world' and its patterns of injustice and dominion, it is a mistake to identify the latter with the whole independent secular realm outside the ecclesiastical orbit. At the same time the Church itself as a vast institution is obviously bound to be contaminated with its own kinds of worldliness.

The absolutizing and sacralizing of the institution in the Middle Ages were themselves part of a great power struggle in which the Church achieved considerable success. But its strength was badly weakened by the Reformation and, despite all the efforts at retrenchment, it was eventually to face after the French Revolution a 'runaway world' in the words of Bill McSweeney, a new secular order that seemed to have escaped its control completely.[8] Different ways of reacting to this threatening situation are possible, but one very central response, as McSweeney shows, was the condemnation of the modern order as a whole and a more deeply defensive absolutizing of the Church, the withdrawal into a 'siege mentality' of the kind described in a famous essay by Wilfred Ward.[9] There is a tragic failure of insight here, the tendency to reject the modern political world not because, like all political systems, it incorporates elements incompatible with the Kingdom of God but rather because it is modern and secular as such and thus a threat to the old, idealized order of Church hegemony.

The genres of historical fiction and to a lesser extent future fantasy are especially useful for Catholic writers in asserting and enforcing this vision of an unchanging Church as the great bastion against the modern secular world. The exigencies of specific controversy with Anglicans lead Wiseman in *Fabiola*, for example, to identify the Roman Catholic Church of his own time completely with the heroic Church of the martyrs. He speaks anachronistically as if the doctrine of the Real Presence, auricular confession and Marian devotion were firmly established in the fourth century and calls the Papal See in ultramontane fashion the chair of an 'immortal race of sovereigns, spiritual and temporal'.[10]

More general but equally blatant ideological purposes contribute to William

Faithful fictions

McCabe's picture of the Church of earlier eras heroically embattled against evils analogous to those of the modern age. *Adelaide, Queen of Italy* (1856) parallels the nineteenth-century controversy about the Papal States with the period in the tenth century when the Pope was deprived of temporal sovereignty under the Alberics: 'It is strange that there should be the same tendencies, and the same dispositions exhibited in this epoch of boasted civilisation which characterised the worse and most barbarous century of this so-called "dark ages"' (p. XI). For modern socialists are only the last and the worst in a long line of the Church's enemies,

> the idolatrous Northmen who despoiled Churches and murdered ecclesiastics . . . the No-Popery intolerance of the Puritans . . . the ruthless cruelty of the first French revolutionists . . . and, so representing those enemies of religion, combine in themselves all the vices and wickedness of their predecessors . . .
>
> (p. XVII)

'Above all the babble of her age and ours, she makes one blunt assertion. And there alone lies Hope', writes Evelyn Waugh of his heroine in *Helena* (1950) and by extension of Christianity as a whole. He uses deliberate anachronisms, arch parallels and anticipations and contemporary slang to enforce this view of the Church as the eternal antidote to modern follies. The heretical Empress Fausta is like an Anglican modernist – 'I mean, we must have Progress' (1963, reprint: 96), and Lactantius is made, in an unsubtle authorial pun, to point to a gibbon when predicting that there might one day arise an apostate historian, 'with the mind of a Cicero or Tacitus and the soul of an animal' (p. 80).

A less deliberate yet very revealing anachronism also occurs, however, when Waugh used the peculiarly English, passive and dated phrase of 'hearing Mass' for Helena's worship at a fourth-century basilica. For, as his future fantasy 'Out of Depth' from *Mr Loveday's Little Outing* (1936) clearly shows, Waugh finds it hard to conceive of a situation in which *all* of the reassuring non-essentials of Roman Catholicism might change. At one level this dream of a future black Catholic civilization is a valiant attempt on Waugh's part to go beyond the European aspects of Catholicism, but John Gray is able to create a sense of strangeness and timelessness about the liturgy in *Park* that shows its transcendence in *every* age. Waugh on the other hand cannot resist the revealing imagery of familiarity: 'something that twenty-five centuries had not altered; something of his own childhood which survived the age of the world.'[11]

Robert Hugh Benson's powerful fantasies, *Lord of the World* and *The Dawn of All*, present contrasting visions of a world in which Catholicism has been reduced to a tiny faithful remnant and a world which has entirely submitted to the faith. If in one sense the difference between the two visions could hardly be more extreme, in another they are parallel in that they both completely identify the Church with the institution. *Lord of the World* is an account of the coming of the Antichrist, the political leader Julian Felsenburgh, who eventually orders the destruction of the city of Rome. The Church nevertheless survives through the election of a new pope and the Holy See is moved to Jerusalem. This is a sign that the last days are here, and the book itself indeed ends melodramatically with the end of the world at the very moment that Jerusalem too is about to be bombed.

The novel is also an allegorical rendition of absolute ultramontanism, for the fate of the Church and the whole world depends on the personal fate of the pope. In a particularly purple piece of triumphalism earlier the hero sees the pope carried in procession through Rome:

> Far ahead, seeming to cleave its way through the surging heads, like the poop of an ancient ship, moved the canopy beneath which sat the Lord of the World, and between him and the priest, as if it were the wake of that same ship, swayed the gorgeous procession – Pronotaries Apostolic, Generals of Religious Orders and the rest – making its way along with white, gold, scarlet and silver foam between the living banks on either side. Overhead hung the splendid barrel of the roof, and far in front the heaven of God's altar reared its monstrous pillars, beneath which burned the seven yellow stars that were the harbour lights of sanctity. It was an astonishing sight, but too vast and bewildering to do anything but oppress the observers with a consciousness of their own futility. The enormous enclosed air, the giant statues, the dim and distant roofs, the indescribable concert of sound – of the movement of feet, the murmur of ten thousand voices, the peal of organs like the crying of gnats, the thin celestial music – the faint suggestive smell of incense and men and bruised bay and myrtle – and, supreme above all, the vibrant atmosphere of human emotion, shot with supernatural aspiration, as the Hope of the World, the holder of Divine Vice-Royalty, passed on his way to stand between God and man . . .
>
> (1944 reprint: 105)

If this is the papacy fallen on hard times, then one wonders what things must have been like at their height. There is obviously much that a full analysis could pick out here – the traditional imagery of ship, haven and harbour; the appeal to the senses and human emotion and yet the weird imagery of transcendence and the dehumanizing note in 'oppress the observers with a consciousness of their own futility'. Most startling of all is the fact that the 'Lord of the World' opposed to the Antichrist who usurps the title is not, as one might at first think, Christ, but the pope, the 'Hope of the World, the holder of Divine Vice-Royalty'.[12]

The Dawn of All describes the alternative scenario in which virtually the whole world has come to accept Catholicism. The priest-hero, like John Gray's Mungo Park, has lost his memory and wakes up in a world in which it is explained to him that in recent history the Church had been

> found to be eternally right in every plane. . . . From every single point she had been justified and vindicated. Men had thought to invent a new religion, a new art, a new social order, a new philosophy; they had burrowed and explored and digged in every direction; and, at the end, when they had worked out their theories and found, as they thought, the

reward of their labours, they found themselves looking once more into the serene, smiling face of Catholicism.

(p. 41)

Benson seems to claim infallibility here not only for the central doctrines of the Church but for all the secondary social thought, aesthetics and philosophy with which Catholicism has been associated. He devotes the main portion of the book to a chilling internal debate about the persecution of heretics, which is justified as the work not of the 'serene, smiling' Church as such but of the secular arm. The final submission of the world to the pope at the end of the novel becomes an enactment of the Second Coming of Christ, and the pope's title 'Vicar of Christ' has come to amount to a virtual identification: the hero had 'seen with his own eyes Christ in His Vicar – *Princeps gloriosus* come at last – take the power and reign' (p. 268).

The 'power and the glory': Rolfe and Greene

Much more nuanced theologically is the thinking of Benson's former friend Frederick Rolfe. His temperament and personal experiences were such as to create a very clear sense of the gap between the individual and the institution and the institution and the ideal, the 'Fallibility of the Machine'. Throughout *Hadrian VII* there is a strong sense of the human weaknesses of Church figures and the political machinations of cardinals. But in this book at least Rolfe seems to be able to go beyond his purely personal frustration and attain a theologically meaningful balance.

For Rolfe's fundamental reverence and loyalty to the Church is not in doubt here, and he is far from being a modernist or even a liberal. Pope Hadrian begins his radical Bull *Regnum Meum* 'with an unwavering defence of the Divine Revelation, the Church, Peter, and the Power of the Keys' (1958 reprint: 148). He calls the pope the 'father of princes and kings' and St Peter's 'Mother and Mistress of All Churches in the City and the World' (p. 106). But Rolfe's attraction to the renaissance gives him a vantage point for rejecting or purifying post-Tridentine Catholicism. Like his author, Hadrian is a conservative radical with a strong sense of tradition. He believes that the 'Barque of Peter' has been beset by storms, and that it is the job of 'the new captain' to 'set the course again from the old chart. His look is no longer backward but onward' (p. 131). He is unusually clear about the Church's need to avoid undue centralization and to purify itself from worldly power. Refreshingly he commands 'the sacrifice of that phantom uniformity which had been the curse of Catholicism for four centuries, and the retention and cultivation of national and local rites and uses' (p. 188). To the great horror of the curia, he also renounces altogether the claim to the Papal States, quoting 'My Kingdom is not of this world' (p. 149).

Opinionated and at times outrageous as Rolfe is, there is not the sense that he is battering against a completely closed door. He speaks with extreme confidence by temperament anyway, but his assurance also comes from an awareness that the prevailing theological options are not the only ones. The consensus of triumphalism and ultramontanism has not yet become completely rigid. Loyal dissent remains possible. From very soon after the date of *Hadrian VII* that situation was to change because of Pius X's campaign against modernism.

In order to ask the questions he does ask, Graham Greene, for example, seems to be forced to make a cult of what he calls 'disloyalty' and declares to be essential for a Catholic writer.[13] Throughout his whole career he has displayed an overpowering awareness of the tension between the individual and the institutional Church. His most famous 'Catholic' novels insistently raise the question of escape clauses and the fallibility of the institutional rules. *The Heart of the Matter* is deliberately provocative, almost teasing in this respect. Early in the book Scobie speaks mercifully about the suicide of Pemberton because he was not a Catholic, but says to Father Clay that it would obviously be different 'If you or I did it, it would be despair – I grant you anything with us. We'd be damned all right because we know, but *he* doesn't know a thing' (p. 88). But the possibility of Scobie's own salvation is nevertheless raised at the end. Father Rank says to Scobie's wife in a famous phrase, 'The Church knows all the rules, but she doesn't know what goes on in a human heart.'

The very title of *The Power and the Glory* evokes the issue that would later come to be called triumphalism. The phrase from the additional clause to the Our Father attributes those qualities to God and His Kingdom, but the Church has throughout its history taken them upon itself as His representative. As John L. McKenzie writes:

> The accretion of pomp and power to the hierarchy and clergy was surely the result of good faith and devotion, of a desire to present the Church to men in a manner becoming to her dignity. Such an impressive institution deserves, one would think, an impressive manifestation of itself. It is precisely here that a danger arises; the Church may present an image of herself which is more the image of a Renaissance princedom than of the suffering Son of Man and the Reign of God.[14]

Political developments in Mexico strip all these accretions away, and the official Church there is reduced by persecution to one corrupt man. Greene, of course, going a long way towards accepting the communist lieutenant's criticisms of the Church before the revolution, suggests that this in a sense is all to the good. It is not only that the new 'Church', purified of its power and riches, can speak now with less hypocrisy about suffering to the poor, but also that it has attained a truer power and glory precisely through being less respectable and ostensibly virtuous than the Church before the revolution:

> He was a man who was supposed to save souls: it had seemed quite simple once, preaching at Benediction, organising the guilds, having coffee with elderly ladies behind barred windows, blessing new houses with a little incense, wearing black gloves . . . it was as easy as saving money: now it was a mystery. He was aware of his own desperate inadequacy.
> (1971 reprint: 95)

Greene's great drama is still bound by its time in certain crucial respects. The whole Church and its future is presented as depending absolutely on the presence, work and survival of priests, as the dramatic ending, the providential arrival of a new priest, makes clear. This clericalism is itself linked with the old individualistic machinery of the 'salvation of the soul' and the elaborate suspense of whether the priest will get there in time with the last sacraments. But we do nevertheless find here the new sense of a paradoxically purified and stripped Church, a Church of the dispossessed: 'As for the Church – the Church is Padre Jose and the whiskey priest – I don't know of any other' (p. 28). This is a Church built perforce on suffering, compassion and 'mutual forgiveness of each vice', a Church whose only power and glory are a weakness and poverty through which God can work. Such a 'Church of the poor' is remarkably prophetic of the ideas of the more sophisticated of the recent liberation theologians. To belong to this suffering Church, Greene says in what seems the deepest strand of the book, is to experience a blessedness that is already a participation in a very real if paradoxical beginning of heaven on earth.

An illuminating analogue to and contrast with *The Power and the Glory* is provided by another radical novel from this period, A. J. Cronin's popular *The Keys of the Kingdom* (1942), the story of the unconventional priest Francis Chisholm. The hero has been influenced by his own Protestant grandfather and by his friendship with the honourable and dedicated Doctor Tulloch, an honest atheist. As his life has progressed,

> my outlook has simplified, clarified with my advancing years. I've tied up, and neatly tucked away, all the complex, pettifogging little quirks of doctrine. Frankly, I can't believe that any of God's creatures will grill for all Eternity because of eating a mutton chop on Friday. If we have the fundamentals – love for God and our neighbour – surely we're all right.
> (1981 reprint: 221)

Coming to believe that all good men can be saved, he reflects that though the 'Church is our great mother, leading us forward . . . a band of pilgrims, through the night . . . , perhaps there are other mothers. And perhaps even some poor solitary pilgrims who stumble home alone' (252).

Such emphases are rare among Roman Catholics at this time, and despite his sentimentality it is impossible not to be moved by Cronin's generous vision. But there is little that is genuinely theological about any of this. By and large these are good-hearted, decent views that simplify the issues and dissolve the distinctiveness of the Christian vision. Greene's paradoxes in *The Power and the Glory* on the contrary suggest the possibility of a new model, a church that is radically differentiated from the values of 'the world' without having to be absolutized in itself, and the way forward seems to lie in that direction.

New perspectives

For deep-rooted changes in attitudes to the Church, the world and politics were on their way, prepared for in the work of a handful of theologians whose views eventually came to dominate the deliberations of the whole Church at the Second Vatican Council. Renewed attention to biblical studies, patristics and church history and to Newman's model of development brought the clearer recognition that the Church is inevitably involved in change through time. The 'constant factor in the history of the Church and of its understanding of itself', as Hans Küng puts it,

> is only revealed in change; its identity exists only in variability, its continuity only in changing circumstances, its permanence only in varying outward appearances. In short, the 'essence' of the Church is not a matter of metaphysical stasis, but exists only in constantly changing historical 'forms'.[15]

New images popular at the Council include the idea of the pilgrim Church and the Church as the people of God. Both incorporate a sense of imperfection as part of the very self-definition of the Church. The pilgrim Church is still on the way: 'at the same time holy and always in need of being purified'.[16] But the most significant change of emphasis has already been referred to in chapter 3, the formula that the true ideal Church *subsists* in the Roman Catholic Church rather than being completely identifiable with it. The traditional ideal norms of the Church: Catholicity, Holiness, Unity and Truth are seen in other words to be eschatological rather than fully realized ones. We live in the interim era of their imperfect embodiment. The Church is not in itself the Kingdom, though it can be its providential herald, agent and even anticipation:

> If the Kingdom preached by Christ had been realized, there would be no need for the Church. Essentially the Church substitutes for the Kingdom and must, theologically, define itself as an instrument for the full realization of the Kingdom and as the sign of a true yet still imperfect realization of this Kingdom in the world.[17]

The deeply unsympathetic Anthony Burgess parodies these new theologies of the Church in the person of his Pope John figure, Carlo, Pope Gregory, who says on a talk-show on American television,

> Until recently, it was assumed that the fraternity of which the Bishop of Rome is the head was sealed off, arrogant in its claim to sole legitimacy, the sole begetter of Christian authority. I think that view is dying now. I think that I and my brothers are helping to kill it. So I say that Christianity is the tin Baptist chapel in Arkansas as well as St Peter's in Rome. . . . We must talk no more of Catholics and Protestants – only of Christians.
>
> (*Earthly Power*, pp. 555–6)

For all the positive implications of the new thinking it would certainly be difficult to deny that there was also the very real danger of a traumatic shock to the traditional sense of Catholic identity. Even in England, where things moved much more slowly than on the continent, ecumenical activities greatly increased, but very considerable bewilderment was generated at the same time:

> The change of posture from the days when the Catholic Church had seen itself as essentially in competition with other, upstart Christian denominations, and set their total submission to its own authority as the price of

unity, was astonishingly swift. Adrian, looking through his combative apologetics textbooks from Catholic Evidence Guild Days, before sending them off to a parish jumble sale, could hardly believe how swift it had been.
(Lodge, *How Far Can You Go?*: 81)

The movement away from the absolutizing of the Church also reflects and at the same time contributes to a breaking down of the absolute dichotomy between the Church and the world. In the Heideggerian theologies of Karl Adam and Karl Rahner a 'transcendental humanism' had been proposed in which the experience of all human beings seen in its deepest perspective could be said to point to God. Considering the ancient problem that used to be called the salvation of the heathen, for example, Rahner comes to the conclusion that those non-Christians who follow their consciences and the dictates of justice should be regarded as anonymous, unrecognized members of the Church. In M. D. Chenu similar thinking had led to a more positive sense of the way God works in human history and politics, and, more famously, Teilhard de Chardin came to see God's immanence at the very heart of the whole process of evolution.[18]

The first British novelist to show any cognizance of these theological developments was, as might have been predicted, Graham Greene. With *A Burnt-out Case* (1961) his interests change from those within the institutional Church, but in paradoxical relationship to it, to those specifically outside it. In this he reflects his own personal development but also, it appears, some of the new insights.

A Burnt-out Case in particular addresses itself to Karl Rahner's influential notion of 'anonymous Christianity'. Querry, the hero, is a famous architect who has given up the faith and come to work in a Catholic leper colony in Africa. The doctor who runs it for a missionary order is an atheist, but one with a certain respect for 'the Christian myth'. He accuses Querry of not being content to have lost his faith, but continuing to agonize about it (p. 248). In a significant incident that several critics comment on they both listen as outsiders to a sermon to the villagers in which the priest rather touchingly says

> Now I tell you that when a man loves, he must be Klistian. When a man is merciful he must be Klistian. In this village do you think you are the only Klistians – you who come to Church? . . . I give back to Yezu only what Yezu made. Yezu made love, he made mercy. Everybody in the world has something that Yezu made. Everybody in the world is that much a Klistian . . .
>
> (p. 101)

Querry says to his friend 'That would make us both Christians. . . . Come away, Colin, before you are converted and believe yourself an unconscious Christian.' Though both strongly deny the suggestion, the impressive Superior who has preached the sermon himself repeats the hint at the close.

The guerilla priest, Father Rivas, in *The Honorary Consul*, treated with considerable sympathy by Greene, uses the same kind of thinking when he passionately denies that he has left the Church, despite appearances:

Father Rivas looked up at him with the inflamed eyes of a dog who defends a bone. 'I never told you I had left the Church. How can I leave the Church? The Church is the world. The Church is this *barrio*, this room. There is only one way any of us can leave the Church and that is to die.' He made the gesture of a man who is tired of useless discussion. 'Not even then, if what we sometimes believe is true.'

(pp. 250–1)

Movingly, despite his great unorthodoxy, he pays tribute to Christ as the herald of what he calls 'the great Church beyond our time and place':

I think sometimes the memory of that man, that carpenter, can lift a few people out of the temporary Church of these terrible years, when the Archbishop sits down to dinner with the General, into the great Church beyond our time and place, and then . . . those lucky ones . . . they have no words to describe the beauty of that Church.

(p. 276)

Always called 'Father', Rivas remains, in a genuine sense, a kind of priest. He dies with this ambiguity about him, going out to be shot perhaps because he wishes to bring absolution like the hero of *The Power and the Glory* or perhaps simply in a gesture of human sympathy. But there remains the hint that Rivas's actual priesthood may serve as a symbolic intensification of this shared human instinct.

There can be no doubt that for many Catholics the new era has brought a considerable relaxation of the institutional sense of the Church. Structures once seen as essential, permanent and definitive have come to be regarded in some quarters as secondary, even provisional. Father Austin Brierley in Lodge's *How Far Can You Go?* prophesies 'a time when the whole elaborate structure of priests and dioceses and parishes would melt away' (p. 142). Edward Schillebeeckx, a far more mainstream Catholic theologian than his troubles with Rome might suggest, goes so far as to say that no more than a provisional identification is possible in our time between believers and the institutional Church.[19]

The ethos of these later novels of Greene's might more properly be termed 'post-Catholic' than Catholic, and there are examples of analogous trends in the more specialized contexts of Catholic gay and feminist fiction as we shall see. A positive expression of the mood is to be found in the ideas of the ex-priest Malachy in John Cornwell's *The Spoiled Priest*, though he is surrounded by other reactions of despair and empty nostalgia there, as we have seen. But if the old ways of the Church are dead, Malachy, whose name is that of the last prophet of the Old Testament, believes that the Holy Spirit will breathe out renewal into the new age and a 'new spirit of the Church' will appear, though he is not sure where or how.

The central problem remains, though, how to preserve the new openness without a disabling loss of identity. One character comments during Lodge's marvellous description of the Easter festival of the 'Catholics for an Open Church' in *How Far Can You Go?*:

> Certainly Catholics are much more tolerant, much more liberal than they used to be. I was brought up as one and the nuns gave us to understand that unless you were a good Catholic your chances of getting to heaven were pretty slim. Most of the people at this affair don't seem to think that they're in any way superior to Protestants or Jews, Hindus or Muslims, or, for that matter, atheists and agnostics. Which is very decent and humble of them, but it does raise the question, why be a Catholic at all, rather than something else or just nothing?
>
> (p. 234)

If the traditional Catholic sense of the institutional Church is allowed to fade too much, it is difficult to see, for example, how the distinction between the Church and the world can be preserved, even at a conceptual level, and without that how a critique of the illegitimate aspects of that 'world' can in turn be sustained. As Küng has said,

> An ecclesiology which takes a *traditionalist* view, which sees itself as something permanent and unchanged from the beginning of time and uncritically allows itself to be enslaved by a particular age or culture now past, misunderstands what historicity is. Historicity is also misrepresented by an ecclesiology which, taking a *modernist* view, adapts itself and becomes enslaved by the present age or culture, and so abandons itself equally uncritically to the disasters of total changeability.[20]

The old ideology had absolutized the Church and oversimplified its relationship with the world. It had nevertheless provided the vantage point for a distinctive vision and critique. There is some question whether the new versions will be able to do the same, and doubts have been expressed not only about the future of Catholic fiction but even about whether a distinctive Catholic contribution of any kind will continue, at least in this country.

Pope John Paul II, of course, has tried to arrest and even reverse some of these processes, but the change of consciousness has been widespread and deep-rooted and it is not easy to reaffirm Catholic identity without encouraging blind conservatism. As noted at the end of chapter 3, the Pope's influence has strengthened those elements in Britain that had proved resistant to the new tendencies, but it is difficult to believe that this will have very great long-term significance. Such positions too have their analogies in the fiction, as we might expect. If it is intellectuals who are most intensely affected by the new trends, it is also from a self-conscious minority of intellectuals that the clearest resistance to them is likely to come. But such resistance is often expressed with a degree of anxiety and defiance that shows it to be a rearguard action. Piers Paul Read's career, for example, has led him further and further away from the relative optimism about the secular world that has dominated much recent Catholic thought. But the political implications of this, explored further in the next chapter, have seemed to lead Read back again to something not far removed from a 'siege mentality'. In their very different way Alice Thomas Ellis's novels also attack secular optimisms of all kinds and combine this with satire on ecumenism and the new Catholicism.

Images of the Church and the world

Some mileage obviously remains both in the post-Catholic and the neo-conservative modes of contemporary 'Catholic' fiction. Yet neither is likely to hold out any lasting answers. If the one runs the risk of dissolving the distinction between the Church and the world, the other seems to go back to oversimplifying it again. There is some evidence to suggest that new ways of preserving the Church's distinctiveness without absolutizing the institution are being worked out in Catholic experience in other parts of the world at the present time, most notably in the so-called 'basic Christian communities' of South America and (it now appears) Eastern Europe.[21] At their best these seem to offer a model for devolving power back to the more immediate Christian community without losing touch with the wider dimensions of the Church and the political implications of Christian commitment. The real question is whether British Catholicism will be able to find analogous solutions in its own very different context and so be able to preserve some of the more valuable Catholic insights while growing closer to other churches. The answer will obviously affect the future of British Catholic fiction, but it also has far wider implications.

· 7 ·
'Mixing themselves up in politics'

In arms against the 'whole modern age'

From the vantage point of Robert Hugh Benson's papocracy in *The Dawn of All* (1911) modern politics as a whole are seen as

> the old dreams of the beginning of the century . . . the phantom of independent thought and the intoxicating nightmare of democratic government. It was certain now that these things were dreams – that it was ludicrously absurd that a man could profitably detach himself from Revelation and the stream of tradition and development that flowed from it; that it was ridiculous to turn creation upside-down and attempt to govern the educated few by the uneducated many.
>
> (p. 122)

By the end the hero has come to the conclusion that there are:

> only two logical theories of government: the one, that power came from below, the other, that power came from above. The infidel, the Socialist, the materialist, the democrat, these maintained the one; the Catholic, the Monarchist, the Imperialist maintained the other.
>
> (p. 220)

Both this novel and its predecessor, *Lord of the World*, enforce Benson's political views with the same powerful obsessiveness as his theological ultramontanism. In *Lord of the World* the rot had set in with the election of a Labour government in England in 1917, and it was then that 'Communism had really began' (1944 reprint: 2). After that, secularism and socialism had taken over the world in preparation for the coming of the Antichrist, and Rome was the only pocket of resistance left.

Such views read like a parody of what were once taken to be traditional

Catholic politics. The whole situation has obviously changed since the Second Vatican Council, but the Catholic Church is not a sect and it is wise to avoid premature generalizations about the Catholic politics of the past as well. Many Roman Catholics keep their political views insulated from their faith, which they regard as an essentially private concern. But even for Catholics who take the political implications of Christianity seriously there has always been more pluralism than might at first seem the case. A variety of alternative ways of interpreting the political demands of that faith are available, and the Bible and church tradition have been taken to legitimize totally antithetical points of view. Piers Paul Read powerfully dramatizes the extremes in *The Free Frenchman* (1986) in his portraits of the worker priest Antoine Dubec who joins the Communist Party, and the *miliciens* who fight to the last to defend Hitler in Berlin, crying out 'long live Christ the King' as they attack tanks with grenades (p. 565).

In Britain the majority of Catholics this century have voted Labour, but this has been essentially for sociological rather than religious reasons. Since many of the novelists have been intellectuals and converts, ideological concerns are much more intensely represented in fiction than in the Catholic community at large, as we have seen, and these concerns have sometimes taken directly political form. Many British Catholic novels are pietistic, private and apolitical, but a wide range of political options are canvassed as well, with fascist novels such as Douglas Jerrold's *Storm over Europe* (1930) and Catholic Marxist ones such as Piers Paul Read's *Game in Heaven with Tussy Marx* (1966). An overall ideological trend towards nostalgic solutions, conservative in a broad sense at least, nevertheless clearly emerges.

For it was natural enough when the Church felt threatened by an overwhelmingly secular world for it to greet modern political developments as a whole with dismay. Nanda's notes from her elderly Jesuit retreat-giver in *Frost in May* are an amusing but revealing summary of a whole complex:

> Rich and poor, however, a divine dispensation. Must not try to alter natural order of things. Abominations of socialism, freemasonry, etc. Trying to do God's work for Him. Women's votes unnecessary. Let her use her great influence in her own sphere. Modesty more effective than desire to shine. Our Lady had no vote and did not want one.
> (1982 reprint: 105)

Not only communism, socialism and the womens' movement but even democracy itself could be regarded with suspicion, for the latter, as Bill McSweeney explains,

> which is now generally conceived as a political arrangement that tolerates and is acceptable to the Catholic Church, appeared in the nineteenth century to be fundamentally anti-Catholic. The rights of man seemed to diminish the rights of God; self-determination was counterposed to hierarchic guidance; moral individualism challenged the whole corpus of Catholic moral teaching.[1]

Faithful fictions

Even in England such writers as William McCabe and Edward Dering portray a definitive confrontation of the old order and the new. For Dering, the Church is 'the only power that could have any chance whatever of stemming the revolutionary torrent that I can see slowly but surely approaching' (*Sherborne*; 504). For William McCabe in *Adelaide, Queen of Italy* it is likewise socialism – 'an attempt on the part of the labouring classes to live in idleness by sharing among themselves the accumulated property of the rich' (p. XIV) – that has to be seen as the greatest threat.

A Church seemingly identified with confrontation against the modern world naturally appeals to those already predisposed in that direction. Dering, the later Belloc, Douglas Jerrold, Evelyn Waugh – these are a formidable array of far-right luminaries, and many other Catholic writers are predictably attracted to a sentimental feudalism and paternalism, a romantic chivalry or Jacobitism. When Waugh announces that the artist must always be a reactionary, he means primarily that, if an artist does not stand out against the spirit of his age, then he will have nothing distinctive to say.[2] But he is deliberately playing with the political meaning of 'reactionary' too. His Guy Crouchbank has taken up arms 'against the whole modern age', an age previously invoked as 'an age for Hoopers' in *Brideshead Revisited*. His Empress Helena, we remember, has had

> a terrible dream of the future. Not now, but presently, people may forget their loyalty to their kings and emperors and take power for themselves. Instead of letting one victim bear this frightful curse they will take it all on themselves, each one of them. Think of the misery of a whole world possessed of Power without Grace.
>
> (*Helena*, 1963 reprint: 122)

It would be misleading, however, to suggest that completely reactionary opposition to modern developments was the whole story. There were always a handful of Catholics like Edmund Randolph whose sympathies were startlingly radical. Even on the official level, as Bill McSweeney goes on to show, simple condemnation was not the only response. Under Leo XIII, in particular, the strategy was rather to compete in a sense by showing that proper social justice could only be won by following Christian tradition. Some later nineteenth-century writers are much more enthusiastic about democracy, and Wilfred Ward and Pearl Craigie, extrapolating from Newman's theological insights, go so far as to say that it is only Rome that can properly sustain and protect democracy by combining it with appropriate authority.[3] Even in this period Catholicism cannot simply be identified as a right-wing influence since the social reformism is often genuine enough within its limits.

The harking back to the past involves an anti-capitalist emphasis that is itself, though conservative in the broadest sense, hard to place along a left–right spectrum. In Chesterton's 'The crime of the communist' (*The Scandal of Father Brown*) it is made very clear that capitalism is the greater enemy of Christianity. Compton Mackenzie's John Ogilvie also says that 'Capitalism was always anti-Christian and could never have established itself without the weakening of the Catholic Church by the Protestant Reformation' (*West to North*, 1942 reprint: 335).

'Mixing themselves up in politics'

Such comments, commonplaces in some circles by the time Mackenzie was writing, look back to medieval condemnations of usury and combine well with a campaign against the modern order. They develop a familiar reading of history drawn partly from William Cobbett and the Catholic priest-historian John Lingard: a view of the pre-Reformation, pre-capitalist order that becomes a potent weapon against the social organization of modern England, which is conveniently associated with Protestantism. The Reformation is itself presented as the root cause of all England's social ills. The dissolution of the monasteries caused great harm to the poor, for, Dering and others claim, the monks did far more for them than the modern Poor Law. At the same time the financial proceeds from the plundered monasteries helped to create and strengthen the position of an oligarchy. In Ford Madox Ford's *The Fifth Queen* it is greed to keep the revenues from the dissolved monasteries that prevents even the Catholic aristocracy and gentry from supporting the queen in restoring Catholicism. The powerful financial interest that had thus been created is seen as the main factor in the Industrial Revolution and the burdensome growth of the Empire.

Chesterton and Belloc, the most famous British Catholic exponents of these theories, themselves began as political radicals, as we have seen. They reject Fabian solutions as too centralizing and bureaucratic and portray socialism and capitalism as the obverse sides of the same steady increase in state power. Parliamentary democracy is condemned, as in Belloc's satire *Mr Clutterbuck's Election*, not because democracy is a bad idea as such but because the modern system is a con-trick that fails to deliver genuine democracy at all. Distributism is a much less paternalistic version of the medieval order than most, and it is presented as the devolution of power back to smallholders, the creation of a true property-owning democracy. The old society, says Michael Herne, in Chesterton's late novel, *The Return of Don Quixote*, was certainly not 'perfect or painless', but it was a time in which 'men were simple and sane and normal and as native to this earth as they can ever be.'

It would be wrong therefore to assume that all those who espouse medievalism are simply reactionaries. Chesterton shows all the appeal of 'the flower of chivalry' in *The Return of Don Quixote*, but he is very careful to distinguish the political essence from the trappings and keen to prevent distributism from being taken over by conservative interests. The novel describes a revival of medievalism in England in reaction to the threat represented by a miners' strike led by the syndicalist, John Braintree. Chesterton's whole point is that by medieval criteria it is the miners who are in the right, not the aristocratic mineowners who have fostered the medieval party and appointed the arbiter. To their great consternation the arbiter in fact awards completely against the establishment. He points out that the introduction of a society run on medieval lines would indeed mean the workers' owning the mines, and Braintree is amazed to find his cause supported 'as a piece of pure medievalism' (p. 289). Above all Chesterton explains the crucial point that though medieval 'ethics and jurisprudence affirmed the principle of private property' it did so

> with rather more elaboration and modification than most modern systems, till we come to the system called Socialism. It was generally

admitted, for example, that a man might be actually or apparently in possession of property to which he had no right, because it had been acquired by methods condemned by Christian morals.

(p. 275)

Medievalism may thus have its uses as an ideological strategy, but its value obviously lies in its critical force rather than its positive content. Even this more nuanced version of Chesterton's has in the last analysis only the invocation of a golden age in the past to oppose against modern injustices. Particular interpretations of Thomism combine in distributism with late Victorian back-to-the-land elements, and Belloc's and Chesterton's associate, the great Dominican, Father Vincent McNabb, refused to use any modern machinery including typewriters.

Catholic medievalism has also played a part in Scots and Welsh nationalism with the work of Fionn MacColla, Compton Mackenzie and Saunders Lewis. It has the advantage of being a potential weapon not only against the dominant culture of England but also against what can be portrayed as the prevailing Protestant ethos in these lands themselves. The Scots writers blend in Jacobite sentiment as well, of course, and Mackenzie's vision has been sympathetically parodied by Lewis Grassic Gibbon as:

a Scots Catholic kingdom, with Mr Compton Mackenzie Prime Minister to some disinterred Jacobite royalty, and all the Scots intellectuals settled out on the land on thirty-acre crofts or sent out to re-colonise St Kilda for the good of their souls and the nation.[4]

In reality this does less than justice to Mackenzie's genuine importance in the movement, and in the ambitious series *Four Winds* at least his role is worthily backed up in the fiction. Jacobitism is carefully redefined there not as loyalty to the Stuarts as such but as the 'longing for a way of life which had been destroyed and to recover which the Stuarts afforded the only chance' (*West to North*, 1942 reprint: 66). Catholicism remains an essential part of Mackenzie's political vision in this work, but its function has changed now to that of preserving an international dimension. John Ogilvie, the hero of *Four Winds*, is said to have 'waited to weave religious and political conviction together with a single gesture of faith. A spiritual imperialism and internationalism was to blend with a political nationalism expressed by many small states.'[5]

If the change of heart produces a new model here, it is still, however, one that itself has a distinctly medieval cast to it. Ogilvie says of himself at one point, 'It's rather unsatisfactory to be a revolutionary whose notion of revolution is putting back the clock' (*The East Wind of Love*, 1973 reprint: 275), and his words may stand as an epitaph on all such strategies. As with most Catholic social thought until very recently, their dynamism comes from a privileging of the past rather than from the perspective of a future Kingdom of Justice.

Real political dangers lay in Belloc's further elaborate ideological identification of 'the faith' with European civilization as a whole. In Bernard Bergonzi's *The Roman Persuasion*, as we have seen, such thinking leads the Catholic publisher Martin Tollybeare to the defence of Mussolini and Franco and eventually, like William Joyce, Lord Haw-Haw, another associate of Belloc, to Germany. As the issues grew more polarized in the late twenties and thirties, it seemed natural to present communism as the enemy of Christian civilization, and it was a dangerously easy next step sometimes therefore to see fascism as its necessary defender. Given what appeared to be a straight choice between fascism or communism, the vast majority of Catholics at this time would certainly choose the former. Gemma, the heroine of Josephine Mary Ward's *In the Shadow of Mussolini* (1927), for example, is a political opponent of Mussolini, but she warns him about an assassination plot because she says Italy is not ready to be without him yet and chaos would result. She tells him she will never accept the loss of democracy, but says that if all authority is to be concentrated in the hands of one man she would prefer it to be him rather than Lenin (p. 222).

The events of the Spanish Civil War obviously sharpened this polarization, and most Catholics, understandably enough at the time, supported Franco. Douglas Jerrold, another associate of Belloc and Chesterton, helped procure a plane to fly Franco back to Spain to lead the rebellion. His earlier Catholic fascist propaganda novel *Storm over Europe* (1930) represents an extreme development of one strand of Catholic political thought that masquerades as the only one. The idea of original sin, for example, is itself turned into an argument for fascism there: 'men are only made happy by recognizing their limitations, and they are only happy in a society whose institutions reflect those limitations' (p. 191).

Throughout the novel Jerrold makes blatant use of Belloc's ideology to indicate that this civil war in 'Cisalpania' between the royalists and the republican 'League of Free Thought' is 'no petty domestic squabble. The fight before us is one which has to be fought out all over Europe sooner or later. The threat to our Civilisation was never graver' (p. 89). The battle lines are drawn up in the clearest possible order. 'Hostility to the Church' is said to be 'an acid test of sincerity among the left-wing movement.' The radical Ravenstein is presented as saying that he hates Europe, and 'the Church is the only solid thing in Europe' (p. 169). Equally, there is an absolute identification between the right-wing party and the Church, and the cardinal gives a broad hint of support to any rebellion caused by a republican attack. 'Rome believes,' says D'Alvarez chillingly, 'that Peace on Earth should be confined very strictly to men of goodwill' (p. 203).

The 'opening to the left'

As George Orwell points out with astonishment, Graham Greene is unusually left-wing in sympathies for a Catholic writer of this time, and he was one of a small handful of Catholic intellectuals that did not support Franco.[6] Greene's early non-religious novels reflect the political and economic pressures of the thirties and display leftist sympathies, though they have no solutions to proffer. The move into specifically Catholic work represents in part at least a turning aside from politics, but *The Power and the Glory* has a political content too and is something of a test-case for Catholic political fiction. For Greene is obviously not without sympathy for his communist lieutenant. His aims are good ones and there is a sense in which Greene shares them. The crucial question is whether Greene's final rejection of his politics has to be seen as a metaphysical obfuscation, a sentimental opting out.

Terry Eagleton, remembering his own Catholic Marxist days, recognizes that the incarnational dimension of Christianity involves a commitment to justice and the poor but says that the doctrine of original sin leads inevitably to pessimism and the rejection of political hopes. Anthony Burgess on the contrary accuses Greene of a political utopianism that results precisely from a failure to recognize the reality of original sin. In Burgess's view Pelagianism is at the root of all liberal, socialist and communist ideas. He writes that 'any political ideology that rejects original sin and believes in moral progress ought strictly to be viewed with suspicion by Catholics.'[7]

Burgess is surely wrong to ignore the strong anti-utopian side to Greene. In *The Heart of the Matter* Scobie says:

> Nobody here could ever talk about a heaven on earth. Heaven remained rigidly in its proper place on the other side of death, and on this side flourished the injustices, the cruelties, the meanness that elsewhere people so cleverly hushed up.
>
> (1950 reprint: 30)

But if original sin is certainly not denied by Greene, as Burgess claims, its implications are far more complex than Eagleton suggest as well. It is compassion caused by the shared sense of human weakness and suffering that itself fuels the desire to improve the situation. Imagery of decay and disease fills *The Power and the Glory*, but the analysis devolves upon different ideas of a cure. The dentist says to the Chief of Police, 'You cure a lot of people in this country, don't you, with bullets?' (1971 reprint: 259). Despite the compassion built into his aims, the lieutenant denies compassion in his means because the revolution is prepared to dispense with individuals for the sake of some apparently greater good. A proper sense of the reality of human weakness, Greene seems to argue, would lead to the recognition that no one is sufficiently unflawed to be able to take the responsibility for such a decision: 'It's no good your working for your end unless you're a good man yourself. And there won't always be good men in your party' (p. 234).

The idea of original sin thus becomes the basis for a critique of what is presented as an ultimately inhuman and impersonal utopianism and of all premature claims to definitive achievement. But that is not simply the end of the matter. In his own weakness the priest feels no temptation to stand above those he is attempting to 'cure'. He cares for individuals too: 'That was the difference, he had always known, between his faith and theirs, the political leaders of the people who cared only for things like the state, the republic: this child was more important than a whole continent' (p. 96).

The implication here has to be that the priest's 'cure' goes far beyond the scope of the lieutenant's. What we see, in other words, is not simply the rejection of revolution but the recommendation of a different, paradoxical kind. A new ecclesiology leads to a new political sense. The Church of the poor brings about a radical new sense of community:

> Again he was touched by an extraordinary affection. He was just one criminal among a herd of criminals . . . he had a sense of companionship which he had never received in the old days when pious people came kissing his black cotton glove.
>
> (p. 153)

The question that has to be asked, though, is whether all this has any genuine political content to it? Speaking again to the lieutenant, the priest says that, if the poor are blessed and the rich are going to find it hard to get into heaven,

> Why should we make it hard for the poor man too? Oh, I know we are told to give to the poor, to see they are not hungry – hunger can make a man do evil just as much as money can. But why should we give the poor power? It's better to let him die in dirt and wake in heaven – so long as we don't push his face in the dirt.
>
> (p. 239)

Is there not evidence here for Greene's complicity in the way the Church has often used its teaching to keep the poor in their place?

It would certainly seem so on the face of it. Greene's own cult of suffering lies behind the passage, and to give the poor all blessings except money and power is open to the accusation of giving them nothing in the end. What can nevertheless be said on Greene's behalf is that, whatever it may sound like here, the book as a whole is not simply preaching pie in the sky. Heaven begins *here*, in the entrance into this new community of the compassionate, forgiving and dispossessed. And if Greene's revolution is a revolution of consciousness rather than a political one, it has political *consequences*, at least for the Church itself, for only those who are prepared to be stripped of everything else can join it: 'For a matter of seconds he felt an immense satisfaction that he could talk of suffering to them now without hypocrisy – it is hard for the sleek and well-fed priest to praise poverty' (p. 82).

Elsewhere Greene shows that he is not against the idea of Catholic political action. Commenting in *The Lawless Roads* (1939) on a strike led by a local priest in Texas, Greene says:

> This strike was the first example I had come across of genuine Catholic action on a social issue. . . . The intention was good, of course, but the performance was deplorable. You compared it mentally with the soap-box orator and the Red Flag and a crowd singing the Internationale. Catholicism, one felt, had got to rediscover the technique of revolution.[8]

In *The Power and the Glory* his point is rather that to learn the worthlessness of all earthly power is more truly revolutionary than giving power to the poor. If this can hardly provide the basis for a full Catholic politics, it is an insight that puts an uncomfortable question to all those involved in Christian political action. If it is obviously a sentiment that has often been manipulated in defence of the status quo, the whole thrust of Greene's work goes to prove that it would be unfair to read it in this way in his case.

Greene meanwhile was coming to seem a little less isolated as official Catholic social thought on the continent itself began to move in more progressive directions, though by very cautious steps at first. Maritain's intellectual influence was important here, but also major practical considerations that amounted to an instinct for self-survival.[9] Even before the Second World War, writes Piers Paul Read in *The Free Frenchman*, 'there was a certain unease that the working classes appeared disaffected from the Catholic religion and gave their loyalties instead to the atheists on the left' (p. 79). The working-class Dominican Antoine Dubec in Read's novel is allowed to work in a textile factory and encouraged in his leftist views. After the war the French worker-priest movement developed further, and it became more organized and better known in the fifties.

Dunstan Thompson's novel, *The Dove with the Bough of Olive* (1955), self-consciously set among wealthy West End Catholics, is a revealing British example of conservative hostility to these developments. The priest hero finds it necessary to assert that

> God loves the well-off, too. Their souls matter just as much as those of Catholic trade unionists. Though you wouldn't think so from the way some of the bishops behave these days. Redder than Cardinals!
>
> (p. 124)

In fact, traditional Catholic anti-communism was intensified during this period by Cold War attitudes and this had far more influence on the majority of Catholics than any 'opening to the left'. Lodge's group of young British Catholics had been brought up to believe that:

> The betrayal of the glorious Allied cause by Soviet Russia, the enslavement of Eastern Europe with its millions of Catholics, the inexorable advance of atheistic communism in the Far East – all showed that Satan was as active in the world as ever. Their hero was Cardinal Mindszenty, who had been imprisoned by the Communists in Hungary . . .
>
> (*How Far Can You Go?* 1982 reprint: 49)

The intensity of contemporary concern for the conversion of Russia is indicated in Ronald Matthews's 1951 novel *Red Sky at Night*. After a miracle there is a crusade to Moscow that succeeds in turning the Russian people back to God. At the end the action proves to have been a dream, but the author passionately encourages his readers to believe that it can become a reality.

In the sixties, however, the previously almost unthinkable change of attitude towards Marxism described in chapter 3 occurred, the desire to make common cause in the search for justice and a general *rapprochement* that turned almost into an identification among a few activists and intellectuals. David Lodge in *How Far Can You Go?* is selecting an admittedly extreme example but not actually making it up or even exaggerating when he cites writers in the Cambridge magazine *Slant* who provocatively identified the Kingdom of God heralded in the New Testament with the Revolution, and characterized the service of Benediction as a capitalist-imperialist liturgical perversion which turned the shared bread of the authentic Eucharist into a reified commodity.

(p. 82)

For the sake of fairness it is worth noting in passing that most theoreticians, however sympathetic, were much more guarded than *Slant* and (in the light of recent events) that there was never any admiration for Eastern-bloc communist regimes as such.[10]

Once again it is Graham Greene that is the first novelist to show much interest in the new Catholic politics. The sympathy for his guerrilla priest Father Rivas in *The Honorary Consul*, who is modelled on Camillo Torres, is also a political sympathy, of course, though it stops far short of complete endorsement. But Rivas is certainly in the last analysis more the victim of violence than its perpetrator. Earlier the same issue had come up in *The Comedians*, where there is a brief liberation-theology-type sermon from a Haitian refugee priest on the text in which St Thomas the Apostle urges the disciples to go up to Jerusalem and die with Christ. The priest says that:

our hearts go out in sympathy to all who are moved to violence by the suffering of others. The Church condemns violence, but it condemns indifference more harshly. Violence can be the expression of love, indifference never. One is an imperfection of charity, the other the perfection of egoism. In the days of fear, doubt and confusion, the simplicity and loyalty of one apostle advocated a political solution. He was wrong, but I would rather be wrong with St Thomas than right with the cold and craven. Let us go up to Jerusalem and die with him.

(pp. 308–9)

Greene's own reactions to this can be gauged only at several removes. Even the priest himself continues to say that violence is wrong, though his heart tells him the opposite. Among the listeners Smith says that he dislikes the sermon because it contains too much of the 'acidity of human passion'. Brown, the ex-Catholic narrator, wonders if the priest will require a very firm repentance from the guerillas who confess to him. But in the letter at the beginning Greene calls the real-life prototypes of these guerillas 'courageous'. He obviously continues to be both sympathetic and evasive himself at the same time.

The more recent *Monsignor Quixote* (1982) is an account of the relationship between the monsignor, a Catholic in spite of the curia, and his friend the mayor, a communist in spite of the *politburo*, but this work too remains evasive in its very whimsicality of tone. The friendship is clearly meant to be of more than purely personal significance, and Greene recapitulates here his own old 'dream of a deepening friendship and a profounder understanding, of a reconciliation even between their respective faiths' (p. 58). But he is not sure himself how much reality the dream can have and therefore seems to assert in contradictory fashion at the same time that the only thing that really matters is the personal love the two men have for each other.

Pope John XXIII's comparative openness to Marxism is echoed in his prototype, Anthony Burgess's Carlo, Pope Gregory, in *Earthly Powers*, 'seventy now, nobly fat, wonderfully ugly' (p. 541). He is accused by an Italian magazine of believing that

> The spirit of man in our age . . . is most nobly manifested in the proletariat. The aspirations of this proletariat, as voiced by the syndicates, are, in his view, totally reconcilable with the Augustinian vision of the City of God. What Marx wanted, God wanted also . . .
>
> (p. 540)

Burgess is parodying the style of the attacker as well as the victim, but the fact that the whole book is in a sense set up to discredit Carlo, despite his sympathetic features, makes it plain where his own political allegiances lie.

John Braine is much less subtle in *The Pious Agent* (1975), an extraordinary, not to say bizarre reworking of James Bond. Conventional spy fiction had reflected the old sense of east and west as absolute black and white. Graham Greene's more ambiguous politics helped make his spy novels among the first to disturb these certainties and show areas of grey, and he has influenced later developments in that direction in such writers as le Carré.[11] Braine's work is a fantasy, but it clearly reflects the desire to return to the old absolutes. The hero is an idealistic assassin who has Braine's sympathy and admiration, a Catholic spy for Britain whose Catholicism, by fuelling his anti-communist zeal, has made him more patriotic, not less like Burgess's Catholic spy in *Tremor of Intent*. Even Braine's hero has to come to the recognition at the end that the old world of moral absolutes has gone for good now, but a great sense of regret remains both on his and the author's part. The fact that the hero's own confessor turns out to have been a communist agent all along is Braine's special paranoid parable of a Church itself contaminated by Marxism.

The early novels of Piers Paul Read show a specific interest in the thinking of the Cambridge *Slant* group. The curious experimental first work *Game in Heaven with Tussy Marx* (1966), taking its cue from a passage also referred to several times by Greene in which Marx defends the monasteries, links revolution with the populist uprisings against the Reformation and the Hanoverian oligarchy by calling it a 'revival of the Forty-Five, of the Levellers, the Chartists and the Pilgrimage of Grace too.' Tussy Marx herself comments that communism and Christianity are 'different sides' of the same coin (1974 reprint: 149), and it is impossible to tell in the procession at the end whether the revolutionaries are carrying guns or crucifixes.

In the second novel, *The Junkers* (1968), the sympathetic character, Edward von Rummelsberg, is a convert to communism because the 'basic assumptions of justice and equality for all men seemed to him compatible with, and part of, Christian belief' (p. 164). But even as early as this a counter-movement has begun in Read and there is a real ambivalence here about the relative moral priorities of public and private life. Because of his love for her, the hero overlooks the presence of Suzi's war-criminal father at his wedding and the possibility that he himself has been unwittingly involved in a right-wing plot to assist the reunification of Germany.

The flawed ethical basis of political action becomes very much the central theme of *The Professor's Daughter*. The young Jesuit, Alan Gray, becomes a revolutionary and in so doing comes to see that he has to split off the religious and ethical realm from the realm of political action, a price he is quite willing to pay. The central character, his teacher Henry Rutledge, liberal Professor of Political Science at Harvard, on the other hand chooses finally to reject political violence and any form of unethical behaviour for political ends. As Father Gray grows away from God, the hero has grown towards Him, and he becomes a martyr figure at the close, being shot as he foils an attempt at a political assassination led by Gray. What the author now seems to affirm is that private life and family love, bolstered by religious faith, are a better way of combating the corruption of society enacted in the compulsive promiscuities of the Professor's daughter, Louisa.

Read's work has moved steadily towards political pessimism. Monk Dawson's optimistic reformism is checked by his discovery that the young Marxist trade-union leader who tells him the case for a strike will not be fairly represented by the press is right. But the world is a fallen one and so the situation will not change. *A Married Man* refines on the lesson of *The Professor's Daughter*. The mid-life crisis of the barrister, John Strickland, leads to a revival of his youthful socialism and he becomes a Labour MP. His Catholic wife, Clare, is unsympathetic to his new ideals and ambitions and writes of him 'I think what irritates me fundamentally about John is that he doesn't believe in God, because how can you assume that justice and equality are good if God isn't there to say so?' (p. 242). Eventually the attempt to gain political justice without God is to lead once more to violence.

The deep stain of contamination incurred in politics is also the central theme of *The Free Frenchman*, a sombre epic about the history of twentieth-century France and the different political options Catholics have adopted. Read's hero, Bertrand de Rouay, leaves France to join de Gaulle, his ex-wife, Madeleine, joins the communists, and his uncle the bishop for a time supports Vichy. The book demonstrates through a complex series of interwoven stories how tangled and corrupted by self-interest the web of politics is. It is Madeleine's lover, for example, who betrays Bertrand and tries to have him killed, whilst an English friend of his unfaithful second wife's family refuses to help save him. When Bertrand himself is finally established as the Free French governor of his province, he finds despite himself that he has to allow the bent police commissioner, Guillot, to continue in office.

Bertrand comes near the end to a major recognition that seems to have Read's own support behind it:

> The madness he ascribed to Dominique when she had become a nun now seemed like the only sense, because the world outside the convent walls was the principality of Satan, and it was impossible to live in it without giving the Devil his due.
>
> In the fading light Bertrand could see farewell messages that had been scratched by former prisoners in this condemned cell. 'A kiss for Elise and the children,' one had written; a second, undoubtedly a defiant *milicien*,

'Long live Christ the King.' How wretched the illusions of those who imagined that it could ever be right to kill for Christ. How mistaken the example of the crusaders; for evil could only be answered with evil, the bombardment of London with the obliteration of Berlin. God took no side in wars, because as Christ himself said, his kingdom is not of this world, and no legions of angels are ever summoned to battle for his cause.

(p. 552)

The deepening pessimism of Read's progress has led him to a kind of stalemate, for these later novels in fact propound a circular argument. Only God can bring about justice and only belief in God makes the struggle for justice worthwhile anyway. But the realm of politics is 'the world' in the biblical sense, by definition the place where God does not reign. It is impossible for Christians to enter this arena without being contaminated by it.

These sombre meditations raise legitimate problems for the new, more positive approaches that have tended to prevail since Vatican II, but they can hardly, of course, be said to exhaust the possibilities. If too ready an adoption of the norms of secular politics represents one extreme, a complete withdrawal surely represents the other. When Rolfe's Pope Hadrian remarks that the world is 'sick for the Church, but she never would confess it as long as the Church posed as her rival' (p. 150), it is clear that the Church's renunciation of the weapons of the world is a preparation for a deeper, more prophetic political role. It seems by no means axiomatic, moreover, that individual Christians should find it impossible, as Read implies, to bring some of the values of the Kingdom with them into their practical politics.

A survey of Catholic fiction certainly shows how easy it is for the faith to be caught up into political ideologies, but there is no reason to speak as if the very real dangers of contamination in the political realm are greater than the opposite dangers of quietism. In a significant dialogue in Compton Mackenzie's *The North Wind* John Ogilvie says to a priest that the German Catholics should make more of a stand against Hitler:

> ... if the clergy believe what they claim to believe, Father Macdonald, how can the clergy help mixing themselves up in politics? I don't mean by that, backing one political party against another. I'm using politics in the sense of all government. It's not mixing in politics to reject National Socialism as a threat to Christianity and as such to fight it.
>
> (p. 169)

The truth seems to lie not in some golden mean between Read's and Mackenzie's views, which both represent respected Christian options, but rather perhaps in an uncomfortable attempt to hold two contradictory opinions in tension at the same time.

Part four

'A drama of good and evil that other writers do not see'

· 8 ·

Good and evil: the providential plot

The supernatural in fiction

Catholic writers, Piers Paul Read has boldly said, see a drama of good and evil that others do not see.[1] Popular Catholicism is a religion full of the supernatural, and popular Catholic fiction often works out the great drama Read refers to by means of miracles, visions, saints, angels and devils. Such fictionalized tracts and hagiographies are usually written for the edification of fellow Catholics and move towards modes of popular romance on the fringes of more respectable fiction. Problems can obviously arise with the direct use of such material in the more realistic kinds of fiction, and even the better authors are not immune. Graham Greene has been attacked for the miracles in *The End of the Affair*, for example, and the recurrent element of the supernatural in Maurice Baring's *The Coat without Seam* (1929) has quite understandably been found unacceptable.[2]

The Only Problem referred to in the title of Muriel Spark's impressive novel (1984) is the ancient philosophical and theological issue of the mystery of evil and its relationship to the goodness and providence of God, the whole question of theodicy. Like the treatment of the supernatural with which it is linked, this is a question with considerable implications for literary form, and this 'only problem' resolves itself in the more immediate sense for Catholic writers into one of literary strategy. In moving beyond a purely Catholic audience the more ambitious Catholic novelists hope for respect from critics and reviewers as well as wider sales. At the same time they have a special sense of their responsibility to emphasize the deeper realities in a complacent liberal Protestant or secular society that has its own vested interest in denying them. But the very origins and *raison d'être* of the novel have been held to lie in secularism, as we have seen, and the liberal realism that is the central tradition of British fiction implies a situation in which human beings are by and large in control of their own moral destinies. In such a climate these writers have to indicate the presence of a fundamental mystery without seeming superstitious or sensationalist and hint at answers to it without being naïvely optimistic or doctrinaire. The successful negotiation of these problems on the literary plane becomes in a sense an analogy to their solution theologically, as will become apparent.

A mode that has appealed to various well-known Christian writers as a possible strategy in this context is fantasy, defined by C. N. Manlove as 'a fiction evoking wonder and containing a substantial and irreducible element of the supernatural with which the mortal characters in the story or the readers become on at least partly familiar terms.'[3] But no simple equation can be made between fantasy and the desire to write on the Christian supernatural. Much of the late eighteenth- and nineteenth-century interest in the mode has been shown on the contrary to relate to the decline of traditional religion and the consequent hunger for alternative experiences. To put it in the bluntest terms, the Christian supernatural claims to be true. The major Catholic fantasists find it imperative therefore to differentiate their work from the speculative dreaminess of other versions.

Chesterton's *The Ball and the Cross* (1909), for example, is highly extravagant in tone, with flying ships piloted by a Professor Lucifer, and the vision of England as one vast lunatic asylum at the close. As so often in Chesterton's work, however, the book contains a manifesto for itself within its own pages. Above all it is the dimension of apocalypse that Chesterton seeks to invoke. The end of the novel is also an end of the world, the lunatic asylum an 'apocalyptic fulfilment' of the logic of the mad, fallen, secular world. Chesterton insists that 'an apocalypse', and hence this form of Christian fantasy, is the opposite of a dream: 'A dream is falser than the outer life. But the end of the world is more actual than the world it ends.' (p. 377)

What is most characteristic of the greatest Catholic fantasists is the use of the mode to indicate a newly grounded vision of the natural, and this is certainly its primary import in Chesterton. The hero's adventures in *Manalive* (1912) are a way of reminding himself and the reader of the wonders of everyday life. This desire to recreate a childlike sense of wonder at the world relates very specifically to his Christian vision, the strong Catholic sense that grace builds on nature, for example, and the belief that God's existence can be established through contemplating the design of the natural world. Chesterton fought contemporary nihilism and pessimism from such a perspective. Even as early as *The Man Who Was Thursday* (1908) he finds beneath all the ambivalence that surrounds Thursday the essential creativity and mystery of nature. Since Christianity is an incarnational religion, this vision is both a prelude to a sense of the supernatural and in a way a part of that sense, though it is at the furthest possible remove from what we would normally think of as 'supernatural' fantasy.

Tolkien disapproved of what he regarded as Chesterton's form of fantasy or at least regarded it as a lesser kind. He himself is a fantasist, to use Christopher Nash's classifications, of the 'neo-cosmic' kind, one who creates a whole alternative world to the real one, yet with the most painstaking realism of detail.[4] Again though, as several critics have said, the worlds Tolkien creates primarily illustrate the processes of Natural Law rather than the supernatural as such. 'Middle-earth' is an alternative to *this* world, and providence works therein as here by secondary causes.

Tolkien writes elsewhere in characteristic fashion:

> *Supernatural* is a dangerous and difficult word in any of its senses, looser or stricter. But to fairies it can hardly be applied, unless *super* is taken merely as a superlative prefix. For it is man who is, in contrast to fairies, supernatural (and often of diminutive stature); whereas they are natural, far more natural than he.[5]

Beneath the whimsy Tolkien is making the important point that the Christian supernatural inverts the usual terms. Peter Hebblethwaite has tried to explain in an article on Catholic fiction that it is a vulgar error (though one to which Christians themselves have often been prone) to identify the supernatural with strange and otherworldly phenomena rather than seeing it as human experience viewed in its deepest and fullest dimensions.[6] 'A supernatural process', in other words, as the priest in Spark's *Mandelbaum Gate* (1965) says, 'is going on under the surface and within the substance of all things' (1980 reprint: 214).

If the desire to write on the supernatural has thus often led Catholic writers to popular modes on the fringes of serious fiction or to a deliberate attempt to subvert the norms of 'secular' realism through high romance or fantasy, there is nothing inevitable about this. The fashionable 'magic realism' of recent South American writers is not specifically Christian, but it provides an interesting analogy that suggests that some modes of realism are not incompatible with the paranormal and the supernatural. The writers of the French Catholic Revival, seen by many as defining the distinctive mode of Catholic fiction, are certainly in reaction against what they saw as the narrow, deliberately anti-Christian naturalism that had preceded them, but it would be wrong to regard them as formal anti-realists as such. They desire to write on the movements of grace, the effects of the supernatural, and they may do so directly at times and violate psychological consistency to some degree, but their claim is that all this is in the interests of a deeper realism. Like the majority of leading Catholic novelists, they preserve a basically realistic mode most of the time. Thinking along similar lines to Peter Hebblethwaite or at least choosing as a matter of literary technique to write as if they do, they usually prefer to show God and the supernatural order working through secondary causes, and they develop a series of special strategies in the attempt to permit even miracles to be treated within the norms of realistic fiction.[7]

The better British Catholic novelists often follow the French in making crafty use of the device of the sceptical third-person narrator, for example, and they seem even more careful to preserve the saving ambiguity of the possibility of alternative explanations. This is true even in the controversial case of *The End of the Affair*, though Greene admittedly loads the dice very much in the other direction and shows Bendrix to be grasping at straws in his desire *not* to believe. A more typically chastened and ambiguous example occurs at the end of Antonia White's *The Lost Traveller* (1950) at the point when the heroine is about to enter on an unfortunate marriage. She prays to Our Lady for miraculous help, and at that very moment her mother providentially comes along and helps her to break the engagement.

'Far too friendly with the Devil'

As well as being full of miraculous answers to prayer, angels and saints, popular Catholicism, at least until the Second Vatican Council, seemed obsessed with supernatural evil and the demonic. The Reverend Mother in Wendy Perriam's *The Stillness, The Dancing* (1985) tells the heroine, a pupil at her school,

> 'I'm sorry to say it, Anne, but you are getting far too friendly with the Devil. Once you give him the smallest crack to put a claw in, he's got you hard and fast, fouling up your mind and then your body.'
> She had seen a programme once about bacteria – microbes swarming on cheese, or crawling into every pore. Devils were as prolific and as dangerous – festering in your body, making dirty footmarks on your soul.
> (p. 22)

Sensationalist modern novels on the demonic such as William Blatty's *The Exorcist* (1971) usually involve Catholic priests, and, if this is mainly because the trappings of Catholicism have the greatest potential for melodrama, there is also perhaps an acknowledgment of the claim to a special insight and expertise on the subject. Keith Thomas records that long past the Reformation English Protestant villages used to call on Papist priests for cases of exorcism since they alone were regarded as having the necessary powers.[8] When Monsignor Masterman in Robert Hugh Benson's *The Dawn of All* wakes up to find himself in a totally Catholic world, he is informed that scientists studying abnormal phenomena have come to understand that 'a body, which had marked and recorded facts with greater accuracy than all the "scientists" put together, at least had some claim to consideration with regard to her hypothesis concerning them.' The way was soon cleared for a 'frank acceptance of the Catholic teaching concerning Possession and Exorcism – teaching which half a century before would have been laughed out of court by all who claimed the name of Scientist' (pp. 32, 33).

The appropriate stance and manner of proceeding for the more respectable Catholic novels on the subject thus appear to be warnings to the naïve, as in Sheila Kaye-Smith's *Gallybird* (1934) and Benson's own famous *The Necromancers* (1909). In the former an elderly Anglican clergyman Gervase Alard marries a young girl but is responsible for her death through misguided jealousy caused by dabbling in spiritualism. This in turn had led him, despite good intentions, into black magic. Kaye-Smith takes the whole of this realm with great seriousness and literalness. Gervase in the climactic scene falls into a trance and his soul is transported to the house of a magician. Only the ministrations of the Catholic priest, Parsons, have the power to exorcize the evil and in a scene of considerable suspense he finally succeeds. Alard repents at the last, though he does not survive the whole ordeal for long.

The Necromancers tells the story of Laurie Baxter, a Catholic convert, who

Good and evil: the providential plot

becomes involved in spiritualism after the death of a girl he loved. The apparent manifestations of the dead Amy prove to be an evil spirit in her guise, taking the opportunity that Laurie's trafficking has presented. In a melodramatic conclusion the evil is exorcized not by the parish priest, whose absence the evil spirit has arranged, but by the devoted Maggie, who has always herself been in love with Laurie.

Once again these warnings are presented with some power and total literalness. It is Benson's whole point indeed that Catholics themselves have foolishly ceased to believe such things literally, even though they are terrifyingly real. Maggie reflects that Catholicism taught

> emphatically that discarnate Personalities existed which desired the ruin of human souls, and, indeed, forbade the practices of spiritualism for this very reason. Yet there was hardly a Catholic she knew who regarded the possibility in these days as more than a theoretical one.
>
> (p. 290)

What is clearly recommended instead is the view of Cathcart, an ex-sprtualist convert to Catholicism, who believes, like Perriam's nun, that 'the air is simply thick with them, all doing their very utmost to get hold of human beings' (p. 318).

It is not always easy of course to distinguish special expertise and proper warnings from morbid obsession. William Blatty, the author of *The Exorcist* himself maintained, after all, that the work was written for purely edifying purposes. Benson himself had a life-long interest in the occult, and *The Necromancers* was famous for its undeniably powerful accounts of phenomena and manifestations, especially the scene of the terrified cats before the seance. The publishers naturally enough made such elements the major selling point in their advertisements.

Even Benson's Cathcart, however, is prepared to concede that these forms of evil may often work through secondary causes. He believes, says Maggie, 'both in indigestion, so to speak, *and* the devil . . . that in one person they produce lunacy . . . and in another just shattered nerves and so on' (p. 319). Most of the more sophisticated modern writers take this kind of approach to the furthest possible limit consistent with any degree of continued belief in this whole realm. Instead of simply assuming all the traditional machinery, they seek to work in almost empirical fashion, suggesting that an unbiased examination of human behaviour in its fullness may perhaps itself imply, without in any way undermining the malice and responsibility of human beings, an element of what is usually termed supernatural influence as part of the total picture.

The demonic dimension in their novels is thus a matter of secondary causes and echo-chamber tracks, and alternative explanations are also proffered. It is only the fact that human activities in the Welsh valley of Alice Thomas Ellis's *Unexplained Laughter* (1985) are so bafflingly self-defeating and absurd that leads her Catholic heroine to become convinced that the being she quaintly calls 'Stan' is walking around. In Waugh's *Ordeal of Gilbert Pinfold* (1957) neither narrator, reader nor perhaps Waugh himself are ever quite sure how much we are dealing with nervous breakdown and hallucinations and how much the devil may be said to play a part, but it is in a church dedicated to the devil's traditional adversary St Michael that the hero begins to become free.

Anne Redmon's third novel *Second Sight* (1987) deals with the evil engendered in the close relationship of a twin brother and sister, Durrand and Mathilde. Durrand haunts Mathilde after his death through the involuntary mediumship of another sister, the Catholic heroine Irene, an epileptic. The latter element brings in the possibility of alternative explanations for Irene's 'sightings' of Durrand here too, and the possibility is also raised that Mathilde's great guilt about her brother's death could have caused the phenomenon by a kind of pyschic projection.

But Redmon is very unusual for a serious recent Catholic novelist in completely rejecting these possibilities and unequivocally asserting the reality of the supernatural in pure form. Reminiscences of Flannery O'Connor and other elements of Southern gothic in the first part of the book combine with Dostoievskian elements in the Russian scenes to provide the literary context for such a bold treatment and to make the supernaturalist assertion plain. At one point there is a reference to an old black Protestant woman who felt it her mission to save white people and who worshipped in a church painted with angels. Now, comments the narrator, the angels have been painted over: 'People do not mention angels now, for fear, perhaps of falling into their grip' (p. 101). Several other characters apart from those directly involved also see Durrand, and Irene says firmly near the end:

> I do not feel qualified to decide what actually happened to me on that journey. But now I have returned and revisited this house, the tree-lined avenue where my brain played neurological pranks, I see it was not that. Not epilepsy. If it was madness, where did it go when I got home? Why do I no longer fear the cold and feral thing that spoke to me in syllables of Durrand?
>
> (p. 204)

The question of theodicy

Exorcisms as literal as any in this fiction are performed by the future Pope, Carlo in Anthony Burgess's *Earthly Powers*, and they are all the more dramatic for being so completely matter-of-fact. Burgess builds Carlo's own impressiveness up thereby, but only in preparation for the horrible deflation of the close. For Carlo's views on the prevalence of demons are a displacement metaphor for his Pelagian denial of original sin, his belief in the essential goodness of man, whose evil can be entirely blamed on these supernatural powers, themselves always defeated by God. The logic of the story instead proposes another more terrible unorthodoxy. Carlo's greatest miracle is the healing of a small boy who has later, we learn at the end, grown up to become the sect leader, 'God Manning', the perpetrator of a Jonesville-style massacre on his deluded followers. Burgess has commented elsewhere: 'I call myself a Manichee. I believe, if you like, that God and the Devil are possibilities, but it is not

Good and evil: the providential plot

foreseeable, it is not inevitable that God should win over the Devil.'[9] The victory of the 'devil' in *Earthly Powers* is a deeper metaphor than Carlo's exorcisms, one meant to signify that evil, however we conceptualize it, can have the last word, and thus to refute misguided optimism about man and God.

Muriel Spark's novels are also full of occultism, spiritualism and supernatural evil. In *The Bachelors* (1960), as in *The Necromancers* and *Gallybird*, spiritualism leads into direct evil, as the name of the medium Seton suggests. But Spark's oblique archness of tone can create a genuinely eerie and suggestive quality, while at the same refusing in entirely orthodox fashion to give evil the tribute of being taken with any *ultimate* seriousness. From first to last in her work the attitude to such subjects is instead so confident as to seem almost dismissive. Caroline in *The Comforters* (1957), for example, calls the Black Mass 'tomfoolery':

> 'I wouldn't dismiss it so lightly as that,' Ernest argued.
> 'It depends on how you regard evil,' Caroline said. 'I mean as compared with the power of goodness. The effectuality of the Black Mass, for instance, must be trivial so long as we have the real Mass.'
>
> (p. 98)

A similar attitude is expressed in the heroine's contempt for the journalist and psuedo-occultist Hector Bartlett in the recent *A Far Cry from Kensington* (1988).

It becomes clear from the havoc caused by Dougal Douglas in Spark's *The Ballad of Peckham Rye* (1960) that he is of demonic origin or at least has a demonic dimension. Through his influence his landlady has a stroke, his friend Humphrey stands up his bride-to-be at the altar and Merle Coverdale is murdered by her lover and employer, Druce. Dougal has two mysterious bumps on his head, cysts presumably, which he maintains to be the remnants of horns. He plots maliciously to destroy people. He is a cheat and a mischievous liar. Yet he is also in some ways a liberating force, a catalyst as well as a destroyer, one who brings evil into the open. Ultimately, he is used by God as a scourge and a test and a purifier, as Satan is in the Book of Job:

> 'I have the powers of exorcism,' Dougal said, 'that's all.'
> 'What's that?'
> 'The ability to drive devils out of people.'
> 'I thought you said you were a devil yourself.'
> 'The two states are not incompatible.'
>
> (1980 reprint: 142)

He embodies the ambivalent fascination with evil that is common in Catholic fiction, but also elements of a completely orthodox kind of theodicy.[10]

For supernatural evil is, of course, only the most dramatic face of the whole theological and philosophical problem of evil and its relationship to the goodness and providence of God that has been endlessly discussed and analysed over the centuries. The combination of the traditional Catholic respect for philosophizing with the demands of apologetical orthodoxy have made the question a central one in Catholic thought. Hillier in Burgess's *Tremor of Intent* (1966) says that the actual doctrines of Catholicism do not matter, 'what counts is the willingness and ability to take evil seriously and to explain it' (p. 32). His friend Roper went to see the concentration camps after the war, but he had jettisoned 'a whole system of thought capable of explaining it – I mean Catholic Christianity' (p. 32).

The whole topic is traditionally organized in what is far from an immediately cogent way around the idea of evil as privation of good, and theologians have produced a variety of different categories in their attempts at definition, clarity and explanation. Supernatural evil itself is to be distinguished from the 'natural evil' of hurricanes and earthquakes, for example, and both again from the moral evil of sin. The 'original sin' into which we are born obviously creates different theoretical problems from the 'actual sin' which we ourselves perpetrate, but the question still has to be asked about why God permits any kind of sin at all.

Such categories, for those with an eye for such matters, may, dimly and unsystematically, be discerned within the fictional worlds too. Spark's *The Only Problem* (1984) is highly unusual, however, in addressing the whole issue of theodicy in a very specific and theoretical, if elegant and ironic, way. The novel is quite deliberately a playful analogy with the Book of Job. Its hero Harvey Gotham is writing a book on Job but, when asked at a press conference if he himself has been put into the same position by the terrorist activities of his wife Effie, he replies that it is true that Job underwent, like him, what was tantamount to an interrogation by the elders of his community. On the other hand, he says, he is not covered in boils!

Related to Job though he is, the answer that Harvey himself reaches to the problem of suffering is the detached, almost aesthetic one apparent in Spark's later work rather than the religious one that is also alluded to. Looking at a refugee in a police station Harvey realizes that at least he found him interesting and reflects 'Is it only by recognizing how flat would be the world without the sufferings of others that we know how desperately becalmed our own lives would be without suffering?' (p. 153). But the concealed aesthetic analogy, the principle of contrast here, itself has traditional implications in the context of theodicy, and these, originally classical, arguments were soon taken up by Christian writers. As an artist uses darkness and shade to provide contrast in his pictures, so God is said to use suffering and evil to make up the harmony of his cosmos.

If Catholic fiction rarely seeks the degree of theoretical pointedness found in *The Only Problem*, and if the answers most writers propose are prefabricated and trite rather than genuinely exploratory like Spark's, at all kinds of levels real issues are still often raised. The interest in these various forms of evil can be obsessive, melodramatic, or masochistic, but the desire to emphasize such realities draws special force for many of these writers, as noted above, from their situation in this country. They have in particular a very strong sense of themselves as engaged in a campaign against an archetypal British complacency and demystification to which both liberal Protestantism and secular scientism have contributed.

The unpleasant Kyril in Alice Thomas Ellis's *The Twenty-seventh Kingdom* (1982), for example, 'knew that there were no gods or ghosts, only taboos and neuroses and $E = MC^2$, and very nice too. The watches of the night held no terror for Kyril, for were not all things concrete and clear, and all mysteries explained?' (110–11). Like Spark's Fleur in *Loitering with Intent* (1981), these writers insist on the contrary that there is such a thing as 'pure evil', realized as it may be 'under the form of disease, injustice, fear, oppression or any other ill element that can afflict living creatures'.[11] In presenting evil as that which limits and negates humanity they point, in other words, to an irreducible element of mystery, but at the same time they suggest that, only when that mystery is recognized, is there any possibility of coming to understand God's providence. In highlighting, as the next chapter will examine, all the Church's lore about suffering, they are also seeking to reaffirm the traditional meaning and purpose that Christians have found in it. For if the existence of evil has always been a stumbling block to the idea of a good God, it has also suggested the need for a saviour to deliver us. It is, in the words of a modern theologian, the 'evil in human life which constitutes the decisive argument against God's reality [that] also gives God the supreme opportunity to manifest his reality.'[12]

Providence and literary plot

The whole idea of theodicy has an intimate connection with matters of literary form. As noted in the last section, it is a deep-rooted human instinct to link the structures of art with God's ordering of the cosmos, and this especially applies to many traditional literary plots and structures. The pattern of a period of trial that ends happily or at least with a sense of meaning and purpose re-established is one of the most basic plots of all literature. Though such happy endings have an obvious element of wish fulfilment and desire to please the reader, benign coincidences and even miracles may contribute to these endings and it is a natural tendency to parallel them with the actions of providence.[13] At the most naïve level of theodicy such plots may be presented as a direct account, instance and thus proof of providence, despite being fictions.

In a stark tractlike version of the paradigm such as Gertrude Parson's *Wrecked and Saved* (1878), for example, the unjustly accused Catholic hero is helped by a benefactor who later proves, unknown at first to either of them, to be his wealthy grandmother. The melodramatic happy ending comes from the staples of Victorian popular fiction but is also obviously presented as a providential reward for the hero's goodness: 'At this time of severest trial Peter reaped the fruit of a life spent in good company, and blessed by habitual acts of piety' (p. 189).

Literary historians and theorists once argued that the genre of the novel served to replace these traditional romance patterns, but this view is obviously an over-simplification. Not only are many popular novels no more than romances with a gloss of realism, but elements at least of romance often remain embedded in some of the greatest novels of classic realism. The more sophisticated writers, of course, present such patterns not as purportedly literal examples of God's providence in a literary plot but rather as deliberate *analogies* to it, as in the classic parallel between the omniscient author and God, both creators of their world, in Henry Fielding's *Tom Jones*.[14] In *imitating* the way God's providence works to bring good out of evil, such works may continue, however, to indicate implicit or even explicit theodicies.

As well as using the traditional providential pattern, Catholic writers time and again enact a more specific providential plot device that thwarts human evil and, in reversing its intention, makes paradoxical good use of it. The heroine of Spark's *The Mandelbaum Gate*, for example, is enabled to get an annulment and marry the man she wants because an enemy of hers passes on a vital piece of information to the Church authorities with the precisely opposite intention of stopping the marriage.

Tolkien makes elaborate use of this idea in his theory of the 'eucatastrophe' or good disaster. The most famous instance is at the end of *The Lord of the Rings* when Gollum's final greedy snatch at the ring is what leads to its destruction and the saving of Middle-earth. Such a device achieves its power and validity for Tolkien, like fairy story as a whole, only because the paradigm has once really happened in the Christian story of redemption:

> The Gospels contain a fairy-story or, a story of a larger kind which embraces all the essence of fairy-stories. They contain many marvels – peculiarly artistic, beautiful and moving: 'mythical' in their perfect, self-contained significance; and among the marvels is the greatest and most complete conceivable eucatastrophe. But this story has entered History and the primary world; the desire and aspiration of sub-creation has been raised to the fulfilment of Creation. The Birth of Christ is the eucatastrophe of Man's history. The Resurrection is the eucatastrophe of the story of the Incarnation.[15]

Tolkien, like various other self-conscious and sophisticated writers in romance and fantasy modes, thus attempts to turn the tables on conventional realism. Romance in a sense, they argue, is the only 'realistic' mode, for life itself seen from the deepest perspective, as Chesterton says, is like a fairy story. There is an attempted justification for the improbable in fiction here, which is at the same time turned in a completely circular argument into an apology or justification for belief in the marvels of providence. The trappings of romance are both supported by a theological dimension and made into a theological assertion. John Ayscough writes that it is 'from the pages of high romance' that we 'may draw a more serene patience, and a more practical remembrance that it is by God, and not by us, that the world is ruled; that somehow, after all our boggling and our crossness, His providence unties our knots and may correct our blunders.'[16] 'Story-bookey' things have happened in Enid Dinnis's whimsical *The Road to Somewhere*, and these marvels on the narrative level are analogues to the marvellous truths of the faith.

Another popular genre of a very different kind than romance that has often been seen as having an inbuilt element of theodicy is detective fiction. According to P. D. James, for example, the very plot structure of such fiction itself implies the 'affirmation of a generally benevolent and understandable universe'.[17]

Many Catholics and high Anglicans have been successful in the genre, and

Catholic motifs and locales are very popular. The closed communities of convents and monasteries make an excellent setting, and the sacriligious juxtaposition of crime and holiness is piquant. The better Catholic practitioners – Pauline King in *The Snares of the Enemy* (1985), for example, or Mary Kelly in *The Spoilt Kill* (1961) – may deepen the accounts of crime with certain Catholic paradoxes about sin. The latter novel in particular makes impressive use of Catholic teaching on presumption and despair.

The main point nevertheless remains the reassuring way in which evil is usually dealt with. Most crime fiction, particularly the classic British type, carries the implication, as Robert Parker puts it, that crime is really 'a deviation from the norm, and man, a creature of reason, could use that reason to find out the deviant, correct the deviation, and return society to its natural, orderly mode.'[18] But this can only be a comforting fiction, the creation of a world, as P. D. James says of such novels, in which 'problems could be solved, evil overcome, justice vindicated and death itself [was] only a mystery which would be solved in the final chapter' (*Devices and Desires*, 1989: 377). Any genuine belief in the Fall is incompatible with such a vision, as the greater writers have always understood. These novels may more properly be said to serve as man-made salves, reassuring substitutes for God, according to Father Rivas in Greene's *The Honorary Consul* (1973), an improbable expert on British detective fiction,

> . . . there is a sort of comfort in reading a story where one knows what the end will be. The story of a dream world where justice is always done. There were no detective stories in the age of faith – an interesting point when you think of it. God used to be the only detective when people believed in Him. He was law. He was order. He was good. Like your Sherlock Holmes. It was He who pursued the wicked man for punishment and discovered all. But now people like the General make law and order.
>
> (p. 260)

Muriel Spark in *The Comforters* (1957) adopts instead the strategy of *contrasting* God's own mysterious and complex 'plot' with a melodramatic jewel-smuggling one on the human level. Her retired police inspector in *Memento Mori* (1959) says that people would like to think of the CID as God. The implication is that they want the police to solve all the problems and mysteries of guilt and evil. But the search for the perpetrator of the anonymous phone-calls leads only to the figure of Death itself, who cannot be caught and tried.

The greatest Catholic writers have always tried thus to defamiliarize and subvert the norms of the genre in a kind of parody, reintroducing the genuine element of mystery and asking much more radical questions. Is crime the same as sin? How much is human justice and law worth and can we really find justice on earth at all? If we are all guilty, then what is the point of looking for the criminal anyway?

The endings of G. K. Chesterton's Father Brown stories clearly have their own reassuring element of explanation of a mystery or unnaturalness and the re-establishment of order, but Chesterton is careful to differentiate the priest's Christian rationality from both the worldly rationalism and the pseudo-mysteries with which he has had to deal. At the same time the author subverts the conventional logic of detective stories by refusing to make his priest–detective the saintly opposite of the criminal. The contrary in fact is the case. Father Brown is a great detective in part because he is humble enough to recognize that he too is a sinner with 'all devils in his heart' and he thus has a deep knowledge of the criminal nature. What he really seeks to establish, as Chesterton says of Browning in *The Ring and the Book*, is 'not the centre of criminal guilt, but the centre of spiritual guilt'.[19]

Very much the same point has often been made about Graham Greene's first Catholic novel, *Brighton Rock* (1938), where the world of human right and wrong represented by the pseudo-detective Ida is totally transcended by Pinky's world of good and evil. We are left in no doubt at the end that the real chase has not been the law's pursuit of Pinky, the criminal, but God's pursuit of the sinner's soul.

At a more concealed but also more fundamental level, questions of providence, plot and the novel are inseparably involved as well with ideas of literary time. The etymology of the word 'providence' implies divine foresight and planning from outside time, even if the more anthropomorphic and thus in fact time-*bound* conceptualizations of this have fallen out of favour with theologians. A modern secular sense of 'transitory human time' on the other hand, especially Locke's view of human identity as consciousness extended through time, has often been said to be of the essence of the new 'realistic' novel, and even to have replaced the 'timeless revealed plots' of religion there.[20]

Here obviously is another source of the attraction some Catholic writers feel for the mythic recurrent structures of romance, where God may reveal Himself as the real 'Lord of the Rings' in the ultimate sense. But Catholic writers of more realistic fictions may also seek to collapse the assumptions on which secular time rests and point to ways in which it may be assimilated to the 'timeless revealed plots'. Father Crompton in Greene's *The End of the Affair*, for example, is made the spokesman for a sense of mystery about time, which the book itself to some degree enacts, despite its basically 'realistic' mode, through the strange implications of Sarah's childhood baptism:

> Saint Augustine asked where time came from. He said it came out of the future which didn't exist yet, into the present that had no duration, and went into the past which had ceased to exist. I don't know that we can understand time any better than a child.
>
> (p. 176)

Flashbacks, anticipations and premonitions like Fitzgerald's vision of his own death in Compton Mackenzie's *The Four Winds of Love* are frequent in Catholic fiction, and Catholic historical novelists have special reasons, as we have seen, for using deliberate anachronisms and flashes forward like Waugh in *Helena*. The desire to go beyond the realities of secular time may lead to specific technical experiments. The flashbacks in Piers Paul Read's experimental first novel *Game in Heaven with Tussy Marx* (1966) are legitimized by the idea of the characters themselves waiting outside time for judgement, and Pamela Frankeau's *The Bridge* (1957) is based on a similar idea.

Good and evil: the providential plot

The remarkable short stories and novels of George Mackay Brown merge together a wide range of styles from different periods, but the effects are far from the ethereal quality of romance. The Mass becomes the central symbol:

> It takes place both in time, wherein time's conditions obtain, and also wholly outside time; or rather, it is time's purest essence, a concentration of the unimaginably complex events of time into the ritual words and movements of a half-hour. . . . The end and the beginning. All time was gathered up into that ritual half-hour, the entire history of mankind, as well the events that have not yet happened as the things recorded in chronicles and sagas.
>
> (*Magnus*, 1973: 139)

The lesser ritual of art has to partake of this same quality. Instead of a timeless realm we find a concentration of the whole history of Greenvoe into the present, or a sudden abolition of chronological distinctions to parallel the death of Magnus with the slaughter of a Bonhoeffer-type figure in Nazi Germany.

The pattern hidden and problematized: 'How far can you go?'

Frank Kermode has pointed out in *The Sense of an Ending* (1967) that the reader wants reassuring patterns of order in literature but that, if these are too neat and predictable, they will defeat their purpose by failing to convince.[21] This has especial relevance to the idea of literary plots as theodicies. If there is an analogy between literary patterning and the affirmation of providence, then the more sophisticated Catholic writers have developed various strategies, as we have seen, to deal with the problem Kermode describes. They may attempt to reverse our normal expectations by presenting romance as ultimately the more 'life-like' mode or subvert the conventional literary patterns to suggest profounder, more mysterious ones. Often the better Catholic fiction simply gives the impression of concealing the providential plot more than popular romance, working it out on the psychological plane, by secondary causes, though, of course, revealing it thereby at the same time as masking it.

Waugh, for example, tries to subsume all the great history of suffering and disappointment in *Brideshead Revisited* into Ryder's providential conversion:

> Something quite remote from anything the builders intended, has come out of their work, and out of the fierce little human tragedy in which I played; something none of us thought about at the time; a small red flame – a beaten-copper lamp of deplorable design relit before the beaten-copper doors of a tabernacle; the flame which the old knights saw from their tombs, which they saw put out; that flame burns again for other soldiers, far from home, farther, in heart, than Acre or Jerusalem. It could not have been lit but for the builders and the tragedians, and there I found it this morning, burning anew among the old stones.
>
> (p. 304)

Here Waugh to some degree succeeds in creating the impression of a pattern emerging through and behind events, and it works itself out in the life of a resistant narrator. If such patterns can be made to seem not so much truly realistic in themselves as at least convincing within the world of the fiction, then they may indeed assume a quasi-demonstrative force. By the kind of paradox that Kermode identifies, this may be all the more so if the patterns are not in fact completed, as in Anne Redmon's *Emily Stone* (1974) where the heroine adamantly refuses conversion or *The End of the Affair* (1951), where Bendrix's resistance has by no means yet been overcome as we finish reading.[22] It is Bendrix himself who is made to explain at least some of the mysterious ways in which 'the affair' cannot really be said to have ended yet. With enormous skill Greene makes the incompleteness of his own authorial pattern a means of highlighting the superior plotting of God, while at the same time contrasting the 'truth' of his fiction with the more predictable patterns of conventional fiction: 'If I were writing a novel I would end it here: a novel, I used to think, has to end somewhere, but I'm beginning to believe my realism has been at fault all these years, for nothing in life now ever seems to end . . .' (p. 144).

Muriel Spark's early novels, as critics have often pointed out, show a special interest in the distinctively Catholic doctrine that God's providential patterns work themselves out in and through human free will.[23] In *The Comforters* (1957), for example, the heroine Caroline, a recent convert to Catholicism as well as a student of fictional form, begins to hear voices and imagines herself part of a novel written by someone else. Eventually she is able to make the crucial distinction between her free acquiescence to God and determinism, and she parallels this with the autonomy the novelist properly grants her characters.

In *The Prime of Miss Jean Brodie* (1961) similar motif leads into a specific contrast with Calvinism. Miss Brodie tries to manipulate events and control people completely, arranging, for example, that Rose should have an affair with her ex-lover Teddy. Sandy comes to realize that the teacher 'thinks she is Providence . . . she thinks she is the God of Calvin, she sees the beginning and the end' (p. 120). But Miss Brodie's plots are defeated by the ironic providences of a more inventive God who takes human free will fully into account in achieving His own mysterious purposes.

If in the end Spark seems to reach relatively optimistic conclusions about the parallel between God and the novelist in these works, the matter is complicated, as noted in chapter 3, by her strong traditional Christian suspicion of fiction. It is the contrast as well as the parallel between God's providence and the partial and deceitful 'plots' of human beings that her books work out, and these limitations, as in *The End of the Affair*, certainly include the 'plots' of the novelist. The work of the novelist in *The Comforters* is tugged uneasily between an analogy with the trickeries of crime on the one hand and the providences of God on the other. The fact that the deceitful, demonic Dougal Douglas becomes a novelist at the end of *The Ballad of Peckham Rye* is Spark's final joke there, though God may perhaps use the 'lies' of the novelist for the purposes of truth as He uses Dougal as an agent of His providence.

Taken to its logical conclusion, this disapproval of art and fiction would make the traditional analogy between God and the human artist blasphemous, as Anthony Burgess's novelist Toomey says ingratiatingly to the Archbishop of Malta:

> ... writers of fiction often have difficulty in deciding between what really happened and what they imagine as having happened. That is why, in my sad trade, we can never be really devout or pious. We lie for a living. This, as you can imagine, makes us good believers – credulous anyway. But it has nothing to do with *faith*.
>
> (*Earthly Powers*: 17)

Yet the lies of fiction, of course, may have their own kinds of truth, as Toomey, like Spark, later concedes. The steady growth of scepticism and relativism in the last two centuries, even among believers, and the enhanced status of art and the imagination after the romantic movement have helped to break down the divide between the terms of the analogy. Liberalism and romantic theology have reduced the propositional content of faith, and in coming to be seen in more imaginative and emotional terms religious truth has itself come closer to the 'truth' literature attains.

Such developments, as well as his own increasingly paradoxical personal position, are reflected in Graham Greene's striking post-Catholic fable, *Monsignor Quixote*, which plays with and deconstructs the fact/fiction and faith/fiction distinctions:

> 'Monsignor Quixote of El Toboso. A descendant of the great Don Quixote himself.'
>
> 'Don Quixote had no descendants. How could he? He's a fictional character.'
>
> 'Fact and fiction again, professor. So difficult to distinguish,' Father Leopoldo said.
>
> (p. 208)

Greene parallels the two kinds of faith throughout the book in a series of complicated mirror images without pretending to offer any final answers, but the suggestion seems to be that faith, like fiction, has its own, admittedly tentative and provisional, kind of truth.

The development of narrative theology in recent years has itself helped bridge the gap between literature and religious faith and strengthened the more specific analogy between God's providential action and the action of a literary work, though altering it at the same time. Biblical critics have emphasized the narrative quality of the Bible both in its parts and as a whole, and liturgy and spiritual autobiography have been studied as re-enactments of the stories of salvation. Structuralist thought has meanwhile stressed the centrality of mythic narratives in human culture as a whole. We live, as Brian Wicker has written, in a 'story-shaped world', and the framing of narratives to make sense of our lives has come to seem an essential part of the whole religious impulse.[24]

These ways of thinking have a special interest to David Lodge as a Catholic, a novelist and a distinguished literary theorist. *How Far Can You Go?* (1980)

develops a rich parallel between the writing and reading of novels and religious faith. Both are ways of organizing, structuring, making sense of our experience. The question of 'How far can you go?' begins, of course, as a reference to the details of Catholic premarital sexual ethics. But these in turn are only a part of a vast Catholic apparatus of belief and morality, now to a large extent superseded. Its author parallels the process of dismantling it with the technical devices of the very novel he is writing:

> For we all like to believe, do we not, if only in stories? People who find religious belief absurd are often upset if a novelist breaks the illusion of reality he has created. Our friends had started life with too many beliefs – the penalty of a Catholic upbringing. They were weighed down with beliefs, useless answers to non-questions. To work their way back to the fundamental ones – what can we know? why is there anything at all? why not nothing? what may we hope? why are we here? what is it all about? – they had to dismantle all that apparatus of superfluous belief and discard it piece by piece. But in matters of belief (as of literary convention) it is a nice question how far you can go in this process without throwing out something vital.

Just as Lodge's own frequent authorial intrusions and reminders of fiction do not necessarily destroy realism and involvement, however, so believers can perhaps adopt the 'double consciousness' fiction readers need, for we have to accept that

> Christian belief will be different from what it used to be, what it used to be for Catholics, anyway. We must not only believe, but know that we believe, live our belief and yet see it from outside, aware that in another time, another place, we would have believed something different (indeed, did ourselves believe differently at different times and places in our lives) without feeling that this invalidates belief. Just as when reading a novel, or writing one for that matter, we maintain a double consciousness of the characters as both, as it were, real and fictitious, free and determined, and know that however absorbing and convincing we may find it, it is not the only story we shall want to read (or, as the case may be, write) but part of an endless sequence of stories by which man has sought and will always seek to seek to make sense of life. And death.
>
> (p. 240)

Narrative theology has itself taken various forms, and the implications of this narrative element in religion can be interpreted in very different ways. The stress can be put, for example, on the way that we are caught up into God's 'story' or on the way that God in the last analysis eludes all our attempts to contain Him within our patterns, and there are analogues to such approaches in the narrative strategies of novels described earlier in the chapter. The providential patterns of God's action may be seen as having an objective content or, more tentatively and subjectively, God can be thought of as revealing to the believer a providential significance to events of themselves in a sense neutral. Lodge himself seems to present the Christian providential story

Good and evil: the providential plot

as only one valid part of a general anthropological story-making pattern rather than seeing it as having a special revealed status over and above other narratives. He continues to use the traditional analogy between artistic form and faith in God as a justification for the latter here, but his version is of a distinctly contemporary and very provisional kind.

· 9 ·

'The sorrowful mysteries'

God's 'extraordinary trick', death

The drama of good and evil referred to in the last chapter has to work itself out on the human plane through the realities of death, suffering, sin and grace. When the American writer André Dubus entitles a section of a book of his short stories 'The sorrowful mysteries', he is revealing, says a recent reviewer, a specifically Catholic sensibility, a strong emphasis on the miseries of our fallen condition.[1] At the same time the allusion to the Passion of Christ, the subject of the Sorrowful Mysteries of the Rosary, cannot fail to suggest – however ironically in Dubus's own case – the idea of redemption. These are indeed the great Catholic themes, the matters on which the Church claims a special expertise and has a library of traditional lore to contribute. Catholic novelists in this country may write edifyingly on such subjects for their co-religionists, but the more ambitious of them, as noted before, have a special consciousness of the need to emphasize such realities in a complacent society that would much prefer to ignore them.

It is death, of course, the greatest natural evil, that above all puts secular and temporal goods to the question and inevitably raises metaphysical issues that seem to touch on the fringes of the supernatural. Alice Thomas Ellis's bereaved Mary

> thought about what Sam would doubtless describe as 'birf 'n' deaf'. Robin's death, the sudden absolute cessation of vaulting, joyful life, seemed to her quite as astonishing and worthy of remark as that other more widely acclaimed and admired miracle, birth. Despite her anger, she thought that God deserved more notice for this extraordinary trick.
>
> (*The Birds of the Air*: p. 67)

'The sorrowful mysteries'

Personal experience of bereavement sharpens the focus on death in Ellis's work, but throughout the whole range of Catholic literature the same claim is made to this special expertise and inwardness. The constant reminders of death in these writers, though not without morbid and sensationalist elements, are clearly intended in part to counter secular attempts at denial and demystification. In Waugh's *Love Among the Ruins* (1953) euthanasia and legalized state suicide have become the norm. The wonderful satire on the hygienic Californian denial of death in *The Loved One* (1948) makes no reference to Catholicism, but Catholic perspectives obviously underlie it, as Waugh was to spell out elsewhere. In an essay in *Life* in 1947 he commented, for example, on the absence of Christian symbols in the Forest Lawn Memorial Park at Los Angeles: 'by far the commonest feature of other graveyards is still the Cross, a symbol in which previous generations have found more Life and Hope than in the most elaborately watered evergreen shrub.'[2]

For, if death is to be swallowed up in life, it is only after the full recognition of its import. It is only after the sting has been felt that it may be removed. This is the recognition that John Braine's Vincent Dungarvan comes to:

> just as his grandmother's house had come into its own for her death, so did St Maurice's come into its own. The thick walls, the small high windows, the darkness and the coolness, admitted death without demur, perhaps even deceived death into the belief of victory; the profusion of memorial tablets, the realism of the Stations of the Cross, were proof enough that here were no illusions about death being a friend. Jesus's face was human; as He took up the Cross He was shocked at its weight, even the grain of the wood was palpable; and when Veronica wiped his face there was not upon it the lightning sketch of the stories but blood and sweat.
>
> (*The Jealous God*: 248–9)

In Muriel Spark's *Memento Mori* (1959) there intrudes into the lives of a mixed group of old people an anonymous phone-caller who announces 'Remember you must die.' Through the course of the pseudo-detective story or theological detective story of which Catholic novelists are so fond, it becomes clear that the retired police inspector Henry Mortimer and the old Catholic woman Jean Taylor are right – the real 'caller' is death itself. The proper recognition is that death, as Henry Mortimer says, is part of the 'full expectancy of life. Without an ever-present sense of death life is insipid. You might as well live on the whites of eggs' (1988 reprint: 150). We end the book with the focus on the more specifically Christian answer of Jean Taylor, who 'lingered for a time, employing her pain to magnify the Lord, and meditating sometimes on Death, the first of the four last things to be ever remembered' (p. 220).

To go beyond the threshold of this first of 'the last things' into 'Judgement, Heaven or Hell', as the writers of popular pious romances and fictionalized tracts often do, is to enter the realm of vision or assertion. The better novelists usually prefer to offer hints towards a completed pattern instead. They describe, for example, not resurrection itself, but the tantalizing suggestion of new life in the remarkable continued influence of a dead character, as with John Strickland's wife Clare in Piers Paul Read's *A Married Man* (1979), to whom the hero clearly thinks of himself as still married. An analogy is suggested here with the very bottom line of what Christians want to say about Christ: the power and action of this One who was dead continue to be so remarkable that they measure a presence as well as an absence, and He has truly to be said to be alive.

The continued influence of Sarah Miles in *The End of the Affair* extends to the working of miracles, and Greene's is the most famous and explicit development of the motif:

> I've got to be reasonable, I told myself going upstairs. Sarah has been dead a long time now: one doesn't go on loving the dead with this intensity, only the living, and she's not alive, she can't be alive. I mustn't believe that she's alive.
>
> (p. 178)

Sasha, the heroine of Anne Redmon's *Emily Stone*, is another, equally unconventional example of these saint figures whose influence continue after death. She had made herself totally vulnerable to Boris, only to be betrayed by him, a betrayal conveyed to her with some malice by her supposed friend Emily Stone. The trauma gives Sasha cancer, from which she eventually dies. In her suffering she is taken completely out of herself into love, though the book is not sentimental and does not baulk at her hair falling out and the other details of her long illness. Her death includes the offer of forgiveness and expiation for Emily, and Sasha is a Catholic heroine of death and suffering as well as of possible resurrection, an archetypal sacrificial victim.

The contrast between Catholic realism and secular attitudes to death lies at the heart of the book and the motif is carefully anticipated and generalized before the heroine's own lingering sickness and death. The Albert Memorial is proposed as the archetypally English and non-Catholic symbol. How little must Victoria have loved Albert, says Sasha, to need such a thing to memorialize him! Against this is set the attitude of the nuns at St Clare's tomb in Assisi. Emily finds horrific the way the body is decked out in flowers and finery, but Sasha says:

> 'But Emily, we are all going to die,' . . . as if explaining something to a child. 'They have simply accepted the fact. It is we who run away . . . those nuns . . . *they're* not afraid of corpses or the dead. They must believe in life almost fanatically to keep that mummy there. They've decked her out for the Last Day when God will make her live. Don't you *see* the life in there?'
>
> (p. 50)

'The law of life'

A contrast is also worked out here between Sasha and the Pelagian views of Emily Stone's mother, a Hampstead Garden suburb socialist who believes that 'suffering, if it in fact exists, is there for her to eliminate'. Mrs Stone was good at mathematics at school:

Not, I think, from an innate talent for the subject, but because she accepted without question that one was one. Her whole life has been unperturbed by questions, but disorder troubles her extremely. She could not have borne to leave an equation unfulfilled. If suffering looks ugly, then it is ugly.

(p. 22)

Catholic writers on the contrary insist that 'suffering is the law of life', as Pearl Craigie puts it in *The Dream and the Business* (1906). It cannot be eradicated in a fallen world and thus teaches us indispensable truths about our condition. In developing all the Church's traditional lore and mystique of suffering these writers seek to appropriate the very word as their own in a secular society. A character in Greene's *A Burnt-out Case* (1961) comments that 'suffering puts you on the side of the Christian myth'. Emily Stone herself seems to grasp that the full recognition of the meaning of suffering demands a religious dimension, for 'Suffering requires the audience of God' (p. 167).

Greene sets at the beginning of *The End of the Affair* the marvellous quotation from Leon Bloy, 'Man has places in his heart which do not yet exist, and into them enters suffering in order that they may have existence.' But the legitimate Christian interest is not always easy, of course, to distinguish from its various distortions. Christian ideas naturally enough appeal to those who make a cult of suffering for its own sake and glorify it with a degree of obsession and masochism. Victorian delight in sentimentality, pathos and the suffering of the innocent, for example, proves to overlap very well with specifically Catholic motifs of martyrdom, expiation and sexual renunciation.

Greene's own specifically Catholic novels privilege suffering as a means to insight. Sarah thanks God in *The End of the Affair* for the very grace of suffering. But her tone is suspiciously extreme. In kissing the rationalist Richard on his defacing birthmark, she thinks of God, and feels

> I am kissing pain and pain belongs to You as happiness never does. I love You in Your pain. I could almost taste metal and salt in the skin, and I thought, How good You are. You might have killed us with happiness, but You let us be with You in pain.

(p. 120)

Greene himself is well aware of pity as a kind of indulgence, and he tries to distance himself from it in the figure of Scobie, in *The Heart of the Matter*, who sins through pity not lust. Yet the differentiation between Greene's and Scobie's voice remains notoriously incomplete: 'If one knew, he wondered, the facts, would one have to feel pity even for the planets? If one reached what they call the heart of the matter?' (p. 125).

The emphasis on suffering may also constitute under the guise of Christianity an essentially non-Christian cult of tragic self-assertion and glorification of the human soul. All the trappings of Hitchens's *Garden of Allah*, for example, are Catholic, as we have seen, and its conclusion impeccably orthodox in the way that its hero renounces the beautiful Domini and returns to his Trappist monastery. Domini seeks agonizedly to find meaning in the suffering they have undergone:

> I am sure we shall know, we shall all know some day, the meaning of the mystery of pain. And then, perhaps, then surely, we shall each of us be glad that we have suffered. The suffering will make the glory of our happiness. Even now sometimes when I am suffering, Boris, I feel as if there were a kind of splendour, even a kind of nobility in what I am doing, as if I were proving my own soul, proving the force that God has put into me.
>
> (p. 515)

But the theodicy provided has little to do with traditional Christian criteria and seems to be an almost purely romantic impulse, 'proving the force that God has put in me'. It serves to legitimize the attention to suffering and the emotional indulgence at the same time as intensifying the eroticism.

The idea of renunciation is undeniably important in Christianity. To become a Christian at all is to renounce 'the world' and the need to renounce various temptations continues throughout the Christian life. Catholic attitudes to adultery make renunciation the likely conclusion and this is developed at great length in the fiction. Renunciation of earthly love for a religious vocation is another favourite version. Both the popularity of the motif and the potential self-indulgence are nicely caught by Antonia White in *Frost in May*. The thirteen-year-old Nanda writes her own early 'Catholic novel' in her notebook, the story of a decadent hero who 'studied black magic and wrote poetry "wrapped in a dressing-gown of yellow oriental silk, wrought with strange symbols". In the end he was to reject the love of the violet-eyed heroine and to enter a Trappist monastery' (p. 159). Unfortunately the nuns get hold of the document before she manages to get to the hero's edifying conversion and she is expelled.

Pearl Craigie's novels circle obsessively around the motifs of adultery and renunciation, and in *The Dream and the Business*, for example, Tessa, Lady Marlsford's decision to stay with her husband is affirmed. Yet she actually dies as a result of her emotional frustration and, when it is said that Roman Catholicism is the only religion for spirits such as hers, it seems an unintentionally back-handed compliment (p. 316).

Maurice Baring's novels of renunciation also glamorize suffering. In *Overlooked* (1922) the Russian Kranitski is in a complicatedly frustrating love situation from which his Catholicism makes it impossible for him to extricate himself, but Mrs Summers says of him 'All people who are unhappy are generally very happy too' (1929 reprint: 211). Baring's melancholy Edwardian romanticism, however, is given a heart of steel by stoicism and the rigorist version of Christianity he espouses. In *Cat's Cradle* (1925) Mrs Lacy prays that her son will be freed from suffering and protected, but her prayer is an impossible one: 'He would have to go to the school of life like every one else. There was no escape – no escape from life, no escape from sorrow, misery, and pain.'

The saving grace, though, is that suffering, even though inevitable, can still be willingly embraced and thus become potentially redemptive. Blanche has caused enormous suffering in pressurizing Bernard into marrying her, but the recognition which is her punishment can also become her expiation. She prays to be

> saved from herself for what remained of her life, not to do more harm, not to cause further unhappiness . . . and scalding tears poured down her cheeks. And it was then the wound caused by the whole situation seemed to pierce her soul, and, as it pierced it, it healed it. It was as if God took away the venom and replaced it by balm.
>
> (p. 696)

This whole idea has been a central one in traditional Catholic thought and practice. The way that individual human suffering can be caught up into Christ's and thus both be redeemed and – in a sense – itself be made redemptive has been a very distinctive doctrinal and devotional bias of Roman Catholicism as opposed to Protestantism. The extension of this to the teaching that the merits, graces and sufferings of one part of the Church could be applied to another part underlies controversial doctrines such as purgatory and indulgences.

Such ideas are treated with much greater caution by modern Catholic theologians, and they have had to be carefully scaled down and reinterpreted. In unduly emphasizing such beliefs and practices, popular Catholicism had run the risk of pushing subordinate and secondary aspects of redemption to the fore and fostering various kinds of guilt and morbidity.

What cannot be denied, though, is the enormous dramatic appeal such motifs have had for novelists at all levels of merit. The theme of expiation itself is extremely popular. In one particularly dramatic development of the motif, various Catholic heroines join convents to atone for their past sins: Gertrude in Lady Georgiana Fullerton's *Ladybird* (1853), for example, and the beautiful Mrs Houseman in Baring's *Passing By* (1921). When a widow becomes a nun in Christine Brooke-Rose's *The Dear Deceit* (1960) it is suggested that this is an unconscious, providentially arranged atonement for the sins of her dead husband, a religious con-man. The son says he cannot pray at all as a legacy from his father, but he is advised, in a Greene-like touch, to make an offering of this very lack of faith itself.

E. M. Delafield, witty author of *The Diary of a Provincial Lady* (1930), had herself joined the noviciate as a young girl, only to leave a year later. In *Consequences* (1919) her heroine enters a convent because of a crush on a nun, and the morbidity of her whole religious ethos is described: 'Perhaps the only belief which had any real hold upon her was . . . that God was a Supreme Being who must be propitiated by the sacrifice of all that one held dear, lest He strike it from one' (p. 247). After her marriage Delafield herself gave up Catholicism, and her main novel on the subject, *Turn Back the Leaves* (1930), again highlights morbid elements. At the end the neurotic Helen enters a convent to atone for the sins of her mother who has had a child out of wedlock and her sister who has married outside the faith. Her decision means that her lively sister Cassie has to stay at home in the deadly secluded house of Yardley with her mad father and pious mother.

In late nineteenth-century France the traditional Catholic emphasis on the possibility of vicarious suffering to win salvation for sinners was highlighted and exaggerated, particularly through the teachings of Boullan, who was later condemned for heresy. Such teachings had a special appeal for Huysmans and the novelists of the Catholic Revival, and in England it was given a special centrality by Robert Hugh Benson, who admired Huysmans.[3] *Initiation* (1914), for example, shows Sir Nevill learning the meaning of suffering from a beautiful young woman, whilst the whole plot of *A Winnowing* (1910) depends upon a striking example of the bargain-with-God motif that is the most extreme development of the idea of vicarious suffering. The typically English, cricket-playing, lax Catholic Jack Weston dies suddenly of a heart attack. His wife Mary promises to give her whole life to God if He will let Jack live, and Jack recovers. In the shock of his experience he wishes to become a monk and suggests that Mary herself might become a nun. She refuses, but is gradually drawn round. Meanwhile, however, Jack himself grows lukewarm again. Then he dies – a second time, and Mary does take up her religious vocation.

This motif, of course, has a special appeal for Graham Greene. The play *The Potting Shed* (1957) depends on the idea of a priest's sacrificing his own gift of faith to save his nephew. There are slightly more ambiguous examples in *The Power and the Glory* (1940) and *The Heart of the Matter* (1948), but the most famous version of the bargain is central to *The End of the Affair*. After an explosion in the blitz Sarah fears that Bendrix is dead and promises that she will give him up if only He will spare him: ' . . . and then he came in at the door, and he was alive, and I thought now the agony of being without him starts, and I wished he was safely back dead again under the door' (p. 93).

Naturally enough, as here, the presence of death in the plot always intensifies the suspense and melodrama of these traditional motifs. Expiation, renunciation and vicarious suffering combine to take their most dramatic form in the idea of martyrdom, which has a very special place in English Catholic mythology. 'I had my first breeding and conversation', wrote Donne, 'with men of suppressed and afflicted religion, accustomed to the despite of death and hungry of an imagined martyrdom.'[4] The most famous treatments, Wiseman's *Fabiola*, Benson's *Come Rack, Come Rope*, for example, have very obvious elements of morbidity and sensationalism. Greene in *The Power and the Glory* takes care to counterpoint its unheroic, unpious and reluctant hero with the conventional hagiography that Luis's mother reads to him, but Greene's work, of course, has an inverted melodrama of its own.

The sacrificial victim is a martyr in a less formal sense, and the motif is common both in the popular Catholic sentimental fiction and in the better novels. Several of Piers Paul Read's works contain the idea, for example. Henry Routledge's death in *The Professor's Daughter* is both a kind of expiation for his past mistakes and a saving death to protect others. In Gabriel Fielding's *Gentlemen in their Season* (1966) the murderer Hotchkiss is shot by the police and becomes a kind of scapegoat to purify marriages. Another impressive modern example in which the sacrifice is specifically assimilated to Christ's is Anne Redmon's *Music and Silence* (1979) where a cellist who has attracted the attentions of a homicidal maniac is saved by the sacrificial death of the mystical heroine. When the murderer approaches his substitutionary victim,

> Curiously, as he saw her, he was ever so moved by beauty, never so touched or moved by anything so beautiful in his life. Never was there creature like this one who was like violets; never was there anyone like this one clothed in white, her eyes open and afraid and grave.
>
> (1980 reprint: 244)

The 'aboriginal calamity'

If Catholic writers seek to appropriate the word 'suffering', they are well known to be on their home territory with 'sin', 'obsessed with good and evil and guilt and redemption' like Hilary Fletcher, the hero of Piers Paul Read's *The Upstart* (London, 1975 reprint: 280). Josephine Mary Ward writes of her Father Gabriel in *One Poor Scruple*,

> Then there had been some, too, who came there weighted with great sins, horrid cruelties, moral and physical, murders of the body or murders of the soul. All this had been poured into his ears. He knew of things stranger than any fiction had imagined; he knew the secret sins of the respectable; he knew the secret remorse of the speculator haunted by his victims; he knew the secrets of women of every kind and sort.[5]

The actual theme of confession and the confessional is predictably common in Catholic fiction, and part of the mystique attached to the figure of the priest is this privileged insight that the confessional is held to give into the hidden depths of evil in the human heart. By extension, though, the Catholic novelist, like Ward herself in this passage, obviously lays claim to the same priestlike knowledge and intimacy with sin, and its presence is everywhere in their works.

The hero of Gabriel Fielding's *In the Time of Greenbloom* (1956) comments at one point that he feels he needs to be forgiven for something he never did.[6] At the end of the same writer's *The Birthday King* (1962) the saintly Frau Waitzmann points out that it is too simple to blame the Nazis alone for the concentration camps, 'No one can dissociate themselves . . . Not Germany, nor Europe nor America' (p. 320). John Braine takes this motif further at the end of *A Jealous God* (1964) with a powerful assertion – only superficially unCatholic – of a kind of priesthood of all human beings in this need of mutual forgiveness. The hero, a layman, absolves his own mistress:

> 'But what more can I do than say I'm sorry? Where does it end?'
> 'It ends here,' Vincent said. The door of the confessional closed behind the penitent; but, he thought, the priest is a penitent too, we absolve each other as soldiers once did on the battlefield.
>
> (p. 286)

What underlies such emphases, of course, is a pervasive sense of the implications of original sin. Newman's eloquent paragraphs on the doctrine in chapter 5 of the *Apologia* make up one of the most famous passages in all Catholic literature, and various novelists refer specifically to it. Any objective survey of human history and human society in its enormous potential and tragic falling short would lead empirically, Newman urges, to the recognition that '*if* there be a God, *since* there is a God, the human race is implicated in some terrible aboriginal calamity.'[7]

Evelyn Waugh's comments in a review of Graham Greene are another well-known statement of the implications of the doctrine, but in his version Newman's dignified cadences have turned into a significantly less humane emphasis:

> The children of Adam are not a race of noble savages who need only a divine spark to perfect them. They are aboriginally corrupt. Their tiny relative advantages of intelligence and taste and good looks and good manners are quite insignificant. The compassion and condescension of the Word becoming flesh are glorified in the depths.[8]

As Waugh and many other critics have suggested, the whole terrain of 'Greeneland' – criminal Brighton, the Mexico of *The Power and the Glory* – , consists of an extreme vision of this universal corruption, though it is expressed with a much greater compassion than in Waugh himself. The Africa of *The Heart of the Matter* with its terrible heat, its dead dogs and rats, and its all-pervasive guilt is perhaps the most precise externalization of this region of the spirit:

> There was a retort in this colony to every accusation. There was always a blacker corruption elsewhere to be pointed at. The scandalmongers of the secretariat fulfilled a useful purpose – they kept alive the idea that no one was to be trusted. That was better than complacence.
>
> (p. 30)

A special sense of original sin may on the other hand contribute to a less obviously exaggerated, more fashionable tone of sceptical detachment that may still strike some readers as pessimistic and anti-humane. Muriel Spark's work, for example, takes the presence of human evil, lust and violence for granted as part of the norms of this fallen world. In so doing, in a sense she also refuses to take them seriously, and such elements are thus – notoriously – almost understated.

The comedy, for example, of the old man in *Memento Mori* who pays a girl to show him her stocking tops has a curious quality in that nothing much is made of it. It suggests the inveteracy of lust, but there is no heavy-handed moralizing. On the other hand there is no prurience to the humour either and no permissive denial of the presence of sin. The tone rather is curiously arch and fastidious, arch in that the recognition of perversity and evil is a witty and knowing one, fastidious in that its description is detached and a little disdainful.

A similar tone is present to some degree in Beryl Bainbridge. Here too Catholicism seems to contribute, though much more ambiguously than in

'The sorrowful mysteries'

Spark.[9] In Bainbridge there is the same almost cynical acceptance of the radically flawed nature of human relationships and activities and this obviously relates to a sense of the Fall. In *A Quiet Life* (1976), in particular, apparently casual mention is made near the beginning of a statue of Adam and Eve. When the doctor comes at the end after the father's heart attack, he hangs his hat on the statue by mistake and rocks the pedestal on which it stands.

The supernatural dimension in Spark, however, is used to judge the secular order. It exists with its own over-riding reality and even shows flashes of its presence here. She writes, for example, of 'The solemn crowds with their aimless purposes, their eternal life not far away.'[10] Bainbridge's work on the other hand is purely of this world. If the hero of *Sweet William* (1975) is a charismatic and mischievous deceiver like Dougal Douglas, there is none of that sense of the supernatural that surrounds the latter figure. Another dimension, different terms of reference, are sometimes invoked in Bainbridge's novels, as with the Adam and Eve statue, but they work in a completely different way.

Another Part of the Wood (1968; 1979 reprint), for example, depends on a series of ironic contrasts, but they measure not a presence but an absence, a gap so unbridgeable as to make them irrelevant even as a criterion of judgment. The weekend away in a pastoral place, 'the Glen', only confirms that there is no such thing as pastoral. George believes that 'Evil lay beyond the Glen' (p. 100), but it proves in the end, of course, to be only 'another part of the wood', thus confirming the unalterable rule in Bainbridge's work that the more special the place and the occasion the more inevitable it is that it will go horribly wrong.

In this case though the motif is strengthened by what is for her an unusually sustained and deliberate, if still totally teasing and ironic and in a sense inconsequential biblical parallel. The idea of pastoral is given a specifically religious dimension through one character's obsession with the Jews and the Promised Land. The character Joseph is interested in dreams and their interpretation like his biblical prototype. All this reaches its climax when Joseph's small son, Roland, climbs a hill and is reminded of the story of Abraham and Isaac: '"My Dad would never sacrifice me," shouted Roland. "He doesn't believe in God"' (p. 149). Yet Roland's life is soon to be pointlessly sacrificed by his father's complete neglect, and the contrast is between an inconsequential and mundane world and a spiritual one.

Yet there is no bridging the gap, no epiphany to be provided. When Balfour later discovers Roland to be dead:

> He couldn't feel surprised or shocked. He had always, it seemed, been on the threshold of some experience that would open a door, and now here was just such an experience and there was no sudden illumination, no revelation such as he had imagined. Indeed it appeared to him that the door had closed for ever. He was quite untouched, it wasn't his loss.
>
> (p. 176)

A rhetoric of paradox and exaggeration

Spark has commented that 'The Christian economy . . . seems so ordered that original sin is necessary to salvation.'[11] Unlike the famous Victorian preacher, it seems, these writers are not simply 'against' sin. If the recognition of sin in its various forms is indispensable, then there is a sense in which sin itself can be regarded as useful. In Spark's most brilliant novel, *The Girls of Slender Means* (1963), the hero, Nicholas, is converted by his horror at witnessing an act of astounding selfishness. In the midst of a terrible fire the lovely Selina has gone back to rescue a Schiaparelli dress rather than one of her friends. In involuntary horror Nicholas makes the sign of the cross at the sight and in his notebook there is found later the comment that a vision of evil is as powerful for conversion as a vision of good. Such a truth appears to apply to one's own sins as well as to those of others. It was the evil of his own imagination, according to Piers Paul Read, that first taught him the need for God.[12]

Such paradoxes have a strong presence in the New Testament itself, of course, where the sinful woman of Luke 7 loves much because she is forgiven much and it is the publican who recognizes his sin who is justified, not the respectable Pharisee. They often accompany the emphasis on sin and the Fall even in the most orthodox of these novelists and are so pervasive indeed as to become almost a reflex at times in Catholic fiction. The story of a French convent for reformed prostitutes in Rumer Godden's *Five for Sorrow, Ten for Joy*, for example, is based on fact, but also provides the opportunity for exploring such motifs: '"They tell me that often the worst criminals make the best nuns." Louis was quite serene. "Because they have known the depths. 'Out of the depths, I cried to Thee' . . ."' (p. 59). In the Father Brown stories the priest comments likewise on the conversion of the thief Flambeau: '"Odd, isn't it," he said, "that a thief and a vagabond should repent when so many who are rich and secure remain hard and frivolous and without fruit for God and man?"'[13]

Through Dostoievsky and Huysmans, as Roger Sharrock has commented, the paradoxes of the holy sinner influence the novelists of the French Catholic Revival, to whose own anti-bourgeois bias they make a special appeal. Certain important shifts of emphasis occur. We begin to find a considerable stress on the idea that the great sinner may reveal, as Eliot says in his essay on Baudelaire, a greatness of aspiration that makes him akin to the saint. There is therefore perhaps a way, directly as it were, rather than by a mystery of God's providential grace, through sin to God. Huysmans's 'way down and out' meant down into sin and even Satanism, out into grace. In the works of Peguy, Bernanos, Julian Green and others such paradoxes are powerfully emphasized in reaction against the respectable Catholicism of *les bien-pensants*.[14]

This is another theme that Graham Greene has made peculiarly his own, as all commentators have noted. At the front of *The Heart of the Matter* he puts the startling assertion from Péguy that the sinner 'is at the very heart of Christianity. No one is such an expert on Christianity as the sinner: no one, that is, except the saint.' In *The Power and the Glory* and *The End of the Affair* there is very much the suggestion that the priest and Sarah become saints not despite but *because* they were sinners:

The brandy was musty on the tongue with his own corruption. He remembered the woman in the prison and how impossible it had been to shake her complacency: it seemed to him that he was another of the same kind. He drank the brandy down like damnation: men like the half-caste could be saved: salvation could strike like lightning at the evil heart, but the habit of piety excluded everything but the evening prayer and the Guild meeting and the feel of humble lips on your gloved hand.

(p. 202)

As the prologue to his own imitation of Graham Greene in *The Upstart*, Piers Paul Read quotes a passage from Julian Green to the effect that in each of us there is a saint and a sinner,

> The one and the other, not the one or the other. Both at the same time. While the saint develops – if the man is a saint – the sinner in him develops on the imaginative plane. . . . If the man is a sinner – that is to say, if the sinner gets the better of the saint – the saint develops as best he can on the imaginative plane (a yearning for holiness).

What follows, encouraged by such teaching, is Read's most violent novel, the story of the vengeance the spurned hero, Hilary Fletcher, takes on the upper-class family the Metheralls by gaining possession of the family seat after ruining the other heirs. To achieve this he has prayed to the devil, he claims later, that the ball will fall on red in the crucial roulette game. The rogue's progress involves *en route* the seduction of the youngest daughter of the family, the murder of a new-born baby and the crippling of another enemy.

The conversion, when it comes, is equally violent and prepared for not by obvious psychological factors but, in accordance with Julian Green's dictum, by a reaction towards good, the violence of which is in direct proportion to the degree of evil already committed:

> Clear images of my actions started to wrap me like a lunatic's straitjacket. I could see the man's grizzled chin on the concrete floor, his wrinkled lids half-opened; I could hear the spasmodic exhalations of his dead lungs. And then again I could feel the baby's legs in my left hand and its little neck between the two fingers of my right hand: I could feel its wriggling movements as if electric shocks were passing into me and, reliving that ghastly moment, I felt more and more intolerably what I must call remorse. I wished, I wished even to God, that I had not done these things.

(p. 260)

Inspired by a 'good thief' Irishman in his cell, Fletcher, though not yet a Catholic, goes to confession and makes a complete repentance. By a special irony of God his 'penance' is that he must keep the estate he has won, even though he would prefer to give it up.

The attempt is often made to justify all this emphasis on sin in Catholic fiction in terms of realism. Newman had written, after all, that it is impossible for there to be a sinless literature of sinful man.[15] In a nice moment in John Braine's *The Jealous God* Vincent Dangarvin brings library books by Waugh and Greene for his grandmother and she at first complains:

'I'd never give you an immoral book, Grandmother. Why, these are good Catholic authors.'

'They're the worst,' she said. 'That man Greene's terrible. Mind you, he knows about life.'

That was the escape clause, Vincent thought. He'd been changing her library books for ten years now; invariably she'd expressed her distaste for immoral books and just as invariably on the few occasions when he'd brought her something innocuous, had rejected it out of hand as being wishy-washy and untrue to life.

(p. 16)

But the extremism of such developments of the traditional paradoxes as Greene's and Read's hardly needs underlining. As with the old lady the excuse of 'realism' is a disingenuous one, for the tone of these works is often over-intense, sensationalist and pessimistic, the paradoxes unfortunately by no means an inevitable index of moral and theological profundity. Indeed the contrary may be thought to be the case. Commenting on the famous death-bed repentance of Lord Marchmain in *Brideshead Revisited*, Orwell says rudely that it shows the 'veneer is bound to crack sooner or later. One cannot really be Catholic and grown up.' Other influential critics have found this whole emphasis on the Fall, sin and the paradoxes of grace in the characteristic Catholic novelists so extreme as to undercut the normal modes of human responsibility and morality on which the novel genre depends. Martin Green, for example, has written eloquently of the sense of original sin in these writers as creating

> That grey accumulation of defeat and decay, that atmosphere of hope and energy being buried in the (humanly) meagre and meaningless . . . the malignancy of the human environment – which extends into the human psyche itself – rendered as suffocating dullness and pettiness.

More generally he has said that

> human achievements and modes of being are consistently and triumphantly shown to be inadequate, egotistic, evil, just in being themselves, in being human. Under stress all natural goodness breaks down; only grace-assisted goodness is valid, and grace-assisted badness is perhaps even better.[16]

Treading as carefully as possible here, it would be difficult to deny that elements of 'Catholic neurosis' have contributed to the attitude to sin in these writers. A traditional Catholic upbringing may obviously help to create both guilt and a sense of forbidden fruits. What often seems especially characteristic, though, is an odd combination of scrupulosity – so many things are sins! – with a certain casualness – sin is so easily forgiven!

In a finely ironic passage in Bergonzi's *Roman Persuasion*, for example, Martin Tolleybeare goes with a prostitute in London during his wife's absence on a trip. Almost immediately afterwards he goes to confession in Westminster Cathedral and then forgets the whole incident as if it had never occurred:

'The sorrowful mysteries'

Martin said what he needed to say, the priest replied in a few kindly but conventional phrases, and told him what prayers to say as a penance. Then came a rapid mutter in Latin, culminating in the act of absolution, *Ego te absolvo*. The Sacrament of Penance had been administered as briskly and impersonally as the renewal of a season ticket. Martin saw no reason for it to be otherwise. Confession was a matter of objectively recognizing one's failings before God and establishing that recognition by telling them to God's representative. There was no occasion for emotional soul-searching, or ecstasies of remorse, merely a dry, even cold recognition of what was so and what should be so, and an intention, however faltering, to do better in future. It was an efficacious mechanism. After leaving the confessional Martin knelt before the Blessed Sacrament again and said the few simple prayers that formed his penance. As always after confession Martin felt serene, and the serenity blended with the physical release following the act in Half Moon Street to produce a suffused calm of mind and body.

(p. 111)

Here, without any overt authorial comment, Bergonzi skilfully diagnoses the way that a degree of moral irresponsibility may come to be combined with the greatest knowledgeableness and sophistication about sin. Joined with the New Testament paradoxes these aspects of the traditional Catholic ethos of sin and forgiveness may have dramatic appeal for converts with their own special reasons for hostility to the conventional codes. Oscar Wilde, not yet a Catholic, writes at the end of a famous letter to Lord Alfred Douglas from France: 'I have been to Mass at ten o'clock and Vespers at three o'clock. . . . I am seated in the Choir! I suppose sinners should have high places near Christ's altar? I know at any rate Christ would not turn me out.'[17] But in developing these traditional motifs in anti-bourgeois and even decadent directions some Catholic novelists, as the critics have said, give the impression of self-consciously flaunting or cynically downgrading morality rather than transcending it.

Granted all this, it cannot be denied that, however obsessive, over-intense or mannered these writers are, they are correct at least in asserting that both the doctrine of original sin and an element of moral paradox are at the heart of Christianity. If we are not lost in a situation from which we are unable to rescue ourselves, then there is no need for a saviour, and the very core of the gospel is missing. Such a belief necessarily transcends and relativizes ordinary human morality, since the latter is not sufficient to extricate us. The very idea of sin in itself, of course, implies a supernatural rather than a purely human or secular standard of measurement. Sylvie's comment in Alice Thomas Ellis's *The Other Side of the Fire* (1983) that to be moral and to be religious are two quite different things is thus not only an essential theme in Catholic fiction, but also central to Christianity as a whole (1988 reprint: 24). As the theologian John L. McKenzie writes magisterially, 'The morality of reason and nature is not the morality which constitutes the life of Christ; and therefore the Christian repents of this morality also.'[18]

None of this is meant, of course, to lead in an antinomian direction that denies that Christians should lead moral lives at all. The process of salvation is to be *from* sin to a new life in Christ, a life that includes a new Christian ethics. But for all their exaggerations, these novelists seem to have grasped an essential element in the gospel. It is a distinctively British tendency to believe that Christianity is simply a matter of being an ordinary decent individual, and it is peculiarly apt therefore that the originator of what might be taken as the formal version of the heresy should be the British monk Pelagius in his great controversy with St Augustine about original sin and the role of human morality in salvation. Like the themes of suffering and death, the idea of sin constitutes a radical threat to human self-sufficiency, and, whatever contribution the variant forms of the 'Catholic neurosis' make, the great emphasis on the subject in these writers comes in part at least from their special consciousness of being in the midst of what they regard as a blind and complacent Pelagian society. In Chesterton's *The Ball and the Cross* a vaguely benign figure tries to intervene to stop the fighting between the Catholic MacIan and his atheist opponent Trumbull. But Chesterton's point, a constant one in British Catholic fiction, is that the two foes are at least not among the lukewarm:

> Give up fighting, and you will become like That. Give up vows and dogmas and fixed things, and you may grow like That. You may learn also that fog of false philosophy. You may grow fond of that mire of crawling, cowardly morals . . .
>
> (p. 101)

The special rhetoric of exaggeration and paradox has itself therefore to be understood as part of a campaign. If the mode of normal 'realistic' fiction suggests that human morality is not only very much under human control but also the real 'heart of the matter', then anything that disturbs that tone may seem worthwhile, even when these novelists are themselves writing within basically 'realistic' constraints. Their antinomian paradoxes and pessimism, their baroque melodrama or worldly-seeming wit, if not without the elements of immaturity and sensationalism which Orwell long ago pointed out, may still at least serve to enforce the distinction between grace and morality and suggest another dimension to human behaviour, the presence of mystery.

For alongside the 'common-or garden life' of this society with its 'much thinner reality', not at all 'concerned with eternal damnation', as Greene says in an essay on Rolfe, these writers believe that a great battle for the soul is taking place.[19] An easy contempt for normal life may sometimes, it is true, seem to result, and the appeal to the drama of salvation and damnation may offer too cheap a resource to sensation and suspense under the guise of spiritual profundity. But, from a more sympathetic perspective, it can be seen to work the other way around as well: the melodrama and extremism that these novelists cultivate serve the function of emphasis in the attempt to bring home the profound reality and significance of this drama in a society that ignores it to its own peril.

All the Church's traditional motifs of expiation, sacrifice and suffering may be called upon in this enterprise, as we have seen, and these novelists often seek to wind up the tension to the highest degree. The bargain-with-God theme, for example, gives the whole great issue of salvation a melodramatic concentration of focus on one appallingly costly central offer, and enormous suspense as to the outcome results. This is even more true of the idea of death-bed repentance, which writers of the highest stature are not afraid to exploit. The most famous example is the one Orwell so savagely attacks, Lord Marchmain in *Brideshead Revisited*. What cannot be questioned, however, is the skill Waugh displays in working up the drama. Suspense is created by the fact that Marchmain has already turned the priest away once. Now he is in the very throes of death and has been annointed with no sign of repentance. Even the hostile Charles finds himself praying for such a sign, and the moment marks the beginning of his own conversion:

> Suddenly Lord Marchmain moved his hand to his forehead; I thought he had felt the touch of the chrism and was wiping it away. 'O God,' I prayed, 'don't let him do that.' But there was no need for fear; the hand moved slowly down his breast, then to his shoulder, and Lord Marchmain made the sign of the cross. Then I knew the sign I had asked for was not a little thing, not a passing nod of recognition, and a phrase came back to me from my childhood of the veil of the temple being rent from top to bottom.
>
> (1949 reprint: 296–7)

A stunning modern version of the motif occurs in Piers Paul Read's *A Married Man* (1979). The hero's Catholic wife Clare, murdered directly after the act of adultery to which she has finally succumbed after a long campaign of temptation, is able to make the sign of the cross on the wall in her own blood as a mark of last-minute contrition. Once again this begins the process of the hero's own conversion.

Even more powerful in the last analysis perhaps, however, is the terrifying rejection of grace, love and conversion at the conclusion of Anne Redmon's *Emily Stone*. Here the 'supernatural' mysteries of good and evil, grace and final destiny work themselves out completely on the human plane, as Peter Hebblethwaite suggests they should. Though there is no reason whatsoever for sternly refusing to enjoy the spiritual melodramas in Catholic fiction, Redmon's novel is a reminder that the treatment of these mysteries does not *have* to take such a very inflated form. Sasha pours herself out in love and in death for Emily, but the crisis has been prepared for so that it makes perfect sense in psychological terms:

> She was as vulnerable in this look as if she existed there without skin. Everything she ever was offered itself forward, even though everything she had ever tried to be had fallen into complete disuse. . . .
>
> She looked at me, and looked at me, and from the mere presentation of herself, her expression deepened and held itself open to me as if she understood me with an indescribable gentleness and delicacy.
>
> And this is what I have never been able to admit even to myself: I felt starved and gross in my starvation, like a repulsive bony animal that sucks the fur off its paws for nourishment.
>
> (1980 reprint: 225)

But the point is that the sacrifice fails. The central character's name, Stone, carrying on the theme of attitudes to death described earlier in the chapter, suggests a tidy English tombstone but also the unrepentant heart of stone of which the bible speaks. Emily is finally invulnerable to Sasha's appeals, and this, of course, is their last meeting.

Redmon has made skilful use here of the popular Catholic device of the sceptical or non-believing narrator. Instead of showing the usual defeat of unbelief the device works in the opposite way here to show how the calls of love and grace can go unheeded and, if this prevents much of the melodrama and sentimentality usually associated with the sacrificial death and the last-minute repentance, it also creates a profounder horror, a demonstration of the ultimate cost of such a rejection.

If there is no sense of the intrusion of anything extraneous in *Emily Stone*, the consideration of human behaviour still seems to point beyond itself, has an *ultimate* dimension, an area of mystery. In one sense Emily's free will, the significance of human moral choice is surely highlighted in such an approach. Yet there is another sense in which it is itself only part of the story, for Emily's choice is clearly a response or rather refusal of response to an unconditional love, something given.

· 10 ·
Sin, sex and adultery

Sin and Catholic sex

For most people 'sin' means sex, and this is perhaps more true for Catholics than anyone else. Muriel Spark's heroine in *A Far Cry from Kensington* (1988) recalls

> reading a book about one of the martyred Elizabethan recusant priests. The author wrote, 'He was accused of lying, stealing and even immorality.' I noted the quaint statement because although by immorality he meant extramarital sex as many people do, I had always thought that lying and stealing, no less, constituted immorality.
>
> (p. 53)

In David Lodge's *The British Museum Is Falling Down* (1965) the hero composes an article on Catholicism for a Martian encyclopaedia and describes it as a religion mainly characterized by curious sex rituals, adding wryly, 'Other doctrines of the Roman Catholics included a belief in a Divine Redeemer and in a life after death.'

The traditional triad of temptations facing the Christian, drawn from Christ's testing in the wilderness, consists of the world, the flesh and the devil. More scholarly modern exegesis has clarified that St Paul does not mean by the 'flesh' (*sarx*), that wars against the spirit, flesh in any purely physical or sexual sense.[1] But usages like 'sins of the flesh' have confirmed the confusion, and popular Catholicism is notorious for its over-attention to sexual matters. The aptly titled Father Byrne in Burgess's *Tremor of Intent* (1966) says to his pupils:

> This damnable sex, boys – ah, you do right to writhe in your beds at the very mention of the word. All the evil of our modern times springs from unholy lust, the act of the dog and the bitch on the bouncing bed, limbs

going like traction engines, the divine gift of articulate speech diminished to squeals and groans and pantings. It is terrible, terrible, an abomination before God and his Holy Mother.

(p. 6)

What we see illustrated here, of course, is the obvious but none the less powerful psychological law that undue attention to chastity reflects undue interest in sex. Freud remarks on a further, paradoxically self-defeating aspect of this:

> It is easy to show that the value the mind sets on erotic needs instantly sinks as soon as satisfaction becomes readily obtainable. Some obstacle is necessary to swell the tide of libido to its height. . . . In this context it may be stated that the ascetic tendency of Christianity had the effect of raising the psychical value of love in a way that heathen antiquity could never achieve; it developed greatest significance in the lives of the ascetic monks, which were almost entirely occupied with struggles against libidinous temptation.[2]

As the ex-monk in *The Garden of Allah* (1904) says forcefully it is the 'starved wolves that devour the villages' (p. 193), and this law is one obvious clue to the sexual preoccupations of Catholic fiction.

Joyce's *Portrait of the Artist as a Young Man* (1916) forever sets the tone for accounts of this struggle between chastity and the flesh, and his influence is apparent, for example, in John Braine's *The Jealous God* (1964), which describes the predicament of an older Catholic bachelor:

> but now at the age of thirty I can only brood over a glimpse of a girl's thighs and toy endlessly with the notion of myself as Father Dungarvan, Society of Jesus, austere and withdrawn but fulfilled at last, rid of the troubles of the flesh . . .

(p. 22)

Vincent, the hero, has affairs with his own sister-in-law and another married woman and the book conveys a brooding sense of frustration and guilt, the oppressive weight of an intense Northern Catholic, Irish-dominated culture.

Such pressures have been intensified by the influence of French Jansenism, the rigorist neo-Augustinian movement that dominated the continental seminaries in which Irish priests were trained and thus indirectly passed into English Catholicism. National temperament may itself play a part, and English Catholicism is often differentiated from Mediterranean brands in this respect. Polly in Lodge's *How Far Can You Go?* comments that 'Italians tolerate adultery and brothels because they're not allowed to divorce. . . . English Catholics have the worst of both worlds. No wonder they're so repressed' (1982 reprint: 40).

At the same time the development of moral theology, casuistry and confessional practice, especially the distinction between mortal and venial sins, encouraged a remarkably detailed attention to matters of sexual morality, the 'how-far-can-you-go mentality' Lodge so brilliantly characterizes. But this has another somewhat paradoxical consequence in that it at least prevents sex from being treated as a total, unspoken taboo, and Michel Foucault has gone so far as to argue in *The History of Sexuality* that the confessional itself helped shape the development of significant erotic narrative.[3]

As noted in the last chapter, there is also an odd combination of scrupulosity and tolerance. Catholicism is after all the most remarkably broad church of all, not in doctrine, but in its readiness to extend its offices to sinners. In Rumer Godden's *Five for Sorrow, Ten for Joy* it is said that French prostitutes are often devoted to the Rosary and some 'would climb up to the Sacre Coeur in Montmartre, all those steep steps, to light a candle. . . . They were far more reverent than many people in the world.' (prelude, 'The pretty beads'). If the sins of the flesh are taken seriously in one way, there is also a strong anti-respectable, anti-bourgeois emphasis that says they are less serious than many other sins. The sympathetic Father Smith in Bruce Marshall's *All Glorious Within* (1941) gives the last sacraments to an old sailor who still on his deathbed cannot say he feels sorry for 'having known all these women because their dresses had made such lovely sounds when they walked' (p. 27). The priest muses later that "Perhaps God didn't take the genial sins too seriously . . . the majority of men who drank to excess and ran wild with the girls were at bottom decent fellows" (1945 reprint: 84).

Less Puritanical medieval and continental attitudes in fact feed into British Catholicism as well as Jansenist trends. Anthony Burgess presents a double aspect to the religion, repressive and frustrating yet at a deeper level life-affirming and robust. In *A Vision of Battlements* (1949) Howarth's wife, Virginia, embodies Catholic timidity about sex and requires abstinence from her husband rather than practising birth control. At the end of the novel she is liberated in the recognition of the way the Church has discriminated against women. Yet Howarth himself also tries to affirm a more medieval and Rabelaisian version, as we have seen. The birth-control question is itself an ambivalent one in Burgess. In *The Wanting Seed* (1962) a new Catholicism so glorifies fertility as to celebrate orgiastic sexuality.

In the Scots Catholic campaign against Calvinism it is essential for Catholicism to be presented as the antithesis of the Puritan ethos, as George Mackay Brown's historical retrospective shows:

> The flame burned high in him when he sat time and again throughout the eighteenth century on the stool of penitence in the crowded kirk, to be publicly rebuked for, it might be, fornication, or playing football on the Sabbath, or getting drunk at the Hellya horse market, 'to the disturbance of the peace and the outraging of the lieges . . .' In this way those gloomy men, the minister and the elders, sought to constrict him and restrain him. But Mansie Hellyman, hemmed in by bigotry, was also in this true to the light; for the man of reason is not an enemy of natural joy. The earth is his and all the goodness thereof. Our mouths are made for kisses and honey and song.
>
> (*Greenvoe*, 1975 reprint: 160)

Various other writers pointedly emphasize that Catholicism is not a dualistic religion but has a high respect for the body. In Muriel Spark's *Robinson* (1958) the schismatic hero has a horror of any material manifestation of grace and it is because of this very unCatholic bias that he has left the Church. Several writers emphasize the contrary view to justify devotion to relics, for example. This is a major emphasis in Waugh's *Helena* (1950) and it lies behind Waugh's sense of the importance of the finding of the actual physical cross on which Christ died. Spark's *The Bachelors* (1960) compares Catholicism to the ethereal spiritualist ethos and presents marriage as an essential assertion of the goodness of the physical. Greene's Sarah in *The End of the Affair* (1951) finds even the vulgarity of popular Catholic art meaningful, as we have seen, in the way it emphasizes the sacramental physical reality of the truths of the religion, and she links this insight with her sexual love for Bendrix's body:

> Suppose God did exist, suppose he was a body like that, what's wrong with believing that his body existed as much as mine? Could anybody love him or hate him if he hadn't got a body? I can't love a vapour that was Maurice. That's coarse, that's beastly, that's materialist, I know, but why shouldn't I be beastly and coarse and materialist . . .
>
> (1971 reprint: 110)

Later she prays, 'Could I have touched You if I hadn't touched him first, touched him as I never touched Henry, anybody?' (p. 120).

When critics therefore argue that the most distinctive mode of Catholic fiction presents a God 'who sets an absolute wedge between the best in human love and love of Himself,'[4] they are oversimplifying Catholic ambivalences and paradoxes about love and sexuality. D. H. Lawrence himself paid eloquent tribute to the more positive attitudes in Catholic tradition in *A Propos of Lady Chatterley's Lover* (1930). In a purple passage in M. C. Bishop's *Elizabeth Eden* (1878) the Catholic millionaire, Rudolph Dene, appeals to the heroine: 'Let us pass together through the portal of human love, and together – what shall I say, Elizabeth? – shall we together find the love that lights up a new Heaven and a new Earth' (p. 214). This may seem no more than Victorian romanticism in a Catholic guise, but the whole idea that secular and even sexual love is a preparation for and analogy to divine love has a long legitimate pedigree going back at least as far as early interpretations of the Song of Songs.

Even in *Brideshead Revisited*, the novel to which the critic quoted above refers, the matter is much more complicated than may at first seem the case. It cannot surely be so surprising that the adulterous relationship finally has to be rejected in a novel written from an orthodox Catholic perspective, but it is made clear at the same time that, if Charles had not loved Julia and for that matter Sebastian, he would not have come to God:

> 'It's frightening,' Julia once said, 'to think how completely you have forgotten Sebastian.'
> 'He was the forerunner.'
> 'That's what you said in the storm. I've thought since; perhaps I am only a forerunner, too.'

'Perhaps,' I thought, while her words still hung in the air between us like a wisp of tobacco smoke – a thought to fade and vanish like smoke without a trace – 'perhaps all our loves are merely hints and symbols . . .'

(1949 reprint: 265)

Obsessive and prurient perhaps at times, these writers may be evasive on other sexual topics as we shall see. But, if they seem puritanical in permissive eras, they may appear permissive themselves in contrast to bourgeois Protestant respectability. What increasingly emerges as a major theme after the mid point of this century is the attempt to counter the secular demystification and trivialization of sex, which these novelists regard as only another form of the British tendency to Pelagianism.

Emily Stone's mother in Anne Redmon's novel, for example, makes Emily and her boyfriend attend an embarrassing sex discussion for teenagers: 'We started on diagrams and a little biology,' my mother said to Peter, filling him in, "and we are now at the stage of talking seriously about responsibility."' (1980 reprint: 96) For Miles, 'child of the State', in Waugh's *Love Among the Ruins*:

> Sex had been part of the curriculum at every stage of his education; first in diagrams, then in demonstrations, then in application, he had mastered all the antics of procreation. Love was a word seldom used except by politicians and by them only in moments of pure fatuity. Nothing that he had been taught prepared him for Clara.
>
> (1953: 29)

In John Braine's *Room at the Top* (1957) Joe Lampton gives up the mistress, Alice, he really loves to marry the wealthy young Susan, but his attempt to trivialize sex has gone against his own deepest moral self. Now, when he makes love he feels like 'one of the characters in a magazine advertisement' (1987 reprint: 183). Earlier he picks up a girl casually in a pub. She means nothing to him, but he is surprised to find that his experiences with Alice have forced him 'to tone down the raw rhythms of copulation . . . to give sex a nodding acquaintance with kindness and tenderness' (p. 229). Braine's sense of the personal and moral cost of the trivialization of sex seems a distinctively Catholic one here, despite the lack of any specifically Catholic reference points, and this is confirmed, as we have seen, in later work.

Sex as subject matter

Novelists obviously find sex and religion a sensational combination, and Catholicism has always seemed to have the greatest appeal of all religions in this regard. From Gothic fantasies to flamboyant modern examples like Colleen McCullough's *The Thornbirds* (1977) such motifs have been exploited. John Braine's bizarre spy novel, *The Pious Agent* (1975), for example, combines the sensationalist sex of the Bond stories with Catholicism by the simple expedient of having his womanizing hero go very frequently to confession!

'Though our population practises no kind of religion,' writes Piers Paul Read in *Monk Dawson* (1969: 45), 'it is left with a curiosity about those who try', and this is one very obvious reason for the remarkable popularity of Catholic fiction. Catholic writers are themselves aware of this fascination which is, of course, especially intense in the area of sexuality. Even what may be considered in some respects as the first British Catholic novel, Elizabeth Inchbald's *A Simple Story* (1791), decorously exploits the *frisson* of sexuality that results when the young Protestant female ward takes up residence in the house of her guardian, a Catholic priest.

Yet if the demands of institutionalized celibacy have always had a special fascination for a Protestant audience, Catholic writers themselves deal surprisingly little with that subject for most of the period, and this was not to change until the sixties. Like most Catholics they seem to find the idea of priests as sexual beings a discomforting one, and even supposedly inward or radical works like Bruce Marshall's or A. J. Cronin's hardly refer to the topic.

The latter's Francis Chisholm in *The Keys of the Kingdom* (1941), for example, spends the night with a prostitute and thus shocks respectable opinion, but he is only talking to her about God. A similar thing happens to E. M. Almedingen's Father Louis in *The Little Stairway* (1960), but he has stayed there merely through fear during the unrest of the Russian revolution. Marshall's Father Smith finds celibacy a sacrifice, but not in the last analysis very much of one.[5] A misogynistic tone masks the whole topic and prevents it from really becoming an issue at all:

> It had not been easy to become a priest, of course. It had not been easy to given up the soft comfortable things of the world which were not sinful in themselves. Girls, too. Almighty God had made their lovely bodies and it had not been easy to give up the hope of some day meeting one whose mind would be as beautiful as her hair; but nowadays when he saw and heard the women he might have married yattering in public places he did not think that God had asked such a tremendous sacrifice from him after all. And then when he had seen a few of them, all wet and dripping in their bathing dresses the practice of chastity did not seem quite as difficult as some of the saints had made out.
>
> (*All Glorious Within*, reprint 1945: 47–8)

Women, the same priest comments elsewhere, 'make themselves even more unattractive than they are by smearing and plastering and painting themselves until they cannot eat or drink without leaving the rust of their beauty on cups and napkins' (p. 121). Celibacy, he reaches the conclusion, is 'perhaps the easiest part of the religious life'.

Even greater embarrassment is evident among Catholic writers at the very idea of the sexuality of nuns. Many novels deal with life in convents, both as schools and as religious communities, but there is rarely anything more than a vague hint of 'crushes'. E. M. Delafield's early novel *Consequences* (1919) was written soon after her own departure from the noviciate and is unusually explicit about its heroine Alex's emotional attachment for her religious superior, 'watching the nun's fervent, flame-like gaze, in which her young idolatry detected none of the resolute fanaticism built up in instinctive self-protection from a temperament no less ardent than her own' (p. 184). It is almost entirely for this reason that Alex joins the order. She is in the convent in Belgium for eight years, 'but the thought that she was summoned to a private interview with Mother Gertrude could still make her heart beat faster' (p. 225). When the superior is moved to another convent Alex comes to some recognition of her plight and she leaves the order herself, but she can find no place back in the world and eventually drowns herself.

George Moore's *Evelyn Innes* (1898) and *Sister Theresa* (1901) are remarkably outspoken and detailed studies of the conflict and interchange between sensuality and spirituality in a talented opera-singer who becomes a nun. Moore had been a Catholic until just before the time of writing and the presentation of emotional attachments within the convent is sensitive and sympathetic. His own new beliefs come across, however, in his heroine's doubts about the Eucharist, and there is a sense of painful defeat in her decision to stay in the convent in the end.

Taboos about such subjects are apparently so severe as to prevent them from being discussed much at all in conventional Catholic fiction, but a remarkably high proportion of Catholic novels, both major and minor, deal with the theme of adultery. Here the prohibition seems only to have increased the fascination of the subject as a special source of both obsessive guilt and tantalizing attraction through the mechanism of 'obstacle love' Freud describes. At the beginning of E. M. Delafield's *Turn Back the Leaves* (1930) the author sympathetically contrasts in this respect the seriousness with which the non-Catholic Craddock and the Catholic Edmunda Floyd regard their affair:

> To Craddock it was a passionate episode: he had loved before, and he was well aware that he would love again. . . . To Edmunda, on the other hand, it was an affair of life and death. She viewed the mutual attraction that had so suddenly and so irresistibly flared up between herself and her lover in terms of tragedy, eternity, mortal sin and renunciation.
>
> (1952 reprint: 1)

The proprieties obviously prevent a full treatment of adultery in the Catholic novels of the Victorian period. Inevitably instead it is the idea of renunciation that dominates, as we have seen. But it requires little psychological sophistication to see that the motif of renunciation often seems to involve not only the rejection but also the guilty, fascinated, masochistic punishment of sexual desire. It may even be used to heighten and highlight the attention to sex, to exploit a certain enjoyment of long prolonged frustration, as in Hitchens's *The Garden of Allah*: 'But the cry of the body, Domini, of the eyes, of the hands, to see, to touch – it's so fierce . . .' (p. 515).

In Maurice Baring's novels love is always unrequited or thwarted in some way, and all this is obviously not without its own sentimentality and romanticism of loss. But what differentiates Baring's approach is an enormously hard and rigorist sense of the futility of secular love. At a crisis in *Daphne Adeadne* (1926) Fanny

> thought of how desperately she had loved Michael, and then of her shattering disillusion.

> But although this passed through her mind, it was not that which was making her miserable, not that which was making her cry.
>
> It was the bitter disillusion. The sense of dust and ashes, and the vanity of everything; 'the frailty of all things here.'
>
> (1927 reprint: 190)

Love, for Baring, has nothing but misery to offer. It is something from which we need to be rescued, but so inveterate is its power that there is 'need of something more than human, and indeed a heavenly force, to confront and vanquish that human passion' (preface to *Cat's Cradle* (1925), quoting Cervantes).

Such motifs would certainly seem to confirm the idea of an absolute gulf between human and divine love in Catholic fiction. But rigorism such as Baring's is very unusual among the novelists, whatever the moral theologians may say. Most of the other famous Catholic novels of adulterous love this century also demand renunciation in the end, but they do so in a much more paradoxical fashion, as noted already with *Brideshead Revisited*. Graham Greene's first major treatment of adultery in *The Heart of the Matter* (1948) is as unglamorous and asexual as it could possibly be, 'that moment of peace and darkness and tenderness and pity "adultery"' (1950 reprint: 235). But if Greene is quite traditional in some respects in seeing Sarah's 'abandonment' in love in *The End of the Affair* (1951) as a preparation for an abandonment to God, he is unusually insistent and explicit about the specifically sexual nature and quality of that abandonment. Sarah is a St Mary Magdalen figure, a repentant sinner turned saint, one who loves much because she has been forgiven much. It is Bendrix's adultery with her that has begun the whole process that is to lead to his final conversion too, though it is a process that will only complete itself outside the boundaries of the text.

The fascination of 'obstacle love' is confirmed by the fact that the negative prohibition receives far more attention than the positive ideal in most of these novels, despite D. H. Lawrence's praise for the affirmation of marriage in Catholicism. Muriel Spark's *The Bachelors* (1960) sees marriage as the central symbol and actualization of Catholicism's unification of spirit and flesh, as mentioned above, but presents it only by contrast to the perilous state of the incomplete bachelors. David Lodge's *The Picturegoers* (1960) includes a warm picture of the Mallorys' marriage, but this is only one aspect of the novel. Catholic family life itself can receive either bleak or sentimental treatment but there are few important novels of marriage as such.

In Gabriel Fielding's *Gentlemen in their Season* (1966) the theme of adultery is for once used to adumbrate the ideal against which it is an offence. The stories of the unsatisfying and unsuccessful adulteries of the Catholic Presage and the atheist Coles are juxtaposed against that of the Catholic criminal Hotchkiss, who, believing in the sanctity of marriage, has killed his wife's lover. Hotchkiss, himself killed by the police near the end of the book, becomes a kind of martyr or scapegoat for marriage, and he is contrasted with the superficiality of Presage and Coles. This sense of the true mystery of marriage, recognized, in a Greeneian touch, only by the murderer, is confirmed by references to the biblical story of Tobias and Sarah, which Milton mentions with similar force just before the first encounter with Adam and Eve in *Paradise Lost*. The Old Testament describes the threat to Sarah's marriage from an evil spirit which had to be driven away by her husband, and Fielding says we must realize that 'in any marriage there might be devils and angels moving about just behind the moods and promises' (p. 287).

Adultery in Piers Paul Read's impressive *A Married Man* (1979) also leads literally to death, as we have seen. The mistress of its hero, John Strickland, arranges the murder of his Catholic wife, Clare, who is herself killed in the act of adultery, though she has time to repent. But the book, as its title suggests, is an affirmation of the power of Catholic marriage, even though John himself is at first a complacent non-believer who feels that his ethics are more robust than Clare's Catholic morals. As John slowly comes to realize what has happened, so he comes to realize what his wife has meant to him. He still feels married to her despite her death and gives up his mistress and his hopes of a political career. He is preparing for conversion, revealing himself to be one of those unbelieving husbands whom St Paul says can be saved by their wives (I Corinthians 7: 14, 16).

Stereotypes and exclusions

It will not have escaped notice that most of these novels are by male writers, and their bias and stereotyping are often apparent. The question of attitudes to women in Catholicism and in Catholic fiction is obviously too vast for full consideration here. It is a topic with enormous ideological, economic and political implications, as we have already seen, as well as sexual and psychological ones. It is hardly necessary to underline the patriarchal and sexist dimension to the elaborate machinery of archetypes, symbols and stereotypes of the feminine in Catholicism or the way that it reflects the prejudices and yearnings of a celibate clergy.[6]

In the more immediate context it is obvious that the ambivalent attitudes to the flesh and to sex described above reflect and contribute to ambivalent attitudes to women. Bertrand de Roujay, the hero of Piers Paul Read's *The Free Frenchman* (1986)

> like many men from a Catholic culture . . . found it difficult to combine respect and desire for the same woman. For his fleeting liaisons in Paris he had always chosen women who had already 'fallen', and he was delighted and horrified in equal measure by their transports of sexual rapture. The concept of purity, inculcated by the Jesuits, had confused his reaction to sexual desire; and because purity was associated with girls of his religion, he only found himself attracted to non-Catholic women.
>
> (p. 48)

What we find here is a particularly self-defeating version of the famous Virgin/Whore antithesis, which has taken definitive form in Catholicism. As Michèle Roberts has said, the Church has never been comfortable with female sexuality and therefore, for example, 'has no women saints who were sexually active *and* involved with spirituality'.[7] Anthony Burgess's Virginia in *The Worm and the Ring* (1961) comes to realize that the Church had presented 'virginity and maternity' as the 'only two desirable states for a woman' (p. 183).

Idealized images of both states naturally abound therefore in the fiction, and it is easy enough to see how they are assimilated to the traditional icons. Father Smith in *All Glorious Within* prays, 'make women more demure but not less beautiful; mould their maidenhood upon Thy Blessed Mother's and place their feet in her pattern' (1945 reprint: 80). Even when the emphasis is on child-bearing and fertility there is little sense of female sexuality as such, though there is a memorable exception in Lodge's affectionate parody of Molly Bloom's soliloquy in the speech of Barbara Appleby that concludes *The British Museum is Falling Down*.

Auberon Waugh devotes the whole of *The Foxglove Saga* (1960) to the hunting down and destruction of the popular chaste-madonna stereotype, a brilliant parody of his own father's near definitive version in Lady Marchmain. The younger Waugh's Julia Foxglove still possesses, at the age of forty-five,

> the extraordinary, sublime beauty of a quattrocento madonna. Her smile, so kind, so understanding, seemed to emanate from a soul in repose. Her obvious chastity added lustre to her grace. Her only child, Martin, had had to be delivered by Caesarean section, and it was feared that another might endanger her life. Sir Derek had accepted the situation humbly. He was a good, simple man, and if he seemed at times to be a trifle brusque with his wife, it must be remembered that beside her St Simon Stylites would have appeared impatient, St Aloysius lecherous, St Francis Xavier brutal.
>
> (p. 24)

Anne Redmon is highly unusual in that, with a full awareness of the force of the feminist critique, she still wishes to affirm the image of Mary the Virgin Mother as 'this chaste, incarnating woman, strong and profound' (*Second Sight*, 1987: 73). It was Mathilde's tormented need 'for a mother who was consecrated, wise, dignified and effective' that lay behind her obsessive interest in Marian icons, for it had 'compelled her towards the truest image she could find of a woman'. Redmon's whole approach depends on the firm differentiation of chastity from sexlessness. If her virgin martyr figure in *Music and Silence* (1979), for example, in one way conforms to a stereotype, she is also made to redefine it, since she is seeking to come out of her isolation, including her sexual isolation, into love. Irene in *Second Sight* comes likewise to realize that 'It was I who had locked and bolted the door and called it integrity; I who chose a withering virginity from a terror of love . . .' (p. 245).

The figure of St Mary Magdalen remains the quintessential Catholic heroine: the mythic transmutation of whore into virgin, the fallen woman who becomes the saint. For many years scholars have been explaining that the idea of the penitent prostitute bears no relationship to the New Testament figure, but the myth has an obvious capacity for combining the fascination of the supposedly lurid past with the utmost edification. Rumer Godden's *Five For Sorrow, Ten for Joy* (1979), for example, sets a modern version of the myth within its own virtual institutionalization in a Magdalen, a religious house for reformed prostitutes. In Robert Keable's best-seller from the 1920s, *Simon Called Peter*, the secular whore-with-the-heart-of-gold stereotype takes Catholic form when the pagan Julie gives her lover up to God, 'And thus did Julie, who knew no God, but Julie of the brave, clean, steadfast heart give Peter to Him' (p. 347). Michèle Roberts provides a revisionist, post-Catholic, and feminist rewriting in her own novel of Mary Magdalen, *The Wild Girl* (1984), where she attempts to bring together again the Magdalen's sexuality and religious devotion, split off in the traditional version.

When the more general attitudes of British culture are taken into account, however, there seems little evidence to suggest that Catholic women writers are themselves unusually modest and repressed on the subject of sexuality. The more distinguished of them at any rate certainly are not, though this is perhaps a circular argument in that it is, of course, partly in their relative honesty and openness that their distinction lies. As Redmon says, the received imagery is itself richer than it is sometimes given credit for. The relative explicitness of confessional practice (even for women) may also have had an effect, or it may simply be that the very existence of the rules creates the potential tendency to defiance.

Edna O'Brien is the most obvious example to come to mind here, but the terms of reference for her poignant accounts of the sexual pressures on Catholic girls come primarily from Southern Ireland, a culture from which she is, of course, in conscious revolt. Muriel Spark makes it clear her heroines do not feel bound by the conventional Catholic restraints. Barbara Vaughan in *The Mandelbaum Gate* (1965) has recently had a passionate affair for which she feels no guilt, and she has made up her mind to marry her lover even if he cannot get an annulment for his first marriage. Antonia White's painful sequence following on from *Frost in May* is a treatment of various emotional and sexual feelings: the poignant eroticism of Clara's desire for the actor, Stephen, her horror at the idea of sex with her future husband, and her later over-intense relationship with Richard after the collapse of her marriage. Overshadowing it all is the special closeness between Clara and her father. This is itself complicated by Catholicism and Catholicism has obviously contributed to her sexual ignorance, but it is not clear to what extent her religion is in itself responsible for her sexual problems, and her friend, the wild Catholic actress, Maidie, is presented in contrast as very free in her own attitudes and language.

Radclyffe Hall, herself a Catholic convert, comments on 'that curious craving for religion which so often went hand in hand with inversion. Many such people were deeply religious . . .' (*The Well of Loneliness*, (1928; 1949 reprint: 454)). Despite this there are relatively few treatments of the subject in British Catholic fiction. John Gray, Rolfe and Firbank were homosexual by orientation and for some periods of their lives practice, but legal and other constraints prevent more than a few hints in their works. The tone and implications of Firbank's novels often seem homosexual, but the perfect lover that the hero of Rolfe's *Desire and Pursuit of the Whole* finds is an androgynous girl. Muriel Spark treats Ernest Manders in *The Comforters* (1957) with deliberately unconventional gentleness. Toomey in Burgess's *Earthly Powers* (1980) shows the pressures of the predicament for Catholics in the scene in which he consults a Jesuit confessor at Farm Street but leaves without obtaining absolution. There is nothing in British Catholic fiction on the topic as powerful as Morris West's portrayal of Nicholas Black in *The Devil's Advocate* (1959) or the more recent work of David Plante in Canada.

With one stunning exception that is – Radclyffe Hall's own *The Well of Loneliness*. For it has not usually been noted that this famous work is in some senses a 'Catholic novel'. The heroine, Stephen, is not a Catholic, but Hall's own personal piety is well recorded. Gradually the theme of the Church's attitude to those in her situation forces itself to the fore. Hall projects her own suffering as a lesbian Catholic on to the Polish painter Wanda, painfully afraid to go to communion even on Christmas Day. But the heroine Stephen herself has also come to believe in God and thus joined the company of those many 'deeply religious' ones like Wanda, who

> believed, and believing they craved a blessing on what to some of them seemed very sacred – a faithful and deeply devoted union. But the Church's blessing was not for them. Faithful they might be, leading orderly lives, harming no one, and yet the Church turned away; her blessings were strictly reserved for the normal.
>
> (1949 reprint: 454)

The book ends with Stephen, having sacrificed herself so that her lover might marry, receiving a terrible vision of millions of 'marred and reproachful faces with the haunted melancholy eyes of the invert' who ask her to demand of God why He has left them forsaken. She prays, 'We have not denied You, then rise up and defend us. Acknowledge us, oh God, before the whole world. Give us also the right to our existence!' (490–1).

Changing perspectives: the 'liberal hedonistic spirit'?

The culture shock of the sixties obviously at first sharpened the conflict between Catholic mores and those of the surrounding culture. More permissive attitudes to sexual display and behaviour increased temptation for Catholics, and at the same time there was more prurient curiosity among the general public about those in their midst who had such different standards and practices. But the new attitudes also inevitably had their analogies within the Church to some degree, so that a more unequivocally positive view of sexuality as a whole began to emerge:

> when the new theology of marriage began to emerge, in which sexual love was redeemed from the repression and reticence of the past, and celebrated as (in the words of the Catholic Theological Society of America) 'self-liberating, other-enriching, honest, faithful, socially responsible, life-giving and joyous,' the value of celibacy no longer seemed self-evident, and a progressive priest might find himself in the paradoxical position of defending the right of the laity to enjoy pleasures he himself had renounced long ago, on grounds he no longer believed in.
>
> (Lodge, *How Far Can You Go?*, reprint, 1982: 120)

Sin, sex and adultery

Far more explicit treatments of clerical celibacy occur in the aftermath of these developments. Lodge himself, for example, has a comic account in the same novel of a young priest's frustration after catching a glimpse of a girl's leg at a university chaplaincy party. Try as he might he cannot get the sight out of his mind and goes to seek advice from his parish priest. He is startled for a moment when the old priest recommends 'ejaculations', since the pressures of his obsession have temporarily driven from his mind the traditional Catholic meaning of short, fervent appeals to God in prayer:

'"My Jesus, mercy, Mary help!" That's a good one.'
'Oh, yes. I've tried prayers.'
'Pray especially to Our Lady, she'll help you to forget it. It wasn't your fault, you didn't seek the occasion of sin.' The PP sniffed and blew his nose loudly into a handkerchief. 'Some of these young hussies need their bottoms smacked,' he said indignantly, a careless expression in the circumstances, that didn't do anything at all for Austin Brierley's peace of mind.
(p. 29)

Later, Father Brierley, like so many others, is to leave the priesthood, and this itself is the subject of a variety of novels. In John Cornwell's *The Spoiled Priest* (1969) Father Gilbert's first act on leaving is to go to see 'Naked in the Grass' at the local cinema. Piers Paul Read's *Monk Dawson* (1969) contains a compassionate treatment of the naïve idealism of its hero's first relationship with women after his departure. In Jill Paton Walsh's *Lapsing* (1986) the heroine Tessa has a deeply emotional but platonic affair with a priest in Oxford in the mid-1950s and is surprised to find out later that he has left the priesthood and married someone else.

As already described, the birth-control controversy was obviously a crucial focus for the Catholic dilemma about attitudes to sexuality. David Lodge's hero Adam Appleby in *The British Museum Is Falling Down* (1965) says sarcastically that the 'safe period' leads to three weeks of abstinence and a few days of frantic activity: 'This behaviour was known as Rhythm and was in accordance with the Natural Law.' He imagines that he might have a nervous breakdown because of the frustration and strain and thus be granted a special personal dispensation by Rome!

As will have already become clear, the same author's later *How Far Can You Go?* (1980) has a special centrality and inwardness among accounts of the sexual strains of growing up a Catholic and the changes in the sixties. Though the novel contains farcical elements, it avoids the basically farcical mode of *The British Museum Is Falling Down*, and it treats the birth-control motif with a real seriousness, since the rhythm method is suggested as a causal factor in the birth of a handicapped child to one couple. But birth control is only one of the problems that concern Lodge's characters. Beginning with the pre-Vatican II problems of sexual frustration for young unmarried Catholics, Lodge provides a detailed, funny and yet compassionate survey of the elaborate game of 'how far can you go?' which they have to play. As time goes on, they all have to struggle to relate their wider experience of the sexual permissiveness of the culture to their Catholicism. Lodge deals humorously and compassionately with all the usual topics, but he also breaks free of the conventional boundaries in a very matter-of-fact treatment of Miles's homosexuality, for example, and a reference to the sexuality of nuns.

These subjects have subsequently been opened up further. Wendy Perriam's *Devils for a Change* (1989) is a very sensational recent account of the sexual problems and experiences of a nun who leaves her order. Michael Carson's *Sucking Sherbet Lemons* (1988) is the most explicit example of the new phenomenon — at least for this country — of Catholic or post-Catholic gay fiction. The hero, Benson, is in constant danger of mortal sin at his Catholic school because of his homosexuality. He decides to become a Brother in a religious order: 'He would put self to death and save souls and die in the odour of sanctity. And he would escape temptation and bad companions and not become a homo' (p. 72). Unfortunately he finds worse trouble within the order. An older brother tries to seduce him, and another castrates himself like Origen to avoid further temptation. Benson leaves and on his return to the world meets the gay Andy who enables him to come to terms with his sexual nature.

The farcical elements in the earlier part of the book are extreme and reflect the sense of oppression, but the fact that the subject is treated humorously at all marks a change. The tone of the later sections becomes celebratory, the book ending with Benson dancing to a record of the 'Missa Lubis' a black brother from the order had given him. Benson and most of the gay Catholics in fact leave the Church, but this is not presented as the only option. A gay priest is mentioned, and Benson's lover Andy says he is not a lapsed Catholic but a 'collapsed' one 'trying to make the best I can by searching through the rubble for something I can call my own' (p. 188).

In *How Far Can You Go?* the narrator, reflecting on various forms of the new liberalization, comments that we are now in a situation in which we can see that:

> the liberal hedonistic spirit has achieved irresistible momentum within the Church as without, that young Catholics now reaching adulthood have much the same views about the importance of sexual fulfilment and the control of fertility as their non-Catholic peers, and that it is only a matter of time before priests are allowed to marry . . .
>
> (1982 reprint: 120–1)

Once again, in other words, it is the question of the *distinctiveness* of Catholicism that has emerged as the crucial one. Tony Tanner has argued in *Adultery in the Novel* that, as marriage itself ceases to be taken seriously as a social and moral contract, adultery will come to be presented as a relatively inconsequential and routine matter and novels will no longer centre around it. In the second half of the twentieth century it has been Catholic novels on the subject that have been the memorable ones, since it is only there that the full sanctions remain. But being a Catholic as such is perhaps no longer enough.

One point of Fielding's *Gentlemen in their Season*, for example, is to illustrate a loss of the distinctive Catholic perspective, though it also seeks to remedy that situation. The novel shows that the Catholic Presage is just as superficial about marriage as the atheist, Coles. He has been influenced by the secularism of the whole society, a secularism suggested by the fact that it is the latter that is in charge of religious broadcasting at the BBC. Only Hodgkiss avoids this trivialization, and the hope is clearly that his sacrificial example may make a difference in the end.

Laura Knight in Rachel Billington's *Occasion of Sin* (1982) is by no means the first lax Catholic in fiction. Unlike Madge Riversdale in Ward's *One Poor Scruple* or Waugh's Julia Marchmain, however, she no longer even feels the moral pressure of the Church to any significant degree, though it recurs to her mind from time to time. She tries to tell herself before her adultery that 'In terms of 1980s morality, it might be nothing . . . but for her it would be a sin' (p. 73). One of her friends becomes a Catholic, but this only serves to reinforce her own moral confusion. Her affair is a matter of traumatic consequence to her way of life. It could have been avoided, had she not entered into the 'occasion of sin' of seeing Martin again. The wisdom of the Church's terminology is reaffirmed, but the considerations are in fact almost entirely secular ones, and it is the inconsequentiality of the whole business that is so well conveyed. The difference between Laura's reflections and Julia Marchmain's famous comments on living in sin in 'The twitch upon the thread' section of *Brideshead Revisited* is very revealing. The Church is not so much rejected as curiously marginalized in Laura's practice and in a sense in the novel as a whole.

A significant shift is measured even from a relatively recent work such as Braine's *Jealous God* (1964), where everything sexual is a matter of enormous consequence, and the shift is not merely in the general culture but also in the Church's own power to condition and control. But it would be wrong to oversimplify. If such a trend can certainly be observed, then other writers go out of their way to counter it. Alice Thomas Ellis's heroine Rose reacts indignantly to priests leaving to get married, for example, and beneath the apparently trivial fastidiousness of her comment that adultery is like using other peoples' toothbrushes the author's own more serious disapproval can be glimpsed (*The Sin Eater*: 123).

Piers Paul Read's recent work has also set itself against fashionable permissiveness. In an interview he has reasserted the traditional Catholic perspective on the moral significance of sexual acts, and several novels are specifically devoted to demonstrating this.[8] It is the threatened seduction of Teofil's innocent fiancée in *Polonaise* (1976), for example, that leads the nihilistic hero to murder in her defence and in so doing at least to affirm that morality does matter. In *The Villa Golitsyn* (1981) Willy, deciding long ago that God does not exist and therefore that morality is unimportant, has reneged on any political commitment and lived in incest with his beautiful sister, Prissy. In rejecting a sexual encounter with the schoolgirl, Helen, however, he makes what is clearly intended to be a highly representative, final recantation and expiation.

In *The Free Frenchman* (1986) the mood is one of radical sexual disgust and pessimism. The hero had taken a Spanish refugee as his mistress and also seduced the sister of a friend:

His shame for this adultery and the suicide of Lucia now reacted with the pain he himself had suffered from the infidelity of his two wives, so that as he made his way through the crowds in the streets he felt that sexual love was a monstrosity which led only to suffering and sin.

(pp. 519–20)

Much more unequivocally positive approaches to human sexuality have become normal within the Church since the Second Vatican Council, as we have seen. Read's own recent comments, on the contrary, echo his hero's here in their extremism. The very exaggeration of the rhetoric seems to suggest the urgency of the need to counter contemporary permissiveness and relativism, and this sense can only have been increased by a feeling of the Church's own partial dereliction of its traditional role.

· 11 ·

Conclusions

If the rise of the novel and the privileging of realistic fiction can be related to secularist values, various pressures may lead Catholic novelists, as we have seen, either to direct confrontation with such modes or to ways of writing that put them on the fringes of the more respected kinds of novel. 'Realism', Chesterton announces boldly in *The Return of Don Quixote,* 'is dull'. The desire to write on the supernatural may lead in the direction of fantasy and romance, and the wish to reach the widest possible audience contributes to an attraction to the popular kinds of romance fiction. Works of the latter type may in the broadest sense subscribe to conventional realism but are obviously formulaic in their sentimentality and stereotyping.

If religiously motivated writers do not produce 'fable', according to W. J. Harvey, they will tend instead towards novels of ideas, again at some distance from classic realism. Neither these works nor the popular romances are properly considered 'experimental' as such, of course, though the more self-conscious high romances may very well be. Some evidence has nevertheless emerged to support Malcolm Bradbury's contention about the specifically Catholic role in aesthetic speculation in the English novel: the characteristic Catholic versions of the strategy of the unreliable narrator, for example; the experiments with time; and occasional instances of what might be considered a quasi-liturgical attitude to language. But such examples are few and far between, and an intriguing overlap between traditional Catholic and fashionable modern concerns is much more common than conscious experimentalism. If George Mackay Brown, for example, is an 'experimentalist', his perspectives come largely from a return to the pre-novel era rather than from modernism or post-modernism.

All the attempts to link Catholic fiction with any narrow or specific formal approach have to be treated with great caution. A revealing anecdote that illustrates the naïvely realist expectations of most readers – whether Catholic or not – is the way that Cardinal Vaughan was horrified to find that the book he had taken to be a straightforward, edifying biography, the *Life of John William Walshe FSA* (1902) by Montgomery Carmichael, was actually a work of fiction.[1] Despite all that the critics have said, the majority of Catholic novels adhere to broadly realistic norms. Some well-known Catholic novelists are themselves traditionally classed as realists of the most conventional kind, such as A. J. Cronin or Compton Mackenzie in most of his work. The most famous and distinctive English Catholic novelists, Waugh and Greene, are both largely anti-modernists in their formal approach and both follow realistic conventions in their best-known 'Catholic' fiction.

If the Christian supernatural is normal human experience seen at its deepest depths, as Peter Hebblethwaite says, then even an interest in the supernatural dimension as such has no inevitable formal concomitants and does not necessarily lead into fantasy or anti-realist modes. Graham Greene has sought indeed to reverse the whole critical argument about religion and the novel:

> With the death of James, the religious sense was lost to the English novel, and with the religious sense went the sense of the importance of the human act. It was as if the world of fiction had lost a dimension; the characters of such distinguished writers as Virginia Woolf and E. M. Forster wandered like cardboard characters through a world that was paper thin. Even in the most materialistic of our novelists – Trollope – we are aware of another world against which the actions of the characters are thrown into relief.[2]

In truth, though, the matter is a complex one. It may very well be that the greatest achievements of classic realist fiction such as George Eliot's *Middlemarch* depend on a view of the world that makes human moral choice and character the absolute final arbiter. The secularized and liberalized Protestant ethos behind such fiction may in the last analysis be inimical to Catholic beliefs. Such an assurance about character and moral choice, however, may itself seem to us now to belong to a giant race before the flood. What recent radical theorists want us to accept, after all, is that 'the very idea of character', in real life as much as in fiction, is 'essentially an ideological construct'.[3]

The new critical thinking has widened the range of fictions regarded as acceptable in recent years, and this can only be to the good. But the recognition that classic realism is not the only valid mode has obviously involved questioning the whole value system on which classic realism depends. If there is a link, in other words, between an attraction to fable and caricature and a refusal to adopt the full and 'adult' morality of classic realist fiction, then we have to recognize that that morality, even when expressed in a work as great as *Middlemarch*, is not sacrosanct, but itself the product of a particular time and place and a particular ideology. It is not always easy or relevant to seek to distinguish the childish from the childlike in the refusal to accept such norms. If the form and ethics of Dickens (say) are in some senses less responsible and 'adult' than George Eliot, he is equally great as a novelist and perhaps closer to the heart of fiction. Catholic writers may themselves be influenced away from the novel's traditional privileging of character and individual morality by a variety of factors, as we have seen, including their own immaturities and 'Catholic neurosis', ideological antipathy to the British status quo and a genuine grasp of the way the gospel transcends the normal codes. But, whatever the impulses behind them, such fictions may have their own interest and value.

At the same time it still has to be repeated that there is no inevitable reason why Catholic writers should not succeed in the classic realist modes. Belloc at the end of *The Green Overcoat* (1912) writes dismissively of all his characters: 'for the whole boiling of them are only people in a story, and there is an end of them' (p. 334), but this is not because he is a Catholic and therefore unable to take human character and morality seriously, but because he is a professional writer writing a potboiler in a quasi-thriller form with metaphysical overtones. And if the attraction to such a form is itself symptomatic, it is symptomatic of Belloc and of his kind of Catholicism rather than of the religion as a whole.

The treatment of Catholicism as a system or of Catholics in their normal social lives requires no special paradoxes and, if Christianity implies a transcendence and relativizing of ordinary human moral codes, it also leads into a renewed ethics on the other side of conversion. Catholic tradition itself puts far more weight on free will and human co-operation than Lutheranism or Calvinism, and this defence of free will is at the heart of Burgess's *A Clockwork Orange* (1962), for example. Catholic novelists have not only been found to write with great moral subtlety but have sometimes quite clearly privileged character as the centre of the novel in the most traditional fashion. Josephine Mary Ward, for example, writes that

> the working out of character is the ordinary story of our lives and is the most appropriate subject of art – because it falls completely within the scope of human action. *Anna Karenina* is a supreme instance of this method of construction arising out of character.[4]

The movements of grace in her *One Poor Scruple* are themselves carefully presented as falling 'completely within the sphere of human action' and this obviously contributes to the very real achievement this novel represents.

In the last analysis the distinctive Catholic tendency may be said to be to *problematize* human moral behaviour by placing it in the context of a realm that transcends that morality and yet also makes use of it. The emphasis on grace in this tradition may be said both to diminish and to heighten the importance of the human act, depending which way you look at it, and both realist and anti-realist strategies may thus have their own appropriateness. In the best of this fiction human moral acts are characteristically portrayed as only a part of the whole story, as essentially a matter of *response*. Yet the terrifying possibilities of salvation or damnation attach an enormous weight to that response, and it is a response that characteristically takes the form of a crucial human decision, as at the end of *One Poor Scruple* or Redmon's *Emily Stone*.

There is more than one way of being a Catholic, as this book may have helped to demonstrate, and no narrow conception of 'Catholic fiction' can therefore be valid. Certain shared themes and concerns, however, have given Catholics a distinctive voice in British fiction. Developments in the international Church have led to a change in the Catholic sense of identity, and in many quarters even to its loss, and attempts to arrest and reverse this process have had only very partial success. Reflecting this, British Catholic fiction is itself at present split into 'post-Catholic' and neo-conservative modes. Interesting novels of both types are being produced, but neither model, as we have seen, is likely to be able to provide any permanent answers.

It was surely both inevitable and proper that international Catholicism should eventually come to put the emphasis more on what it had in common with other forms of Christianity than what differentiated it. Catholic fiction here bears a significant, if necessarily oblique, relationship to the life and beliefs of the British Catholic community, but it is not entirely clear what the future holds. Catholic conservatism will no doubt retain a real power and significance of its own for a long time to come, but its influence as a cultural base for Catholic fiction must surely continue to shrink. Specifically Catholic insights will presumably come in the end to be assimilated into a more general Christian witness. The hope must be that the best of those insights will retain something of their old power under a new form rather than simply being dissolved in a bland ecumenical consensus that offers no real Christian challenge to the status quo.

Notes

Introduction

1 Walpole cited by Robert Speaight, *Ronald Knox the Writer*, London, Sheed and Ward, 1966: 100; George Orwell, *Inside the Whale*, 1940: 173, cited by David Lodge, 'Catholic fiction since the Oxford Movement: its literary form and religious content', unpublished MA thesis, University College, London, 1959: 8.
2 Georg Lukács, *The Theory of the Novel*, 1920; reprint, London, Merlin, 1978: 88; Peter Faulkner, *Humanism in the English Novel*, London, Elek, 1976: 11; Ian Watt, *The Rise of the Novel*, London, Chatto & Windus, 1957.
3 Lawrence Lerner, 'Graham Greene', *The Critical Quarterly*, 5, 1963, 3: 217–31, cited Faulkner, *Humanism*: 156; W. J. Harvey, *Character and the Novel*, London, Chatto & Windus, 1965: 28.
4 Peter Brook, *Reading for the Plot*, Oxford, Clarendon Press, 1984: 5–6; David Lodge, 'The human nature of narrative', *Write On: Occasional Essays 1965–1985*, London, Penguin, 1988: 198–9.
5 Harvey: 27.
6 For brief guides see Raman Selden, *Contemporary Literary Theory*, Brighton, Harvester, 1983; Shlomith Rimmon-Kenan, *Narrative Fictions: Contemporary Poetics*, London, Methuen, 1983; Patricia Waugh, *Metafiction*, London, Methuen, 1984.
7 Albert J. Menendez, *The Catholic Novel, An Annotated Bibliography*, New York and London, Garland, 1988.
8 'Educating Anthea: classic fiction for the Filofax', *Sunday Times*, Books, 9 July 1989: G9.
9 Donat O'Donnell (Conor Cruise O'Brien), *Maria Cross: Imaginative Patterns in a Group of Modern Catholic Writers*, London, Chatto & Windus, 1953; Albert Sonnenfeld, *Crossroads: Essays on the Catholic Novelists*, York, South Carolina, French Literature Publications, 1982; Martin Green, *Essays on Literature and Religion: Yeats's Blessings on von Hügel*, London, Longman, 1967. For a more general definition see Sister Mariella

Garbley, 'The Novel', *The Catholic Bookman's Guide*, Sister M. Regis (ed.), New York, Hawthorn Books, 1962: 411.
10 For a full survey of the evidence see John Lester, *Conrad and Religion*, London, Macmillan, 1988.
11 In Robert Nowell (ed.), *Why I Am Still a Catholic*, London, Fount, 1983: 62.
12 *Brideshead Revisited*, 1945; reprint, London, Chapman & Hall, 1949: 80; J. C. H. Aveling, *The Handle and the Axe: The Catholic Recusants in England from Reformation to Emancipation*, London, Blond & Briggs, 1976: 19; John Coventry, 'Roman Catholicism', Rupert Davies (ed.), *The Testing of the Churches, 1932–1982: A Symposium*, London, Epworth Press, 1982: 30.
13 *The Lost Traveller*, part 3, chapter 3, *Frost in May*, vol. I, reprint, London, Fontana, 1982: 326; *Brideshead Revisited*: 195.
14 John Bossy, *The English Catholic Community, 1570–1850*, London, Darton, Longman & Todd, 1975.
15 Adrian Hastings, *A History of English Christianity, 1920–1985*, London, Collins, 1986: 227.
16 Cited Menendez, Introduction, *Catholic Novel*: x.
17 Malcolm Bradbury, *Possibilities: Essays on the State of the Novel*, Oxford, Oxford University Press, 1973: 247; Bryan Appleyard, 'Aspects of Ackroyd', *Sunday Times Magazine*, 9 April 1989: 53.

Chapter 1

1 *One Poor Scruple*, London, Longmans, Green, 1899: 100.
2 David Lodge, 'An earlier Foxglove Saga: the first English Catholic novel?' *Dublin Review*, 486, 1960–61: 365–71; Roger Manvell, *Elizabeth Inchbald*, Lanham, Maryland, University Press of America, 1988.
3 Edward Norman, *Roman Catholicism in England from the Elizabethan Settlement to the Second Vatican Council*, Oxford, Oxford University Press, 1985: 41.
4 P. 369, cited Lodge, 'Catholic Fiction': 27.
5 Edward Norman, *The English Catholic Church in the Nineteenth Century*, Oxford, Clarendon Press, 1984: 29.
6 See Irene Bostrom, 'The novel and Catholic emancipation', *Studies in Romanticism*, II, 1962: 155–76.
7 For a useful account see Kevin L. Morris, *The Image of the Middle Ages in Romantic and Victorian Literature*, London, Croom Helm, 1984: 112–17.
8 For a good account see Norman, *The English Catholic Church in the Nineteenth Century*.
9 David Matthew, *Catholicism in England*, London, Eyre & Spottiswood, 1948: 200.
10 *Poverty and the Baronet's Family*, cited Robert Lee Wolff, *Gains and Losses: Novels of Faith and Doubt in Victorian England*, London, John Murray, 1977: 30.
11 This is true at the end of Newman's *Loss and Gain*, for example.
12 For a full account see Joseph Ellis Baker, *The Novel and the Oxford Movement*, Princeton Studies in English, no. 8, 1932, and Raymond Chapman, *Faith and Revolt: Studies in the Literary Influence of the Oxford Movement*, London, Weidenfeld & Nicolson, 1970.
13 See *The Genius of John Henry Newman: Selections from his Writings*, Ian Ker (ed.), Oxford, Clarendon Press, 1990.
14 See Chapman: 121–9, for example. For a good account see 'Newman as novelist: *Loss and Gain*' by the editor in T. R. Wright (ed.), *John Henry Newman, A Man for Our Time?*, Newcastle, Grevatt, 1983: 7–15.
15 P. 262. On the question of anachronism see Chapman: 149 and Andrew Sanders, *The*

Notes

    Victorian Historical Novel, 1840–1880, London, Macmillan, 'and New York, St Martin's Press, 1979: 137.
16 E. C. Agnew, *Rome and the Abbey*, 1849: 25, cited Margaret M. Maison, *The Victorian Vision: Studies in the Religious Novel*, New York, Sheed & Ward, 1961: 149.
17 Tony Tanner, *Adultery in the Novel: Contract and Transgression*, Baltimore, Johns Hopkins University Press, 1979.
18 Bernard Bergonzi, Introduction, *One Poor Scruple*, Encore Series reprint, Padstow, Cornwall, Tabb House, 1985: x.
19 A good brief account of these and the following trends may be found in the introduction to Ian Fletcher's *British Poetry and Prose 1870–1905*, Oxford, Oxford University Press, 1987.
20 Richard Shannon, *The Crisis of Imperialism, 1865–1915*, London, Hart-Davis MacGibbon, 1974: 217; see too Elizabeth K. Helsinger, Robin Lauterbach Sheets and William Veeder, *The Woman Question: Society and Literature in Britain and America, 1837–1883*, 3 vols., Chicago, University of Chicago Press, 1989.
21 For comments, see Fletcher, Introduction, *British Poetry and Prose 1870–1905*.
22 R. M. Scheider, 'Loss and gain? The theme of conversion in late Victorian fiction', *Victorian Studies*, IX, 1965: 29–44.
23 Norman, *Nineteenth Century*: 333. For Mallock's Father Stanley see, for example, *The Old Order Changes* (1886).

Chapter 2

1 *The Condition of England* (1909), cited John Batchelor, *The Edwardian Novelists*, London, Duckworth, 1982: 22.
2 *Return to Yesterday*, cited Robert Green, *Ford Maddox Ford: Prose and Politics*, Cambridge, Cambridge University Press, 1981: 41.
3 David Matthew, *Catholicism in England*: 238.
4 For the whole phenomenon, with accounts of *The Garden of Allah* and *Simon Called Peter* see Claude Cockburn, *Bestseller, The Books that Everyone Read, 1900–1939*, London, Sidgwick & Jackson, 1972.
5 Cited Lodge, 'Catholic fiction': 479.
6 Cyril Martindale, *The Life of Monsignor Robert Hugh Benson*, London, Longman, 1916, II: 364–5.
7 *Desire and Pursuit*: 20, cited Miriam Benkovitz, *Frederick Rolfe, Baron Corvo: A Biography*, London, Hamish Hamilton, 1977: 185.
8 Lodge 'Rolfe's Bestiary', in Cecil Woolf and Brocard Sewell (eds) *New Quests for Corvo*, London, Icon Books, 1965: 74; Benkovitz: 79.
9 For good accounts see: A. N. Wilson, *Hilaire Belloc*, London, Hamish Hamilton, 1984; John P. McCarthy, *Hilaire Belloc, Edwardian Radical*, Indianapolis, Liberty Press, 1978; Alzina Stone Dale, *The Outline of Sanity: A Life of G. K. Chesterton*, Grand Rapids, Eerdmans, 1982; Jay P. Corrin, *G. K. Chesterton and Hilaire Belloc: The Battle Against Modernity*, London, Ohio University Press, 1981; Bernard Bergonzi, 'Chesterton and/or Belloc', *Critical Quarterly*, I, 1959: 64–71.
10 Cited and discussed by Gene Kellogg, *The Vital Tradition: The Catholic Novel in an Age of Convergence*, Chicago, Loyola University Press, 1970: 97.
11 For a representative selection see D. J. Conlon, *G. K. Chesterton, A Half-Century of Views*, Oxford, Oxford University Press, 1987. For a full study of the fiction see Ian Boyd, *The Novels of G. K. Chesterton*, London, Elek, 1975.
12 'A defence of penny dreadfuls', *The Defendent*, 1901, cited John D. Coates, *Chesterton and the Edwardian Cultural Crisis*, Hull, University of Hull Press, 1984: 160.

13 Corrin: 171.
14 The best account is David Lodge's 'Maurice Baring, novelist, a reappraisal', *Dublin Review*, 485, 1960: 262–70.
15 Cited Andro Linklater, *Compton Mackenzie: A Life*, London, Chatto & Windus, 1987: 133.
16 Anthony Burgess, 'Warring Fictions', *Observer*, 14 October 1990: 63; Malcolm Bradbury, *Possibilities*: 137; J. K. L. Walker, 'Mad about writing', *Times Literary Supplement*, 19 December 1986: 1427.
17 Hastings, *English Christianity*: 232.
18 'Come inside', John O'Brien (ed.) *The Road to Damascus: The Spiritual Pilgrimage of Fifteen Converts to Catholicism*, New York, Doubleday, 1949: 14–15, cited Lodge, 'Catholic fiction': 594.
19 Hastings, *English Christianity*: 279, 290, 487.
20 Norman, *Roman Catholicism in England from the Elizabethan Settlement to the Second Vatican Council*: 109.
21 See, for example, Sebastian Moore, *God is a New Language*, London, Darton, Longman & Todd, 1967, chapters 1 and 2, and Martin Green, *Yeats's Blessings*, especially 'The Catholic as psychological type'.
22 'Absolute and Abitofhell', cited Speaight, *Ronald Knox*: 47.
23 Cited Valentine Cunningham, *British Writers of the Thirties*, Oxford, Oxford University Press, 1988: 23.
24 Bernard Bergonzi, *Reading the Thirties: Texts and Contexts*, London, Macmillan, 1978: 64.
25 *The Times*, 15 April, 1966, cited Gene D. Phillips, *Evelyn Waugh's Officers, Gentlemen and Rogues*, Chicago, Nelson-Hall, 1975: 155.
26 See Richard Johnstone, *The Will to Believe: Novelists of the 1930s*, Oxford, Oxford University Press, 1982: 135.
27 *Write On*: 33.

Chapter 3

1 Hastings, *English Christianity*: 444.
2 Alistair Davies and Peter Sander, 'Literature, politics and society', in Alan Sinfield (ed.), *Society and Literature, 1945–1970*, London, Methuen, 1983: 17.
3 Cited Randall Stevenson, *The British Novel Since the Thirties, An Introduction*, London, Batsford, 1986: 169.
4 *Letters*, C. Tolkien (ed.), London, Allen & Unwin, 1981: 172, cited Shelagh Price, 'Sources, Analogues, Characterization and Use of Language in the Fictional Works of J. R. R. Tolkien', Reading English Department Long Essay, 1989.
5 Cited Ruth Whittaker, *The Faith and Fiction of Muriel Spark*, London, Macmillan, 1982: 59.
6 *Memento Mori*, 1959: 210; 'The house of fiction', *Partisan Review*, Spring, 1963: 80: both quoted Peter Kemp, *Muriel Spark, Novelists and their World*, London, Elek, 1974: 8; Patrick Parrinder, 'Muriel Spark and her critics', *Critical Quarterly*, 25, 1983: 23–32.
7 *Write On*: 31.
8 Anthony Archer, *The Two Catholic Churches: A Study in Oppression*, London, SCM Press, 1986: 127–30; Hastings: 562–3.
9 *Write On*: 31.
10 Harry Richie, *Success Stories: Literature and the Media in England, 1950–1959*, London, Faber: 1988.

Notes

11 *Orkney Tapestry*, 1973 reprint: 20, cited Alan Bold, *George Mackay Brown*, Edinburgh, Olive & Boyd, 1978: 10.
12 *The History of Scottish Literature*, vol. 4, Cairns Craig (ed.), Aberdeen, University Press, 1987: 394, 125.
13 *English Christianity*: 525.
14 *Lumen Gentium* 8. See, e.g., Leonardo Boff, *Church, Charism and Power*, London, SCM Press, 1985: 75.
15 Preface to *Sword of Honour*, 1965: 9.
16 Charles Davis, *A Question of Conscience*, London, Hodder & Stoughton, 1967; Gregory Baum, *The Credibility of the Church Today: A Reply to Charles Davis*, New York, Herder & Herder, 1968.
17 See especially Karl Rahner, *Theological Investigations*, vol. 5, Baltimore, Helicon, and London, Darton, Longman & Todd, 1966.
18 Karl Rahner, 'The theological position of Christians in the modern world', *Christian Commitment*, London, Sheed & Ward, 1963; Anthony Archer, *The Two Catholic Churches*; Eamonn Bredin, *Disturbing the Peace*, Dublin, Columba Press, 1985: 33. See too Michael P. Hornsby-Smith, *Roman Catholics in England: Studies in Social Structure since the Second World War*, Cambridge, Cambridge University Press, 1987.
19 Bernard Bergonzi, 'The decline and fall of the Catholic novel', in *The Myth of Modernism and Twentieth Century Literature*, Hassocks, Sussex, Harvester, 1986; David Lodge, 'The Catholic Church and cultural life', *Write On*: 37.

Chapter 4

1 The translation that most aptly makes my point is the New International Version. (Elsewhere I have preferred the Jerusalem Bible.) Fergus Kerr, paraphrasing Marcuse, 'Ataraxy and Utopia', *New Blackfriars*, 50, 1969: 312, cited by Simon Tugwell, *Did You Receive the Spirit*, London, Darton, Longman & Todd, 1972: 46.
2 *Epistle to Diognetus*, cited Jaroslav Pelikan, *Jesus Through the Centuries*, London and New Haven, Yale University Press, 1985: 50.
3 *Beatrice: or, The Unknown Relatives* (1852), cited Maison: 173.
4 Carol M. Dix, *Anthony Burgess*, London, Longman for the British Council, 1971: 4.
5 Graham Greene, *The Lawless Roads*, 1939; reprint London, Heinemann & Bodley Head, 1978: 221.
6 See John P. McCarthy, *Hilaire Belloc*: 320–1; A. N. Wilson, *Hilaire Belloc*: 226.
7 *Urgent Copy: Literary Studies*, New York, Norton, 1968: 271.
8 *Exiles and Emigrés: Studies in Modern Literature*, London, Chatto & Windus, 1970.
9 Edward Norman, *Roman Catholicism*: 2. Adrian Hastings argues in similar fashion that Roman Catholicism here has always been more English than Protestants have recognized, *English Christianity*: 667.
10 T. W. Burke, 'Father Burke's answer to Froude', n.p., P. J. Kennedy, n.d., cited Archer: 49.
11 See Bergonzi, 'Decline and fall of the Catholic novel'.
12 Isobel Murray, 'Novelists of the Renaissance', in Cairns Craig (ed.), *The History of Scottish Literature*, vol. 4: 114.
13 Prologue to *The Storm*, cited Bold, *George Mackay Brown*: 11; *Spell for Green Corn*: 90–1, cited Bold: 72.

Chapter 5

1 See, for example, the photo essays by Anthony Burgess, 'The smart sect' and Jonathan Glancey, 'Jiggery popery' in *The Tatler*, vol. 282, 6 June, 1987.
2 Cited A. N. Wilson, *Belloc*: 243.
3 Hans Kung, *The Church*, translated R. and R. Ockenden, Tunbridge Wells, Burns & Oates, 1967: 25.
4 *Urgent Copy*: 30.
5 Ian Littlewood, *The Novels of Evelyn Waugh*, Oxford, Blackwell, 1983: 42.
6 *Urgent Copy*: 27.
7 Marlowe, cited Lodge, *The Picturegoers*: 150; A. J. A. Symons, cited Kevin L. Morris, *Image of the Middle Ages*: 132.
8 Benkovitz: 105, 102.
9 'Come inside', O'Brien (ed.), *Road to Damascus*: 18–20, cited Phillips, *Officers and Gentlemen*: 53.
10 Wilson, *Belloc*: 243.
11 C. S. Lewis, 'The inner ring', 1944, in *Transposition and other Addresses*, London, Geoffrey Bles, 1949.
12 'My Joyce', *Write On*: 60; 'Memories of a Catholic childhood', *Write On*: 31.
13 Cited Whittaker, *Faith and Fiction*, p. 50.
14 *Sunday Times*, 13 March 1988: G9.
15 Whittaker, *Faith and Fiction*: 15.
16 'Getting her to a nunnery', *Times Literary Supplement*, 16–22 October 1987: 1136.

Chapter 6

1 Christian Duquoc, *Provisional Churches*, London, SCM Press, 1987: 46; Leonardo Boff, *Church, Charism and Power*, London, SCM Press, 1985: 84.
2 *Letters from Baron Friedrich von Hügel to a Niece*, 1928; reprint, London, Dent, 1950: 166.
3 For a critique see Richard P. McBrien, *Do We Need the Church?*, New York, Harper & Row, 1969: chapter 4.
4 P.22, cited Paul Pickering, 'Gilt-ridden faith', *Sunday Times Books*, 10 September 1989: G6.
5 Cited Julian Moynihan, 'Waiting for God in Inglenook', *New York Review of Books*, 8 December 1988: 51.
6 Robert Speaight, *Belloc*: 383.
7 Speaight, *Belloc*: 378.
8 *Roman Catholicism: The Search for Relevance*, Oxford, Blackwell, 1980: 116.
9 Ward first discusses the idea in his famous essay 'The rigidity of Rome' in *Nineteenth Century*, 38, November 1895: 786–804.
10 Part II, chapters 22 and 33: see Sanders, *Victorian Historical Novel*: 137.
11 Littlewood: 149.
12 Benson is in fact reviving the title applied to Pope Innocent III at the Lateran Council of 1215.
13 *Why Do I Write* (1942), cited Lodge 'Catholic fiction': 653.
14 *The Power and the Wisdom*, Milwaukee, Bruce, 1965: 183.
15 Kung, *The Church*: 4.
16 *Lumen Gentium*, cited Avery Dulles, *The Catholicity of the Church*, Oxford, Clarendon Press, 1985: 103.
17 Leonardo Boff, *Church, Charism and Power*: 146.

Notes

18 See McSweeney, *Roman Catholicism*, for a good brief account.
19 Edward Schillebeeckx, *Interim Report on the Books Jesus & Christ*, London, SCM Press, 1980: 103.
20 Kung, *The Church*: 14.
21 See Boff, *Church, Charism and Power*, chapter 9, and for Eastern Europe Walter Schwarz, 'Tremors in the Church triumphant', *Guardian*, 2 June 1990: 23. For a contrary view of south and central American developments see Piers Paul Read, 'Taking Heaven by storm', *The Independent Magazine*, 17 March 1990: 22–9.

Chapter 7

1 McSweeney, *Roman Catholicism*: 54.
2 Interview, Alfred Kazin (ed.), *Writers at Work: The Paris Review Interviews*, 3rd Series, New York, Viking, 1967: 103–14, cited Phillips, *Officers and Gentlemen*: 78.
3 Craigie, *Robert Orange*: 115.
4 Cited Andro Linklater, *Compton Mackenzie, A Life*: 227.
5 *North Wind* (1944): 70, cited David Joseph Dooley, *Compton Mackenzie*, New York, Twayne, 1974: 90.
6 Letter to T. R. Fyvel, 15 April 1949, Sonia Orwell and Ian Angus (eds), in *Collected Essays, Journalism and Letters*, vol. 4, London, Secker & Warburg, 1968: 496.
7 Eagleton, 'From Swiss Cottage to the Sandinistas', *Times Literary Supplement*, 16–22 September 1988: 1033; Burgess, *Urgent Copy*: 14.
8 Cited Richard Johnstone, *The Will to Believe: Novelists of the 1930s*, Oxford, Oxford University Press, 1982: 68.
9 Emmanuel Mounier (1905–51) is another figure with a major role here. See John Cruikshank (ed.), *French Literature and its Background*, vol. 6: *The Late Nineteenth Century*, London, Oxford University Press, 1969: 139.
10 For a carefully nuanced account see Dietrich Weiderkehr, chapters 6 and 7, *Belief in Redemption*, translated J. Moiser, London, SPCK, 1976.
11 See W. M. Chace, 'Spies and God's spies: Greene's espionage fiction', in Jeffrey Meyers (ed.), *Graham Greene: A Revaluation*, London, Macmillan, 1989: 156–80.

Chapter 8

1 Interview with Michael Barber, *Book Choice*, January 1982, No.13: 18.
2 Ian Gregor and Brian Nicholas, 'Grace and morality', *The Novel and the Story*, London, Faber, 1962: 192–206.
3 C. N. Manlove, *Modern Fantasy: Five Studies*, Cambridge, Cambridge University Press, 1975: 1.
4 Cristopher Nash, *World Games: The Tradition of Anti-Realist Revolt*, London, Methuen, 1988: 11.
5 Cited Manlove: 167.
6 Peter Hebblethwaite, 'How Catholic is the Catholic Novel?' *Times Literary Supplement*, 27 July 1967: 678–9.
7 Malcolm Scott, *The Struggle for the Soul of the French Novel: French Catholic and Realist Novelists, 1850–1970*, London, Macmillan, 1990.
8 *Religion and the Decline of Magic*, London, Weidenfeld & Nicolson, 1971: 492.
9 Interview, 1969, Geoffrey Aggeler, *Anthony Burgess: The Artist as Novelist*, University, Alabama, University of Alabama Press, 1979: 28.
10 See Francis Russell Hart, *The Scottish Novel: A Critical Survey*, London, John Murray,

1978: 305, and Richard C. Kane, *Iris Murdoch, Muriel Spark and John Fowles: Didactic Demons in Modern Fiction*, Rutherford, Madison, Teaneck, Fairleigh Dickinson University Press and London, Associated University Presses, 1988: 65–77.

11 P.169, cited Valerie Shaw, 'Muriel Spark', *The History of Scottish Literature*, 4: p. 284.
12 John Knox, *The Church and the Reality of Christ*: 170, cited F. R. Barry, *The Atonement*, London, Hodder & Stoughton, 1968: 82.
13 See, for example, Leopold Damrosch, *God's Plot and Man's Stories: Studies in the Fictional Imagination from Milton to Fielding*, Chicago, University of Chicago Press, 1985.
14 David Lodge, 'The uses and abuses of omniscience', *The Novelist at the Crossroads*, London, Routledge & Kegan Paul, 1971: 119.
15 'Tree and leaf': 71–2, cited by Thomas Egan, 'Tolkien and Chesterton: some analogies', *Mythlore*, 43, autumn, 1985: 30.
16 For Chesterton's comments see, for example, the closing pages of the *Autobiography*, and Coates, *Chesterton and the Edwardian Cultural Crisis*: 145; Ayscough, 'Kings' servants', cited Leo Kettle, 'John Ayscough, Novelist', *Catholic World*, 111, 1920: 165.
17 'P. D. James: the matron saint of murderers', *Sunday Times*, 1 October 1989, Books: G9.
18 Robert Parker, 'Down these mean streets', *Sunday Times Magazine*, 1 October 1989: 69.
19 'The eye of Apollo', *The Innocence of Father Brown*, in *The Father Brown Stories*, London, Cassell, 1947: 130, cited W. W. Robson, 'Father Brown and others', in John Sullivan (ed.), *G. K. Chesterton: A Centenary Appraisal*, London, Elek, 1974: 62. See too prologue and epilogue, *The Secret of Father Brown*.
20 On time in fiction see Wesley A. Kort, chapter 3, 'Plot and process', *Narrative Elements and Religious Meanings*, Philadelphia, Fortress Press, 1975 and *Modern Fiction and Human Time: A Study in Narrative and Belief*, Tampa, Florida: University of South Florida Press, 1985; Watt, *Rise of Novel*: 21.
21 Frank Kermode, *The Sense of an Ending*, New York, Oxford University Press, 1967.
22 Stevenson, *British Novel since the Thirties*: 98.
23 Lodge, 'The uses and abuses of omniscience': 138–44.
24 Brian Wicker, *The Story-Shaped World*, London, Athlone Press, 1975; T. R. Wright, chapter 3, *Theology and Literature*, Oxford, Blackwell, 1988.

Chapter 9

1 Christopher Walker, 'Tales of exile in miniature', review of André Dubus, *Selected Stories*, London, Picador, 1990, *Observer Review*, 18 March 1990: 62.
2 'Death in Hollywood', *Life*, 29 September 1947: 73–84, cited D. Phillips, *Officers and Gentlemen*: 82.
3 Richard Griffiths, *Reactionary Revolution*: 152–3; Jennifer Birkett, 'The ideology of the French Catholic revival', *New Blackfriars*, 58, 1977: 496–505.
4 'Biathanatos', cited Evelyn Hardy, *Donne, A Spirit in Conflict*, London: Constable, 1942: 1.
5 (1899): 371, cited Bergonzi, Introduction, reprint of *One Poor Sample*: xi.
6 This is an incident from *In the Time of Greenbloom*, 1956: 357, cited Alfred Borrello, *Gabriel Fielding*, New York, Twayne, 1974: 65.
7 Geoffrey Tillotson (ed.), *Newman: Prose and Poetry*, London, Hart Davis, 1957: 758.
8 'Felix culpa?', *Commonweal*, 16 July 1948: 322–5, cited Phillips, *Officers and Gentlemen*: 45.
9 Stevenson, *British Novel Since the Thirties*: 185.

10 'The Portabello Road', *Collected Stories*, I: 11, cited Peter Kemp, *Muriel Spark*: 13.
11 Cited Francis Russell Hart, *The Scottish Novel*: 303.
12 Nowell (ed.), *Why I Am Still a Catholic*: 71.
13 'The queer feet', *Innocence of Father Brown*, in *Father Brown Stories*, 1947: 50.
14 *Saints, Sinners and Comedians*, Tunbridge Wells, Burns & Oates, 1984: 88–9; Ian Fletcher, *W. B. Yeats and his Contemporaries*, Brighton, Harvester, 1987: 290.
15 'English Catholic literature', 1854–8, *The Idea of a University*, 1852, 1859 reprint, London, Longman, 1901: 316.
16 Orwell, cited Faulkner, *Humanism in the Novel*: 160; Martin Greene, *Yeats's Blessings on von Hügel*: 116, 74.
17 Bernevel-sur-Mer, 6 June 1897, Rupert Hart-Davis (ed.), in *The Letters of Oscar Wilde*, London, Hart-Davis, 1960: 600.
18 McKenzie, *Power and Wisdom*: 148.
19 'Frederick Rolfe: Edwardian inferno', *Collected Essays*, London, Bodley Head, 1969: 74, cited Whittaker, *Faith and Fiction of Muriel Spark*: 5.

Chapter 10

1 McKenzie, *Power and Wisdom*: 118.
2 Cited Tanner, *Adultery*: 88–9.
3 Michel Foucault, *The History of Sexuality, vol.1, An Introduction*, 1976, translated Robert Hirley, London, Allen Lane, 1979: 19–23.
4 A. E. Dyson, 'Evelyn Waugh and the mysteriously disappearing hero', *Critical Quarterly*, 2, 1960: 72–9, cited Faulkner, *Humanism*: 160.
5 Julia Morris makes this point well in 'The Catholic priest in twentieth-century literature', Reading English Department Long Essay, 1989.
6 See Marina Warner, *Alone of All Her Sex*, London, Weidenfeld & Nicolson, 1976.
7 Michèle Roberts in Olga Kenyon (ed.), *Women Writers Talk*, Oxford, Lennard, 1989: 154; the Burgess passage below is cited by Aggeler: 63; see too Uta Ranke-Heinemann, *Eunuchs for Heaven: The Catholic Church and Sexuality*, London, Deutsch, 1990.
8 *Books and Bookmen*, January 1982: 18.

Chapter 11

1 J. G. Snead-Cox, *The Life of Cardinal Vaughan*, II: 407, cited Lodge, 'Catholic fiction': 396.
2 'Henry James', *Collected Essays*: 91, cited John Spurling, *Graham Greene*, London, Methuen, 1983.
3 Lennard J. Davis, *Resisting Novels: Ideology and Fiction*, New York and London, Methuen, 1987: 120.
4 Maisie Ward, *The Wilfred Wards and the Transition*, London, Sheed & Ward, 1934: 233.

Selected bibliography

(Where writers have used a *nom de plume* I have classified them either by this or real name according to present usage.)

Novels by British Catholic and ex-Catholic writers

Agnew, E. C. (1849). *Rome and the Abbey*. London, Dolman.
Almedingen, E. M. (1960). *The Little Stairway*. London, Hutchinson.
Ayscough, John (Monsignor Bickerstaffe-Drew) (1908). *Dromina*. Bristol, Arrowsmith.
   (1909). *San Celestino*, London, Smith, Elder.
Bainbridge, Beryl (1968). *Another Part of the Wood*. Reprint, London, Duckworth, 1979.
   (1975). *Sweet William*. London, Duckworth.
   (1976). *A Quiet Life*. London, Duckworth.
Baring, Maurice (1921). *Passing By*. London, Secker.
   (1922). *Overlooked*. Reprint, *Passing By* and *Overlooked*, London, Heinemann, 1929.
   (1924). *C*. Reprint, London, Heinemann, 1926.
   (1925). *Cat's Cradle*. London, Heinemann.
   (1926). *Daphne Adeadne*. Reprint, London, Heinemann, 1927.
   (1929). *The Coat Without Seam*. London, Heinemann.
Barry, William (1887). *The New Antigone*, 3 vols. London, Macmillan.
   (1898). *The Two Standards*. London, T. F. Unwin.
   (1900). *Arden Massiter*. London, T. F. Unwin.
Belloc, Hilaire (1904). *Emmanual Burden*. London, Methuen.
   (1908). *Mr Clutterbuck's Election*. London, Everleigh Nash.
   (1912). *The Green Overcoat*. Bristol, Arrowsmith.
Benson, Robert Hugh (1906). *The Sentimentalists*. London, Pitman.
   (1907). *Lord of the World*. London, Burns & Oates, 1944.
   (1908). *The Conventionalists*. London, Burns & Oates.
   (1909). *The Necromancers*. London, Hutchinson.

Selected bibliography

(1910). *A Winnowing*. London, Hutchinson.
(1911). *The Dawn of All*. London, Hutchinson.
(1912). *Come Rack, Come Rope*. London, Hutchinson.
(1913). *An Average Man*. London, Hutchinson.
(1914). *Initiation*. London, Hutchinson.
(1915). *Loneliness*. London, Hutchinson.
Bergonzi, Bernard (1981). *The Roman Persuasion, A Novel*. London, Weidenfeld & Nicolson.
Best[e], Henry Digby (1845). *Poverty and the Baronet's Family, A Catholic Novel*. London, T. Jones.
Beste, J. Richard (1856). *Modern Society in Rome*. London, Hurst & Blackett.
Billington, Rachel (1982). *Occasion of Sin*. Reprint, Harmondsworth, Penguin, 1983.
Bishop, C. Mary (1878). *Elizabeth Eden*. London, Sampson Low, Marston, Searle & Rivington.
Blundell, Mary Elizabeth [M. E. Francis] (1926). *Tyler's Lass*. London, Sands & Co.
Braine, John (1957). *Room at the Top*. Reprint, Harmondsworth, Penguin, 1987.
   (1964). *The Jealous God*. London, Eyre & Spottiswood.
   (1975). *The Pious Agent*. London, Eyre & Spottiswood.
Brooke-Rose, Christine (1960). *The Dear Deceit*. London, Secker & Warburg.
Brown, George Mackay (1972). *Greenvoe*. Reprint, London, Hogarth Press, 1975.
   (1973). *Magnus*. Reprint, London, Hogarth Press, 1974.
Burgess, Anthony (1949). *A Vision of Battlements*. First published 1961; New York, Norton, 1965.
   (1961). *The Worm and the Ring*. London, Heinemann.
   (1962). *The Wanting Seed*. London, Heinemann.
   (1962). *A Clockwork Orange*. London, Heinemann.
   (1966). *Tremor of Intent*. London, Heinemann.
   (1980). *Earthly Powers*. London, Hutchinson.
Caddell, Cecilia M. (1858). *Home and the Homeless*. London, T. C. Newby.
Carmichael, Montgomery [Daniel Maudsley] (1902). *The Life of John William Walsh FSA*. London, John Murray.
Carson, Michael (1988). *Sucking Sherbet Lemons*. London, Gollancz.
Chesterton, G. K. (1908). *The Man Who Was Thursday*. Bristol, Arrowsmith and London, Simpkin, Marshall.
   (1909). *The Ball and the Cross*. London, Wells Gardner.
   (1911–35). *The Father Brown Stories*. Reprint, London, Cassell, 1947.
   (1912). *Manalive*. London, Nelson.
   (1927). *The Return of Don Quixote*. London, Chatto & Windus.
Cornwell, John (1969). *The Spoiled Priest*. London: Longman.
Craigie, Pearl (John Oliver Hobbes) (1897). *The School for Saints*. London, T. F. Unwin.
   (1900). *Robert Orange*. London, T. F. Unwin.
   (1906). *The Dream and the Business*. London, Dent.
Cronin, A. J. (1942). *The Keys of the Kingdom*. Reprint, London, Gollancz, 1981.
Delafield [de la Pasture], E. M. (1919). *Consequences*. London, Hodder & Stoughton.
   (1930). *Turn Back the Leaves*. Reprint, London, Chariot Books, 1952.
Dering, Edward (1875). *Sherborne*. London, Art & Book Co.
   (1894). *The Ban of Mablethorpe*. London, Art & Book Co.
Dinnis, Enid (1927). *The Road to Somewhere*. London, Sands.
Donnolly, Gabrielle (1987). *Holy Mother*. London, Gollancz.
Ellis, Alice Thomas (1977). *The Sin Eater*. Reprint, Harmondsworth, Penguin, 1986.
   (1980). *The Birds of the Air*. Reprint, Harmondsworth, Penguin, 1983.

    (1982). *The Twenty-seventh Kingdom*. Reprint, Harmondsworth, Penguin, 1982.
    (1983). *The Other Side of the Fire*. Reprint, Harmondsworth, Penguin, 1988.
    (1985). *Unexplained Laughter*. Reprint, Harmondsworth, Penguin, 1986.
    (1987). *The Clothes and the Wardrobe*. London, Duckworth.
Fielding, Gabriel [Alan Barnsley] (1956). *In the Time of Greenbloom*. London, Hutchinson.
    (1962). *The Birthday King*. London, Hutchinson.
    (1966). *Gentlemen in their Season*. London, Hutchinson.
Firbank, Ronald (1919). *Valmouth*. Reprint, with following titles, in 1 vol., Harmondsworth, Penguin, 1961.
    (1924). *Prancing Nigger*. See *Valmouth*.
    (1926). *Concerning the Eccentricities of Cardinal Pirelli*. See *Valmouth*.
Ford, Ford Madox. (1906–8). *The Fifth Queen*. Reprint in *The Bodley Head Head Ford Madox Ford*. 5 vols., London, Bodley Head, 1962–71.
    (1908). *Mr Apollo, A Just Possible Story*. London, Methuen.
    (1915). *The Good Soldier*. See *The Fifth Queen*.
    (1924–8). *Parade's End* 4 vols. See *The Fifth Queen*.
Frankeau, Pamela (1957). *The Bridge*. London, Heinemann.
Fullerton, Lady Georgiana (1853). *Ladybird*. London, Moxon.
    (1865). *Constance Sherwood*. London, Moxon.
    (1869). *Mrs Gerald's Niece*. London, Bentley.
Gibbs, Sir Phillip (1961). *The Age of Reason*. London, Hutchinson.
Godden, Rumer (1969). *In This House of Brede*. London, Macmillan.
    (1979). *Five For Sorrow, Ten for Joy*, London, Macmillan.
Gray, John (1932). *Park*. Reprint, with an introduction by Bernard Bergonzi, Aylesford, St Albert's Press, 1966.
Greene, Graham (1938). *Brighton Rock*. London, Heinemann.
    (1940). *The Power and the Glory*. Reprint, London, Bodley Head, 1971.
    (1948). *The Heart of the Matter*. Reprint, London, Reprint Society, 1950.
    (1951). *The End of the Affair*. Reprint, Harmondsworth, Penguin, 1971.
    (1957). *The Potting Shed*. (play) New York, Viking.
    (1961). *A Burnt-out Case*. London, Heinemann.
    (1966). *The Comedians*. London, Bodley Head.
    (1973). *The Honorary Consul*. Reprint, London, Book Club Associates.
    (1982). *Monsignor Quixote*. London, Bodley Head.
Hall, Radclyffe (1928). *The Well of Loneliness*. Reprint, London, Falcon Books, 1949.
Harland, Henry (1900). *The Cardinal's Snuff Box*. London and New York, J. Lane.
Inchbald, Elizabeth (1791). *A Simple Story*. J. M. S. Tomkins (ed.), Oxford, Oxford University Press, 1967.
Jerrold, Douglas (1930). *Storm over Europe*. London, Ernest Benn.
Kaye-Smith, Sheila (1934). *Gallybird*. London, Cassell.
Kelly, Mary (1961). *The Spoilt Kill*. London, Joseph.
King, Pauline (1985). *The Snares of the Enemy*. London, Collins.
Lodge, David (1960). *The Picturegoers*. Reprint, London, Panther, 1970.
    (1965). *The British Museum Is Falling Down*. Reprint, Harmondsworth, Penguin, 1983.
    (1980). *How Far Can You Go?* Reprint, Harmondsworth, Penguin, 1982.
McCabe, William (1856). *Adelaide, Queen of Italy*. London, Dolman.
MacColla, Fionn [T. D. Macdonald] (1932). *The Albannach*. Reprints Edinburgh, Reprographia, 1971.
    (1945). *And the Cock Crew*. Reprint, London, Souvenir Press, 1977.

Selected bibliography

Mackenzie, Compton (1914). *Sinister Street*. 3 vols. Reprint, London, Martin Secker, 1916.
   (1922). *The Altar Steps*. London, Cassell.
   (1923). *The Parson's Progress*. London, Cassell.
   (1924). *The Heavenly Ladder*. London, Cassell.
   (1937). *The East Wind of Love*. Reprint, London, Chatto & Windus.
   (1940). *West to North*. Reprint, London, Book Club Associates, 1942.
   (1944–5). *The North Wind of Love*. 2 vols. Reprint, London, Chatto & Windus, 1968.
   (1957). *Rockets Galore*. London, Chatto & Windus.
Marshall, Bruce (1931). *Father Malachy's Miracle*. London, Heinemann.
   (1941). *All Glorious Within*. London, Constable, 1945.
   (1947). *Vespers in Vienna*. Boston, Riverside Press.
   (1970). *The Bishop*. London, Constable.
Matthews, Roland (1951). *Red Sky at Night*. London, Hollis & Carter.
Moore, George (1898). *Evelyn Innes*. London, T. F. Unwin.
   (1901). *Sister Theresa*. London, T. F. Unwin.
Newman, John Henry (1848). *Loss and Gain*. Reprint, London, Burns & Oates, 1869.
   (1856). *Callista*. London, Burns & Lambert.
Parsons, Gertrude (1878). *Wrecked and Saved*. London, Burns & Oates.
Perriam, Wendy (1985). *The Stillness, The Dancing*. London, Michael Joseph.
   (1989). *Devils for a Change*. London, Grafton Books.
Randolph, Edmund (1886), *Mostly Fools, A Romance of Civilisation*. 3 vols. London, Sampson Low.
Read, Piers Paul (1966). *Game in Heaven with Tussy Marx*. Reprint, London, Alison Press/Secker & Warburg, 1974.
   (1968). *The Junkers*. London, Alison Press/Secker & Warburg.
   (1969). *Monk Dawson*. London, Alison Press/Secker & Warburg.
   (1971). *The Professor's Daughter*. London, Alison Press/Secker & Warburg.
   (1973). *The Upstart*. Reprint, London, Quartet Books, 1975.
   (1976). *Polonaise*. London, Alison Press/Secker & Warburg.
   (1979). *A Married Man*. London, Alison Press/Secker & Warburg.
   (1981). *The Villa Golitsyn*. London, Alison Press/Secker & Warburg.
   (1986). *The Free Frenchman*. London, Alison Press/Secker & Warburg.
Redmon, Anne (1974); *Emily Stone*. Reprint, London, New English Library, 1980.
   (1979). *Music and Silence*. Reprint, London, Magnum Books, 1980.
   (1987). *Second Sight*. London, Secker & Warburg, 1987.
Roberts, Michèle (1984). *The Wild Girl*. London, Methuen.
Rolfe, Frederick (1895–6). *Stories Toto Told Me*. Reprint, London, Collins, 1969.
   (1904). *Hadrian VII*. Reprint, London, Chatto & Windus, 1958.
   (1934). *The Desire and Pursuit of the Whole*. London, Cassell.
   (1958). *Nicholas Crabbe*. Reprint, London, Chatto & Windus.
Spark, Muriel (1957). *The Comforters*. London, Macmillan.
   (1958). *Robinson*. London, Macmillan.
   (1959). *Memento Mori*. London, Macmillan.
   (1960a). *The Bachelors*. London, Macmillan.
   (1960b). *The Ballad of Peckham Rye*. Reprint, London, Macmillan, 1980.
   (1961). *The Prime of Miss Jean Brodie*. Reprint, Harmondsworth, Penguin, 1965.
   (1963). *The Girls of Slender Means*. Reprint, London, Macmillan, 1985.
   (1965). *The Mandelbaum Gate*. Reprint, London, Macmillan, 1980.
   (1974). *The Abbess of Crewe*. London, Macmillan.
   (1976). *The Takeover*. London, Macmillan.

(1981). *Loitering with Intent*. London, Bodley Head.
(1984). *The Only Problem*. London, Bodley Head.
(1988). *A Far Cry from Kensington*. London, Constable.
Stewart, Agnes (1860). *Eustace, or Self-devotion*. London, Catholic Publishing Co.
Thompson, Dunstan (1955). *The Dove with the Bough of Olive*. London, Cassell.
Tolkien, J. R. R. (1954–5). *The Lord of the Rings*. London, Allen & Unwin.
Walsh, Jill Paton (1986). *Lapsing*. London, Weidenfeld & Nicholson.
Ward, Josephine Mary (1899). *One Poor Scruple*. London, Longman, Green. Reprint with an introduction by Bernard Bergonzi. Padstow, Cornwall, Tabb House, 1985.
(1906). *Out of Due Time*. London, Longman.
(1927). *In the Shadow of Mussolini*. London: Sheed & Ward.
Waugh, Auberon (1960). *Foxglove Saga*. London, Chapman & Hall.
Waugh, Evelyn (1930). *Vile Bodies*, Chapman & Hall.
(1936). 'Out of Depth' in *Mr Loveday's Little Outing and Other Sad Stories*. London, Chapman & Hall.
(1945). *Brideshead Revisited*. Reprint, London, Chapman & Hall, 1949.
(1948). *The Loved One*. London, Chapman & Hall.
(1950). *Helena*. Reprint, Harmondsworth, Penguin Books, 1963.
(1952). *Men at Arms*. Reprint, Harmondsworth, Penguin Books, 1988.
(1953). *Love Among the Ruins*. London, Chapman & Hall.
(1957). *The Ordeal of Gilbert Pinfold*. London, Chapman & Hall.
(1961). *Unconditional Surrender*. Reprint, Harmondsworth, Penguin Books, 1983.
(1965). *Sword of Honour*. London, Chapman & Hall.
White, Antonia (1933). *Frost in May*. London, D. Harmsworth. Reprint, *Frost in May*, 2 vols. London, Fontana, 1982.
(1950). *The Lost Traveller*. London, Eyre & Spottiswood. Reprint, see *Frost in May*.
(1952). *The Sugar House*. London, Eyre & Spottiswood. Reprint, see *Frost in May*.
(1954). *Beyond the Glass*. London: Eyre & Spottiswood. Reprint, see *Frost in May*.
Wiseman, Nicholas (1854). *Fabiola*. London, Burns & Lambert.

Other fictional works referred to in the text

Blatty, William (1971). *The Exorcist*. New York, Harper & Row.
Dubus, Andre (1990). *Selected Stories*. London, Picador.
Fielding, Henry (1749). *Tom Jones*. R. P. Mutter (ed.), Harmondsworth, Penguin, 1966.
Hartley, L. P. (1951). *My Fellow Devils*. London, James Barrie.
Hitchens, Robert (1904). *The Garden of Allah*. London, Methuen.
James, P. D. (1989). *Devices and Desires*. London, Faber.
Joyce, James (1916). *Portrait of the Artist as a Young Man*. Chester G. Anderson (ed.), New York, Viking; London, Cape, 1964.
Keable, Robert (1921). *Simon Called Peter*. London, Constable.
Kennedy, Grace (1823). *Father Clement*. Edinburgh, W. Oliphant.
Mallock, W. H. (1886). *The Old Order Changes*. 3 vols. London, Bentley.
Mantel, Hilary (1989). *Fludd*. London, Viking.
McCullough, Colleen (1977). *The Thornbirds*. London, Macdonald & James and Futura, 1977.
Powers, J. F., (1988). *Wheat that Springeth Green*. New York, Knopf.
Sinclair, Catharine (1852). *Beatrice: or, The Unknown Relatives*. 3 vols. London, Bentley.
Trollope, Antony (1857). *Barchester Towers*. 3 vols. London, Longman.
West, Morris (1959). *The Devil's Advocate*. London, Heinemann.
Wilson, A. N. (1988). *Incline Our Hearts*. London, Hutchinson.

Selected bibliography

Secondary sources

Aggeler, Geoffrey (1979). *Anthony Burgess, The Artist as Novelist*. University, Alabama, University of Alabama Press.
Archer, Anthony (1986). *The Two Catholic Churches: A Study in Oppression*. London, SCM Press.
Aveling, J. C. H. (1976). *The Handle and the Axe: The Catholic Recusants in England from Reformation to Emancipation*. London, Blond & Briggs.
Baker, Joseph Ellis (1932). *The Novel and the Oxford Movement*, Princeton Studies in English, no. 8.
Batchelor, John (1982). *The Edwardian Novelists*. London, Duckworth.
Baum, Gregory (1968). *The Credibility of the Church Today: A Reply to Charles Davis*. New York, Herder.
Benkovitz, Miriam (1977). *Frederick Rolfe, Baron Corvo: A Biography*. London, Hamish Hamilton.
Bergonzi, Bernard (1959). 'Chesterton and/or Belloc'. *Critical Quarterly*, I: 64–71.
  (1986). 'The decline and fall of the Catholic novel' in *The Myth of Modernism and Twentieth Century Literature*. Hassocks, Sussex, Harvester.
  (1978). *Reading the Thirties: Texts and Contexts*. London, Macmillan.
Birkett, Jennifer (1977). 'The ideology of the French Catholic Revival', *New Blackfriars*, 58: 496–505.
Boff, Leonardo (1985). *Church, Charism and Power*. Trans. J. W. Diercksmeir. London, SCM Press.
Bold, Alan (1978). *George Mackay Brown*. Edinburgh, Oliver & Boyd.
Borrello, Alfred (1974). *Gabriel Fielding*. New York, Twayne.
Bossy, John (1975). *The English Catholic Community, 1570–1850*. London, Darton, Longman & Todd.
Bostrom, Irene (1962). 'The novel and Catholic Emancipation'. *Studies in Romanticism*, II: 155–76.
Boyd, Ian (1975). *The Novels of G. K. Chesterton*. London, Elek.
Bradbury, Malcolm (1973). *Possibilities: Essays on the State of the Novel*. London, Oxford University Press.
Bredin, Eamonn (1985). *Disturbing the Peace*. Dublin, Columba Press.
Burgess, Anthony (1968). *Urgent Copy: Literary Studies*. New York, Norton.
Chapman, Raymond (1970). *Faith and Revolt: Studies in the Literary Influence of the Oxford Movement*. London, Weidenfeld & Nicolson.
Coates, John D. (1984). *Chesterton and the Edwardian Cultural Crisis*. Hull, University of Hull Press.
Cockburn, Claude (1972). *Bestseller, The Books that Everyone Read, 1900–1939*. London, Sidgwick & Jackson.
Conlon, D. J. (1987). *G. K. Chesterton, A Half-Century of Views*. Oxford, Oxford University Press.
Corrin, Jay P. (1981). *G. K. Chesterton and Hilaire Belloc: The Battle Against Modernity*. London, Ohio University Press.
Couto, Maria (1988). *Graham Greene on the Frontier: Politics and Religion in the Novels*. London, Macmillan.
Coventry, John (1982). 'Roman Catholicism' in Rupert Davis (ed.), *The Testing of the Churches, 1932–1982: A Symposium*. London, Epworth Press.
Craig, Cairns (ed.) (1987). *A History of Scottish Literature*, vol. 4, Aberdeen, Aberdeen University Press.
Cruikshank, John (ed.) (1969). *French Literature and its Background, vol. 6: The Late Nineteenth Century*. London, Oxford University Press.

Cunningham, Valentine (1988). *British Writers of the Thirties*. Oxford, Oxford University Press.
Dale, Alzina Stone (1982). *The Outline of Sanity: A Life of G. K. Chesterton*. Grand Rapids, Eerdmans.
Damrosch, Leopold (1985). *God's Plot and Man's Stories: Studies in the Fictional Imagination from Milton to Fielding*. Chicago: University of Chicago Press.
Davis, Charles (1967). *A Question of Conscience*. London, Hodder & Stoughton.
Davis, Lennard J. (1987). *Resisting Novels: Ideology and Fiction*. London and New York, Methuen.
Dix, Carol M. (1971). *Anthony Burgess*. London, Longman for the British Council.
Dooley, David Joseph (1974). *Compton Mackenzie*. New York: Twayne.
Dulles, Avery (1985). *The Catholicity of the Church*. Oxford, Clarendon Press.
Duquoc, Christian (1987). *Provisional Churches*. Trans. John Bowden. London, SCM Press.
Dyson, A. E. (1960). 'Evelyn Waugh and the Mysteriously Disappearing Hero', *Critical Quarterly*, 2: 72–9.
Eagleton, Terry (1970). *Exiles and Emigrés: Studies in Modern Literature*. London, Chatto & Windus.
Egan, Thomas (1985). 'Tolkien and Chesterton: some analogies'. *Mythlore*, 43 (autumn).
Faulkner, Peter (1976). *Humanism in the English Novel*. London, Elek.
Fletcher, Ian (ed.) (1987). *British Poetry and Prose 1870–1905*. Oxford, Oxford University Press.
(1987). *W. B. Yeats and his Contemporaries*. Brighton, Harvester.
Foucault, Michel (1976). *The History of Sexuality, vol. 1: An Introduction*, trans. Robert Hirley. London, Allen Lane, 1979: 19–23.
Garbley, Sister Mariella (1962). 'The novel', in Sister M. Regis (ed.), *The Catholic Bookman's Guide*. New York, Hawthorn Books.
Green, Martin (1967). *Essays on Literature and Religion: Yeats's Blessings on von Hügel*. London, Longman.
Green, Robert (1981). *Ford Madox Ford: Prose and Politics*. Cambridge, Cambridge University Press.
Greene, Graham (1969). *Collected Essays*. London, Bodley Head.
(1939). *The Lawless Roads*. Reprint, London, Heinemann and Boldey Head, 1978.
Gregor, Ian and Nicholas, Brian (1962). *The Novel and the Story*. London, Faber & Faber.
Griffiths, Richard (1966). *The Reactionary Revolution: The Catholic Revival in French Literature, 1870–1914*. London: Constable.
Hart, Francis Russell (1978). *The Scottish Novel, A Critical Survey*. London: John Murray.
Harvey, W. J. (1965). *Character and the Novel*. London, Chatto & Windus.
Hastings, Adrian (1986). *A History of English Christianity, 1920–1985*. London, Collins.
Hebblethwaite, Peter (1967). 'How Catholic is the Catholic novel?'. *Times Literary Supplement*, 27 July: 678–9.
Helsinger, Elizabeth K., Sheets, Robin Lauterbach and Veeder, William (1989). *The Woman Question: Society and Literature in Britain and America, 1837–1883*. Chicago, University of Chicago Press.
Hornsby-Smith, Michael P. (1987). *Roman Catholics in England: Studies in Social Structure since the Second World War*. Cambridge: Cambridge University Press.
Hügel, Friedrich von (1928). *Letters from Baron Friedrich von Hügel to a Niece*. Reprint, London, Dent, 1950.
Johnstone, Richard (1982). *The Will to Believe: Novelists of the 1930s*. Oxford, Oxford University Press.
Kane, Richard C. (1988). *Iris Murdoch, Muriel Spark and John Fowles: Didactic Demons in*

Selected bibliography

Modern Fiction. Rutherford, Madison, Teaneck, Fairleigh Dickinson University Press, and London, Associated University Presses.
Kellogg, Gene (1970). *The Vital Tradition: The Catholic Novel in an Age of Convergence*. Chicago: Loyola University Press.
Kemp, Peter (1974). *Muriel Spark, Novelists and their World*. London, Elek.
Kenyon, Olga (ed.) (1989). *Women Writers Talk*. Oxford, Lennard.
Kermode, Frank (1967). *The Sense of an Ending*. New York, Oxford University Press.
Kerr, Fergus (1969). 'Ataraxy and Utopia'. *New Blackfriars*, 50: 304–13.
Kettle, Leo (1920). 'John Ayscough, Novelist'. *Catholic World*, 111: 164–73.
Kort, Wesley A. (1975). *Narrative Elements and Religious Meanings*. Philadelphia, Fortress Press.
   (1985). *Modern Fiction and Human Time: A Study in Narrative and Belief*. Tampa, Florida, University of South Florida Press.
Küng, Hans (1967). *The Church*. Trans. R. and R. Ockenden. Tunbridge Wells, Burns & Oates.
Lawrence, D. H. (1930). *A Propos of Lady Chatterley's Lover*. London, Mandrake Press.
Lerner, Lawrence (1963). 'Graham Greene'. *The Critical Quarterly*, 5: 217–31.
Lester, John (1988). *Conrad and Religion*. London, Macmillan.
Lewis, C. S. (1944). 'The Inner Ring'. In *Transposition and other Addresses*. London, Geoffrey Bles, 1949.
Linklater, Andro (1987). *Compton Mackenzie, A Life*. London, Chatto & Windus.
Littlewood, Ian (1983). *The Novels of Evelyn Waugh*. Oxford, Blackwell.
Lodge, David (1959). 'Catholic fiction since the Oxford Movement: its literary form and religious content', unpublished MA thesis, University College, London.
   (1960–1). 'An earlier Foxglove Saga: the first English Catholic novel?'. *Dublin Review*, 486: 365–71.
   (1960). 'Maurice Baring, novelist, a reappraisal'. *Dublin Review*, 485: 262–70.
   (1965). 'Rolfe's Bestiary' in Cecil Woolf and Brocard Sewell (eds), *New Quests for Corvo*. London, Icon Books.
   (1971). *The Novelist at the Crossroads*. London, Routledge & Kegan Paul.
   (1988). *Write On: Occasional Essays 1965–1985*. Harmondsworth, Penguin.
Lukács, Georg (1920). *The Theory of the Novel*. Reprint, London, Merlin Books, 1978.
McBrien, Richard P. (1969). *Do We Need the Church?* New York, Harper & Row.
McCarthy, John P. (1978). *Hilaire Belloc, Edwardian Radical*. Indianapolis, Liberty Press.
Mackenzie, Compton (1936). *Catholicism and Scotland*. London, Routledge.
MacKenzie, John (1965). *The Power and the Wisdom*. Milwaukee, Bruce.
McSweeney, Bill (1980). *Roman Catholicism: The Search for Relevance*. Oxford, Blackwell.
Maison, Margaret M. (1961). *The Victorian Vision: Studies in the Religious Novel*. New York, Sheed & Ward.
Manlove, C. N. (1975). *Modern Fantasy: Five Studies*. Cambridge, Cambridge University Press.
Manvell, Roger (1988). *Elizabeth Inchbald*. Lanham, Maryland, University Press of America.
Martindale, Cyril (1916). *The Life of Monsignor Robert Hugh Benson*. 2 vols. London, Longman.
Matthew, David (1948). *Catholicism in England*. London, Eyre & Spottiswood.
Menendez, Albert J. (1988). *The Catholic Novel, An Annotated Bibliography*. New York and London, Garland.
Meyers, Jeffrey (ed.) (1989). *Graham Greene: A Revaluation*. London, Macmillan.
Moore, Sebastian (1967). *God is a New Language*. London, Darton, Longman & Todd.
Morris, Kevin L. (1984). *The Image of the Middle Ages in Romantic and Victorian Literature*. London, Croom Helm.

Newman, John Henry (1852, 1859). *The Idea of a University*. Reprint, London, Longman, 1901.
 —in Geoffrey Tillotson (ed.) (1957). *Prose and Poetry*. London, Hart Davis.
 —in Ker, Ian (ed.) (1990). *The Genius of John Henry Newman: Selections from his Writings*. Oxford, Clarendon Press.
Norman, Edward (1984). *The English Catholic Church in the Nineteenth Century*. Oxford, Clarendon Press.
 (1985). *Roman Catholicism in England from the Elizabethan Settlement to the Second Vatican Council*. Oxford, Oxford University Press.
Nowell, Robert (ed.) (1983). *Why I Am Still a Catholic*. London, Fount.
O'Donnell, Donat [Conor Cruise O'Brien] (1953). *Maria Cross: Imaginative Patterns in a Group of Modern Catholic Writers*. London, Chatto & Windus.
Orwell, George (1968). *Collected Essays, Journalism and Letters*. 4 vols, ed. Sonia Orwell and Ian Angus. London, Secker & Warburg.
Parrinder, Patrick (1983). 'Muriel Spark and her critics'. *Critical Quarterly*, 25: 23–2.
Pelikan, Jaroslav (1985). *Jesus Through the Centuries*. London and New Haven, Yale University Press.
Phillips, Gene D. (1975). *Evelyn Waugh's Officers, Gentlemen and Rogues*. Chicago, Nelson-Hall.
Rahner, Karl (1963). 'The theological position of Christians in the modern world' in *Christian Commitment*. London, Sheed & Ward.
 (1966). *Theological Investigations*, vol. V. Baltimore, Helicon, and London, Darton, Longman and Todd.
Ranke-Heinemann, Uta (1990). *Eunuchs for Heaven: The Catholic Church and Sexuality*. London, Deutsch.
Rimmon-Kenan, Shlomith (1983). *Narrative Fictions: Contemporary Poetics*. London, Methuen.
Sanders, Andrew (1979). *The Victorian Historical Novel, 1840–1880*. London, Macmillan, and New York, St Martin's Press.
Scheider, R. M. (1965). 'Loss and gain? The theme of conversion in late Victorian fiction'. *Victorian Studies*, IX: 29–44.
Schillebeeckx, Edward (1980). *Interim Report on the Books Jesus & Christ*. London, SCM Press.
Scott, Malcolm (1990). *The Struggle for the Soul of the French Novel: French Catholic and Realist Novelists, 1850–1970*. London, Macmillan.
Selden, Raman (1985). *Contemporary Literary Theory*. Brighton, Harvester.
Shannon, Richard (1974). *The Crisis of Imperialism, 1865–1915*. London, Hart-Davis MacGibbon.
Sharrock, Roger (1984). *Saints, Sinners and Comedians: The Novels of Graham Greene*. Tunbridge Wells, Burns & Oates.
Sinfield, Alan (ed.) (1983). *Society and Literature, 1945–1970*. London, Methuen.
Sonnenfeld, Albert (1982). *Crossroads: Essays on the Catholic Novelists*. York, South Carolina, French Literature Publications.
Speaight, Robert (1957). *Life of Hilaire Belloc*. London, Hollis & Carter.
 (1966). *Ronald Knox the Writer*. London, Sheed & Ward.
Spurling, John (1983). *Graham Greene*. London, Methuen.
Stevenson, Randall (1986). *The British Novel Since the Thirties, An Introduction*. London, Batsford.
Sullivan, John (ed.) (1974). *G. K. Chesterton, A Centenary Celebration*. London, Elek.
A. J. A. Symons (1934). *The Quest for Corvo*. Harmondsworth, Penguin, 1940.
Tanner, Tony (1979). *Adultery in the Novel: Contract and Transgression*. Baltimore, Johns Hopkins University Press.

Selected bibliography

Thomas, Keith (1971). *Religion and the Decline of Magic*. London, Weidenfeld & Nicolson.
Ward, Maisie (1934). *The Wilfred Wards and the Transition*. London, Sheed & Ward.
Ward, Wilfred (1895). 'The rigidity of Rome'. *Nineteenth Century*, 38, November: 786–804.
Warner, Marina (1976). *Alone of All Her Sex*. London, Weidenfeld & Nicolson.
Watt, Ian (1957). *The Rise of the Novel*. London, Chatto & Windus.
Waugh, Patricia (1984). *Metafiction*. London, Methuen.
Weiderkehr, Dietrich (1976). *Belief in Redemption*. Trans. J. Moiser. London, SPCK.
Whittaker, Ruth (1982). *The Faith and Fiction of Muriel Spark*. London, Macmillan.
Wicker, Brian (1975). *The Story-Shaped World*. London, Athlone Press.
Wilson, A. N. (1984). *Hilaire Belloc*. London, Hamish Hamilton.
Wolff, Robert Lee (1977). *Gains and Losses; Novels of Faith and Doubt in Victorian England*. London, John Murray.
Wright, T. R. (1983). 'Newman as novelist: *loss and gain*' in T. R. Wright (ed.) (1983). *John Henry Newman, A Man for Our Time?* Newcastle, Grevatt: 7–17.
  (1988). *Theology and Literature*. Oxford, Blackwell.

Selective glossary of Catholic and theological terminology

Antinomianism: the belief, attributed especially to the sixteenth-century Anabaptists, that the moral law is irrelevant to Christians and (in the extreme form) that they may sin as much as they wish or alternatively that nothing that they do can be a sin.

Apologetics: the technical discipline of arguing for and defending the logic of the faith in controversy with Protestants or unbelievers.

Assumption, the dogma of: the doctrine that the body of Mary, the Mother of Jesus, did not see corruption after death but was assumed immediately into heavenly glory. Defined by Pope Pius XII in 1950.

Augustinianism: the doctrine associated with St Augustine of Hippo (5th century), which stresses how radical the Fall was and how totally dependent on God we are for salvation.

Benediction: a service of adoration of the host (the consecrated communion bread believed to be the real body of Christ). Especially popular after the Council of Trent as an affirmation of this Real Presence.

Blessed Sacrament: the consecrated host (see above).

Charismatic movement: a movement that began in the late 1960s in all the mainstream churches to renew personal devotion and worship through the adoption of Pentecostal modes such as the gift of tongues.

Confession, auricular: the forgiveness of sins through private consultation with and absolution by a priest.

Curia: the administrative organ or bureaucratic headquarters of the papacy and the Vatican.

Distributism: twentieth-century political theory, claiming medieval antecedents, that argues for the devolution of all economic and political power back to smallholders.

Divine office: daily series of services: compline, vespers, etc., the singing in choir or recitation of which is incumbent on monks, nuns and other clergy.

Ecumenism: the pursuit of unity between the churches.

Eschatology: the theology of the final stages of redemption history, the Second Coming of Christ in particular.

Selective glossary of Catholic and theological terminology

Four Last Things: death, judgement, heaven, hell. Traditional Catholic version of the above with especial focus on the fate of the individual soul.

Hagiography: conventionalized narratives of the lives of saints.

Hierarchy: technical term for the clerical offices and officers of the Church, usually referring mainly to the Pope and the bishops.

Humanae Vitae: Encyclical of Pope Paul VI in 1968 reaffirming the ban on artificial methods of birth control.

Jansenism: strongly rigorist theological movement in seventeenth-century France claiming to revive St Augustine's teaching about grace. Named after Cornelius Jansen (d.1638), Bishop of Ypres, Flanders. Often seen as a 'Puritanical Protestant' strand in Catholicism and condemned several times by the papacy, for example, in 1653. Continued nevertheless to exercise an influence, especially on sexual morality.

Liberation theology: belief that the *practical* search for social justice (especially in South American and Third World context) is an inherent part of the gospel. Often influenced by Marxist thought.

Manichaeism: non-Christian doctrine, popular in third – fifth centuries AD, that saw control of the universe divided between two *equal* powers of Good and Evil.

Modernism: theological attempt to accommodate the faith to modern science and biblical criticism. Condemned as heresy by Pope Pius X.

Mortal sin: a grave sin believed to destroy the supernatural life of grace in the soul until restored by contrition and absolution.

Narrative theology: trend in theology to emphasize the structural narrative element in the bible and religious discourse as a whole.

Natural Law: the belief (central to the European tradition) that an innate moral law is built into all aspects of human life and can be known even before the full Christian revelation.

Oxford Movement: attempt to restore the Catholic and sacramental heritage of the Church of England. Began in the University of Oxford in the 1830s. Led eventually to many conversions to Rome.

Patristics: the study of the Fathers of the Church, the major theologians of the first few centuries.

Pelagianism: named after Pelagius, British monk of the fifth century, whose followers minimized the doctrine of original sin and argued that we contribute to our own salvation by proper moral behaviour.

Quietism: technically a form of mysticism that teaches complete passivity before God. In a looser sense a religion of withdrawal from the world.

Theodicy: the attempt to find a theoretical solution to the problem of evil, the question of why there is evil in the world if God is both good and omnipotent.

Thomism and Neo-Thomism: theology and philosophy based on the synthesis of Aristotelianism and Christianity by the thirteenth-century Dominican, St Thomas Aquinas. Revived in the nineteenth century and given an official status as *the* Catholic philosophy. Reworked again this century (in more progressive directions) in the Neo-Thomism of philosophers such as Jacques Maritain and Étienne Gilson.

Trent, Council of: gathering of Roman Catholic bishops of the world in 1545–63 to respond to the threat of the Reformation by authoritatively defining Catholic dogma and inaugurating the official internal reform and counter-attack, the Counter-Reformation.

Triumphalism: the tendency to celebrate and glory in the Church's past history, external achievements and exclusive claims.

Ultramontanism: literally, 'beyond the mountains', the tendency to look to Rome and the Papacy as the absolute, totally centralized source of authority in the Church and to minimize local and national autonomy.

Index

Ackroyd, Peter, xiv
Acton, John Edward Emerich Dahlberg, 1st Baron, 15
Adam, Karl, 92
adultery, 9–10, 72, 132, 151–3, 158–60
aestheticism, see Catholicism and the arts; *fin de siècle*
Agnew, E. C., *Rome and the Abbey*, 8
Almedingen, E. M., *The Little Stairway*, 150
'angry young men', 35
'anonymous' Christianity, 41, 95
antinomianism, see grace and morality, paradoxes of; sin
Archer, Anthony, 42, 43
aristocracy, 3, 30, 58–9, 63–5, 99
art, see Catholicism and the arts
Augustine, St, 33, 34
Aylesford Priory, 34
Ayscough, John, 18, 120
   Dromina, 18
   San Celestino, 18

Bainbridge, Beryl, 136–7
   Another Part of the Wood, xiii, 137
   A Quiet Life, 137
   Sweet William, 137
bargain-with-God motif, 19, 134, 142–3
Baring, Maurice, xi, 22–3, 151–2
   C, 23, 24, 57–8, 81, 85

Cat's Cradle, 82, 132–3, 152
The Coat Without Seam, 111
Daphne Adeadne, 151–2
Overlooked, 132
Passing By, 133
Barry, William, 12
   Arden Massiter, 12, 13–14
   The New Antigone, 13, 14
   The Two Standards, 13–14
Barth, Karl, 26
'basic Christian communities', 95
Beardsley, Aubrey, 14
Bellamine, St Robert, 82
Belloc, Hilaire, xi, 21–2, 25, 29, 51–2, 62, 72, 83, 85, 98–101, 163
   Emmanuel Burden, 21–2, 163
   Mr Clutterbuck's Election, 21, 99
   The Green Overcoat, 163
Benediction, 6
Benson, Archbishop E. W., 6, 19, 50
Benson, Robert Hugh, 14, 19, 20, 21, 54, 134
   A Winnowing, 19, 134
   An Average Man, 53, 61–2
   Come Rack, Come Rope, 19, 134
   Initiation, 134
   Loneliness, 19
   Lord of the World, 19, 66, 86–7, 96
   The Conventionalists, xii
   The Dawn of All, 19, 86, 87–8, 96, 114

Index

The Necromancers, 19, 114–15
The Sentimentalists, 19
Bergonzi, Bernard, 10, 29, 42, 100–101, 140–41
The Roman Persuasion, 29, 51, 53–5, 83, 140–41
Bernanos, George, xi, 138
Beste, Henry Digby, 5, 55
Poverty and the Baronet's Family, 5, 55
Beste, J. Richard, 12
Modern Society in Rome, 12, 83
Billington, Rachel, *Occasion of Sin*, 54, 159
birth control, 39, 157
Bishop, Mary C., 9, 14
Elizabeth Eden, 9, 14, 53, 148
Blatty, William, 115
The Exorcist, 114, 115
Bloy, Leon, 131
Blundell, M. E., *Tyler's Lass*, 65
Bossy, John, xiii
Boullan, Joseph-Antoine, 134
Bradbury, Malcolm, xiv, 161
Braine, John, 35
Room at the Top, 35, 149
The Jealous God, 35, 129, 135, 139–40, 146, 159
The Pious Agent, 40–41, 106, 149
Bredin, Eamonn, 42
British Catholicism
anti-bourgeois emphasis in, 30, 63, 65–6, 71–2, 75
Edwardian, 17–21
eighteenth-century, 3–4
as English, xii, 22, 53–9
and Europe, 51–2
as foreign, 50–53
future of, 94–5, 164
Gothic movement in, 5, 6
and ideology, xiii, 5, 57–8, 56
middle classes and, 4, 9, 35, 65
'old Catholics' and, 3, 5, 6
persecution and, 3, 49, 52, 134
politics and, xi, 12–14, 20–22, 32, 97–8, 99–107
the poor and, 65–6
post-First World War, 25–6
post-Second World War, 31–6
and Second Vatican Council, 37, 43, 91–2
separation in, xiii, 3, 4, 27, 34–6, 48–9

and snobbery, xii, 58, 63
in the thirties, 26–30
Victorian, 4–13
see also aristocracy; Catholic neurosis; Irish influence; liberalism, Catholic; 'post-Catholic' ethos
Brook, Peter, x
Brooke-Rose, Christine, 34
The Dear Deceit, 133
Brown, George Mackay, xi, xii, 36, 60, 69, 123, 147, 161
Greenvoe, 36, 60, 69–70, 147
Magnus, 36, 60, 123
Browning, Robert, 11, 70
'Mr Sludge the Medium', 11
The Ring and the Book, 122
Burgess, Anthony, xi, 32–3, 50, 52, 64, 91, 102, 116–17, 147
A Clockwork Orange, 163
A Vision of Battlements, 32, 50, 147
Earthly Powers, 33, 41, 91, 116–17, 125, 155
The Wanting Seed, 147
The Worm and the Ring, 52, 66, 71, 153–4
Tremor of Intent, 52, 106, 117–18, 145–6
Urgent Copy, 52

Caddell, Cecilia M., 9
Home and the Homeless, 9
Calvinism, 59–60, 124, 147, 163
capitalism, 98–100
Carmichael, Montgomery, *The Life of John William Walsh FSA*, 162
Carson, Michael, *Sucking Sherbet Lemons*, 158
Catholic Emancipation Act, 4, 10
'Catholic neurosis', 27, 82, 140
Catholic novel
defined, xi, 130, 161
see also British Catholicism; French Catholic Novel; neo-conservative fiction; 'post-Catholic' ethos and fiction; rhetoric of exaggeration
Catholic schools, 27, 35, 49, 52, 56–7, 63, 83
Catholicism (general)
and the arts, x, xiii, 4, 14, 28, 49, 62, 67–71
and politics, x, 37–8, 66–71, 85, 96–8, 104–8; *see also* British Catholicism,

Catholicism (general) – *cont.*
  politics of; democracy; distributism; fascism; Marxism; socialism; Spanish Civil War
  sense of identity of, 41–3, 81–2, 93–5, 164
  see also British Catholicism; church, the
celibacy, 38–9, 150
character, *see* novel, the
Chardin, Teilhard de, 92
Chenu, M. D., 92
Chesterton, G. K., xi, xii, 21–2, 25, 99–101, 161
  Manalive, 112
  The Ball and the Cross, 62, 112, 142
  'The Crime of the Communist', 98
  The Father Brown Stories, xii, 121–2, 138
  The Man Who Was Thursday, 112
  The Return of Don Quixote, 58, 66, 99–100, 161
chic, Catholic
  aesthetic, 66–71
  intellectual, 71–7
  social, 61–6
Christianity, 10–11, 26, 61, 163, 164
Church, the
  as institution, 63, 71–2, 74, 84, 94
  new images of, 37–8, 62, 88–95
  old images of, 16, 69, 81–8
  see also Catholicism; post-Catholic ethos and fiction; world, the
Church of England, 6, 7, 13, 15, 25, 43, 82
Clarke, Isabel, 28
Cobbett, William, 5, 21, 29
Communism, *see* Marxism
confession, 135, 140–41, 146–7
Conrad, Joseph, xii
conversion, 6, 14, 26–7
  novels of, 7–9, 14, 28, 31
Cornwell, John, *The Spoiled Priest*, 39, 82, 93, 157
Craigie, Pearl, xii, 10, 13, 14, 98, 132
  Robert Orange, 10, 13, 14
  The Dream and the Business, 54, 131, 132
  The School for Saints, 10
critical theory, x, xiv, 22, 162–3

Cronin, A. J., xi, xiv, 31, 90, 163
  The Keys of the Kingdom, 31, 90, 150
Darwin, Charles, 11
Davis, Charles, 39
death theme, 76, 123, 128–30
death-bed repentances, 9, 140, 143
decadence, 14, 20, 25, 141
  see also fin de siècle; grace and morality, paradoxes of
Delafield, E. M., 133, 150–51
  Consequences, 133, 150–51
  Turn Back the Leaves, 133, 151
democracy, 21, 97–9
Dering, Edward, 13, 15, 54, 58, 98
  Sherborne, 12, 13, 104
  The Ban of Mablethorpe, 11, 12, 13, 58
detective fiction, 22, 120–22
Dickens, Charles, 162
Digby, Sir Kenelm, 5
Dinnis, Enid, 28
  The Road to Somewhere, 28, 120
Diognetus, Epistle of, 48
distributism, 21–2, 99–100
Donne, John, 134
Donnolly, Gabrielle, *Holy Mother*, 48–9, 81
Dostoievsky, Fyodor, 116, 138
Dowson, Ernest, 14
Dubus, Andre, 128
  Selected Stories, 128
Duchêne, Anne, 76

Eagleton, Terry, 53, 102
ecumenism, 37, 91–2
Edwardian period, Edwardian fiction, *see* British Catholicism
Eliot, George, 162
  Middlemarch, 162
Eliot, T. S., 72, 138
Ellis, Alice Thomas, xi, 15, 40, 73, 76–7, 99, 128–9
  The Birds of the Air, 76, 228
  The Clothes and the Wardrobe, 51
  The Other Side of the Fire, 141
  The Sin Eater, 40, 76, 77
  The Twenty-seventh Kingdom, 76, 118–19
  Unexplained Laughter, 76, 115
evil, 33–4
  forms of, 114–19
  problem of (theodicy), 111, 117–19, 132

supernatural, 114–17
  see also providence and literary form
exile, sense of, 52–3
expiation, 23, 24, 132, 135
  see also vicarious suffering

Faber, Frederick William, 5, 6, 9
fable, x, xiv, 161–2
Fall, the, *see* original sin
fantasy, xiv, 33, 85, 112–13, 161
fascism, 26, 29, 100–101
Faulkner, Peter, ix
Fielding, Gabriel, xii, 33, 34
  Gentlemen in their Season, 134, 152–3, 158–9
  In the Time of Greenbloom, 135
  The Birthday King, 33, 135
Fielding, Henry, *Tom Jones*, 120
Fin de siècle, 10, 14, 67
Firbank, Ronald, xi, 25, 50, 67–9, 155
  Concerning the Eccentricities of Cardinal Pirelli, 68–9
  Prancing Nigger, 68
  Valmouth, 67
First World War, the, 24
Ford, Madox Ford, xi, xii, 17–18, 21, 24
  Mr Apollo, 17–18
  Parade's End, 24, 55, 58
  The Fifth Queen, 18, 57, 66, 99
  The Good Soldier, 24, 49
Foucault, Michel, 147
  The History of Sexuality, 147
Franco, General Francisco, 29, 101
Frankeau, Pamela, 31
  The Bridge, 122
free will, 124, 163
French Catholic Novel, xi, xii, 14, 113, 134, 138
Freud, Sigmund, 146
Fullerton, Lady Georgiana, 9
  Constance Sherwood, 9
  Ladybird, 10, 11, 133
  Mrs Gerald's Niece, 9

Gibbon, Lewis Grassic, 100
Gibbs, Sir Philip, 26
  The Age of Reason, 26, 82
Gill, Eric, 28, 29
Gilson, Étienne, 72
Godden, Rumer, 37, 138

Five For Sorrow, Ten for Joy, 138, 147, 154
In This House of Brede, 37, 38, 65
Gothic fiction, 57, 149
Gothic movement, English Catholic, *see* British Catholicism
grace, paradoxes of and morality, xii, 30, 64, 138–41, 163
Gray, John, 14, 28, 69, 155
  Park, 14, 20, 28, 69, 86
Green, Julien, 136
Green, Martin, 140
Greene, Graham, x, xi, xii, 19, 28–30, 35, 41, 50, 71–2, 89–90, 101–5, 131, 134, 138–40, 142, 162–3
  A Burnt-out Case, 41, 92, 131
  Brighton Rock, 29, 122
  Monsignor Quixote, 105, 125
  The Comedians, 41, 105
  The End of the Affair, 24, 70, 72, 111, 113, 122, 124, 130, 131, 134, 139, 149, 152
  The Heart of the Matter, xii, 30, 50–51, 72, 89, 131, 134, 136, 138, 152
  The Honorary Consul, 41, 91–3, 105, 121
  The Lawless Roads, 103
  The Potting Shed, 134
  The Power and the Glory, x, 30, 50, 88–9, 93, 101–4, 134, 136, 138–9

Hall, Radclyffe, 155, 156
  The Well of Loneliness, 155, 156
Harland, Henry, xii, 14, 18–19, 50, 67
  The Cardinal's Snuff Box, 18–19, 67
Hartley, L. P., *My Fellow Devils*, 71
Harvey, W. J., x, 161
Hastings, Adrian, xiii, 26, 35–6, 37
Hebblethwaite, Peter, 113, 162
hierarchy, restoration of the, 5
historical fiction, 8, 13, 85–6
Hitchens, Robert, 18
  The Garden of Allah, 18, 131–2, 146, 151
homosexuality, 155–6, 158
Hügel, Baron Friedrich von, 15, 82
Humanae Vitae, 39
humour, Catholic, 71–2
Huntingdon, Jedidiah, xiii
Huysmans, Joris Karl, 14, 19, 134, 138

Inchbald, Elizabeth, 3
  A Simple Story, 3–4, 150

189

inner ring, 73
Irish Home Rule, 55–6
Irish influence, 4, 5, 6, 55–6, 65
Italianate devotions, 4, 5, 9

Jacobitism, 3, 66, 98, 100
James, P. D., 120, 121
   Devices and Desires, 121
Jansenism, 146
Jerrold, Douglas, 29, 97, 98, 101
   Storm over Europe, 29
John XXIII, Pope, 37, 106
John Paul II, Pope, 37, 42–3, 94
Johnson, Lionel, 14
Jones, David, 28
Joyce, James, 73
   Portrait of the Artist as a Young Man, 146

Kaye-Smith, Sheila, 28, 54
   Gallybird, 54, 114
Keable, Robert, 26, 154–5
   Simon Called Peter, 26
Kelly, Mary, *The Spoilt Kill*, 121
Kennedy, Grace, *Father Clement*, 4
Kermode, Frank, *The Sense of an Ending*, 123
King, Pauline, *The Snares of the Enemy*, 121
Kitsch, 70–71
Knox, Ronald, 15, 28
Küng, Hans, 62, 91, 94

Labour Party, 97
language, literary, xiv, 20, 69, 123
Latin, 36, 38
Lawrence, D. H., 148, 152
   A Propos of Lady Chatterley's Lover, 148
le Carré, John, 106
Leo XIII, Pope, 98
Lerner, Lawrence, ix–x
Lewis, C. S., 73
Lewis, Saunders, 100
liberalism, 26
   Anglican, 6, 15, 82
   Catholic, 12–13, 15
liberation theology, 38, 41, 90
Lingard, John, 5, 21, 99
Lisle, Ambrose Philipps de, 5
Littlewood, Ian, 63, 64, 74
liturgy, 28, 36, 69, 86, 123, 161
Locke, John, 122

Lodge, David, xi, xii, 20, 30, 31, 34–5, 39, 73, 125–7
   How Far Can You Go?, 39, 40, 41, 42, 55, 62, 73, 91–2, 93–4, 104–5, 125–7, 146, 156–7, 157–8
   The British Museum Is Falling Down, 39, 55, 73, 145, 154
   The Picturegoers, 35, 70, 71, 152
Lukács, Georg, ix
Lyell, Sir Charles, 11

McCabe, William, 13, 98
   Adelaide, Queen of Italy, 86, 98
MacColla, Fionn, 59–60, 69
   And the Cock Crew, 59–60, 62
   The Albannach, 59, 71
McCullough, Colleen, *The Thornbirds*, 149
Mackenzie, Compton, xi, xii, 23–4, 25, 28, 29, 60, 100, 108, 162
   Catholicism in Scotland, 60
   Rockets Galore, 60
   Sinister Street, 23–4
   The Altar Steps, 28
   The East Wind of Love, 48, 65, 100
   The Four Winds of Love, 29, 55–6, 100, 122
   The Heavenly Ladder, 25
   The North Wind of Love, 72, 108
   West to North, 29, 85, 98, 100
McKenzie, John, 89
McNabb, Vincent, 100
McSweeney, Bill, 85, 97, 98
magic realism, 113
Maison, Margaret M., 8, 9
Mallock, W. H., 10, 15
Manichaeism, 33, 116–17
Manlove, C. N., 112
Manning, Henry, Cardinal, xi, 5, 6, 7
Mantel, Hilary, *Fludd*, 82
Maritain, Jacques, 26, 72, 104
Marlowe, Christopher, 66
marriage, 152–3
Marshall, Bruce, xii, 30, 32, 83
   All Glorious Within, 18, 25, 51, 59, 65, 71, 147, 150, 154
   Father Malachy's Miracle, 30
   The Bishop, 39
   Vespers in Vienna, 32, 84
martyrdom, 134
Marxism, 29, 38, 41, 97, 100, 104–6

Index

Mary Magdalen, St, 154
Mary the Mother of Jesus, 154
Masterman, C. F. G., *The Condition of England*, 17
Matthews, Roland, *Red Sky at Night*, 154
Mauriac, François, xi, 35
medievalism, 4, 5, 22, 66, 99–100
Menendez, Albert, xi
miracles, 111, 113–14, 119, 130
Mivart, St George J., 15
modernism, literary, 161–2
modernism, theological, 15–16
Moore, George, xi, 10, 151
   Evelyn Innes, 151
   Sister Theresa, 15, 151
   The Lake, xi
Moore, Sebastian, 27
Mounier, Emmanuel, 104n
Mussolini, Benito, 29, 101

narrative theology, 125–7
Nash, Christopher, 112
natural law, 113
nature, Catholic attitudes to, 112
neo-conservative fiction, 94–5, 164
Newman, John Henry, Cardinal, 6–8, 16, 90, 98, 139
   Apologia Pro Vita Sua, 136
   Callista, 6, 8
   Loss and Gain, 7, 61, 63, 81–2
Niebuhr, Reinhold, 26
nineties, the, *see fin de siècle*
Norman, Edward, 4, 15, 27, 53
Northern Irish influence, xii
novel, the (general)
   and character, ix, 162, 163
   of ideas, 7, 161
   and Protestantism, ix, 162
   rise of, ix, x, 161
   and secularism, ix, x, 161
   see also Catholic novel, the; postmodernism; realism; romance
nuns, 51, 133, 150–51, 158

O'Brien, Edna, 155
O'Connor, Flannery, 116
original sin, 33–4, 102, 118, 136–8, 140–41
Orwell, George, ix, x, 101, 140
Oxford Movement, 5, 7

Papal States, 12, 88
Paradox, *see* grace, paradoxes of and morality; rhetoric of exaggeration
Parker, Robert B., 121
Parsons, Gertrude, *Wrecked and Saved*, 119
Pater, Walter, 15
Paul, St, 47, 145
   Epistle to the Corinthians, 61
Paul VI, Pope, 39, 82
Péguy, Charles, 138
Pelagius, Pelagianism, xiii, 142
   see also grace, paradoxes of and morality; original sin; sin
Perriam, Wendy
   Devils for a Change, 158
   The Stillness, The Dancing, 114
Peter, St, First Epistle of, 47
Pius IX, Pope, 12
Pius X, Pope, 88
Plante, David, 156
politics, *see* British Catholicism and politics; Catholicism and politics; democracy; distributism; fascism; Marxism; socialism; Spanish Civil War
'post-Catholic' ethos and fiction, 93–5, 155, 158, 164
post-modernism and literary experiment, x, xiv, 34, 161
   see also critical theory
Powers, J. F., *Wheat that Springeth Green*, 83
priests, 38–9, 54, 89, 150, 157
providence and literary form, xiv, 118–24
psychic phenomena, *see* spiritualism
Pugin, Welby, 4

Rahner, Karl, 42, 92
Randolph, Edmund, 7, 12, 13, 15, 55, 73, 98
   Mostly Fools, 12, 13, 15, 49, 63
Read, Piers Paul, xii, 37, 39, 63, 94, 106–8, 111, 138, 140, 159–60
   A Married Man, 39, 108, 129, 143, 153
   Game in Heaven with Tussy Marx, 39, 97, 106, 122
   Monk Dawson, 37, 39, 42, 48, 55, 56–7, 61, 149–50, 157

Read, Piers Paul – *cont.*
  Polonaise, 39, 159
  The Free Frenchman, 39, 97, 104, 107–8, 153, 159–60
  The Junkers, 106
  The Professor's Daughter, 107, 134
  The Upstart, xi, 39, 135, 139
  The Villa Golitsyn, 159
realism, ix–x, xiv, 22, 34, 36, 111, 139, 161–3
  see also novel, the; magic realism; romance; post-modernism
Redmon, Anne, xii, 116, 154
  Emily Stone, 66, 70, 124, 130–31, 134–5, 143–4, 149, 163
  Music and Silence, 154
  Second Sight, 116, 154
Reformation, the, 21, 59–60, 99
renunciation, 9–19, 132–3
rhetoric of exaggeration, xiv, 30, 43, 140, 142
Roberts, Michèle, 153, 155
  The Wild Girl, 155
Rolfe, Frederick, xi, xii, 7, 14–15, 19–21, 50–51, 66, 70, 71, 88, 142, 155
  Hadrian VII, 20–21, 49, 51, 88, 108
  Nicholas Crabbe, 20
  Stories Toto Told Me, 20
  The Desire and Pursuit of the Whole, 20, 71, 155
romance, x, 22, 111, 119–20, 123, 161

sacrificial victim, 134–5
satire, 7, 83
Schillebeeckx, Edward, 93
Scots Catholicism, xii, 59–60, 69–70
Scots Nationalism, 101
Scott, Sir Walter, 41
Second World War, the, 30–31
sex, Catholic attitudes to, 10, 145–53, 155, 156–60
  and 'obstacle love', 146, 151
  see also adultery; birth control; homosexuality; nuns; priests; sexism and stereotypes of the feminine
sexism and stereotypes of the feminine, 153–6
Sharrock, Roger, 138
Shaw, Bernard, 21

sin, 135–44, 145–7
  see also grace and morality, paradoxes of; original sin; sex, Catholic attitudes to
Sinclair, Catharine, 50
  Beatrice: or, The Unknown Relatives, 50
sixties, the, 36–7, 156
Slant, 38, 104–5
socialism, 11, 13, 38, 97–8, 102
Spanish Civil War, 29, 101
Spark, Muriel, x, xii, xiv, 33–4, 40, 74–6, 84, 117, 136, 138
  A Far Cry from Kensington, 117, 145
  Loitering with Intent, 119
  Memento Mori, 129, 136
  Robinson, 148
  The Abbess of Crewe, 40, 75–6
  The Bachelors, 34, 117, 148, 152
  The Ballad of Peckham Rye, 34, 117, 124
  The Comforters, 34, 74, 117, 121, 124
  The Girls of Slender Means, 31, 33, 74, 75, 138
  The Mandelbaum Gate, 74, 113, 120, 155
  The Only Problem, 111, 118
  The Prime of Miss Jean Brodie, 74, 124
  The Takeover, 40
spiritualism and psychic phenomena, 11–12, 114–16
spy fiction, 22, 52–3
Stewart, Agnes, *Eustace, or Self-devotion*, 9
Strachey, John, 28
  The Coming Struggle for Power, 28
structuralism, 125
suffering, 103, 119, 130–35
  see also vicarious suffering
Sunday Times, x
supernatural, the, 111–16, 161, 162
  fictional strategies for, xiv, 30, 111–16, 161
suspicion of fiction, 34, 74, 124–5
Symons, A. J. A., 66

Tanner, Tony, 9, 158
Tatler, 62
theodicy, *see* evil, problem of
Thomas, Keith, 114
Thomism, 26, 100
Thompson, Dunstan, *The Dove with the Bough of Olive*, 104
Thompson, Francis, 'The Hound of Heaven', 19

Index

time in fiction, 122–3
Tolkien, J. R. R., x, 33, 112–13, 120
  The Lord of the Rings, x, 33, 120
Torres, Camillo, 38, 105
Trent, Council of, 82
Trollope, Anthony, *Barchester Towers*, 4
Tromp, Sebastian, 82
Tyrell, George, 15

ultramontanism, *see* Church, the, old images of
unreliable narrator technique, 24, 144

Vatican Council, Second, 36–9, 90, 97, 108
Vaughan, Herbert, Cardinal, 162
vicarious suffering, 134–5
  see also expiation
Victorian period, Victorian fiction, *see* British Catholicism

Walpole, Sir Hugh, ix
Walsh, Jill Paton, *Lapsing*, 157
Ward, Josephine Mary, 3, 4, 10, 29, 163
  In the Shadow of Mussolini, 29, 101
  One Poor Scruple, 3, 10, 14, 47, 49, 135, 163
  Out of Due Time, 15–16
Ward, Wilfred, 85, 98
Warhol, Andy, 70–71
Watt, Ian, ix
Waugh, Auberon, *Foxglove Saga*, 83, 154
Waugh, Evelyn, x, 15, 25–6, 28–30, 32, 38, 54, 58, 63–5, 70, 98, 129, 136, 162
  Brideshead Revisited, x, xii, 24, 29, 30, 32, 47, 54, 58, 64, 123, 140, 143, 148–9, 159
  Helena, 86, 98, 148
  Love Among the Ruins, 32, 129, 149
  Men at Arms, 64
  'Out of Depth', 86
  Sword of Honour, 32, 38, 64
  The Loved One, 129
  The Ordeal of Gilbert Pinfold, 38, 64, 115–16
  Unconditional Surrender, 56, 64
  Vile Bodies, 25–6, 63–4
Wells, H. G., 19, 21, 26
Welsh influence, xii, 100
West, Morris, *The Devil's Advocate*, 156
White, Antonia, xi, xii, 31
  Beyond the Glass, 135
  Frost in May, xiii, 27–8, 81, 97, 132
  The Lost Traveller, xii, 53–4, 62, 67, 113–14, 155
  The Sugar House, 25, 155
Wicker, Brian, 125
Wilde, Oscar, 14, 141
Wilson, A. N., *Incline Our Hearts*, 71
Wiseman, Nicholas, Cardinal, xi, 4, 5, 6–7, 8
  Fabiola, 6, 8, 85, 134
women, role of, ix, 10, 11, 14, 97
  see also sexism and stereotypes of the feminine
worker priest movement, 104
'world, the', 5, 23, 47–8, 61, 85, 92–5